Published by the
ASSOCIATES OF THE
NATIONAL MARITIME MUSEUM LIBRARY

and

THE GLENCANNON PRESS

With the generous support of
Mystic Seaport Museum

The American Maritime Library: Volume 1

Glory of the Seas

by
MICHAEL JAY MJELDE

THE GLENCANNON PRESS
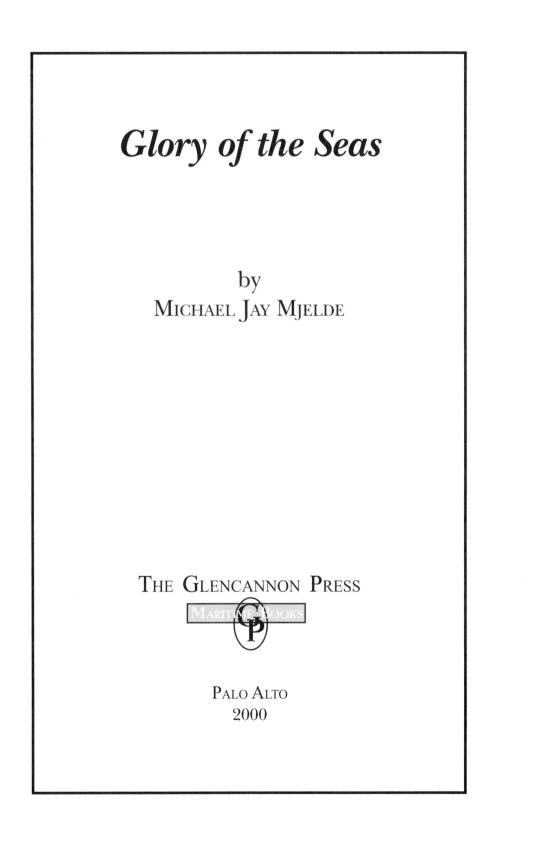
MARITIME BOOKS

PALO ALTO
2000

Preface To the Second Edition

As one who was practically born with a love for ships of sail, it's a pleasure to be asked to write the preface of a book about a ship in which he never sailed; nor did Michael Mjelde, the author.

Wherever Mr. Mjelde acquired his love for one of the finest, wooden, sailing, square rigged ships, he has, in this book, shared that passion with the reader. He carefully researched *Glory of the Seas* from the time Donald McKay, possibly the finest designer of clipper-ships that raced around Cape Horn to San Francisco, built her — the ship that caused his financial ruin but which carried on long after other fast, wooden, square rigged vessels were lost or scrapped.

The book, *Glory of the Seas,* was the first volume published by Mystic Seaport Museum in the American Maritime Library Series, in 1970. No finer representative could have been used to begin this excellent series.

The writer of this foreword never sailed more than a day aboard a square rigger. He still retains apprenticeship papers his father refused to sign. The voyage was for a trip around Cape Horn. However, a number of voyages as seaman, bosun and mate, aboard three-, four-, and five-masted schooners were good training for a young man who would eventually become an officer in steam and captain of a fine schooner converted from yacht to training vessel, Mystic Seaport Museum's *Brilliant,* in which he served as mate and master for twenty-five years.

The days of sail are not forgotten. Year by year more fine books about ships of sail and the men who built and sailed them appear. *Glory of the*

Seas was a heartbreak for Donald McKay, her designer and builder, but this book is an eloquent reminder of his great achievements and keeps alive his place in history.

Sic Transit Gloria Mundi
Capt. Francis E. "Biff" Bowker

✳✳

Table of Contents

List of Illustrations

GLORY OF THE SEAS

CHAPTER I

A Dream Materializes

THURSDAY, October 21, 1869, was launching day for *Glory of the Seas.* Donald McKay went down to his shipyard early that morning to attend to last-minute duties. This was a day of enormous import to him and he had prepared carefully for the grave and proud occasion. Dressed in a black suit, a white shirt with winged collar, a large bow tie, and sporting a black top hat, he was conspicuous among his workmen. During the hours before the crowds started assembling, McKay's men raised long poles at *Glory*'s fore, main, and mizzen mastholes, since she was being launched unrigged, and then decorated her with bright flags and streamers. A United States Jack flew from a pole made fast to the outboard end of her bowsprit. A huge American flag flapped aft in the brisk morning breeze.[1] For nearly five months *Glory of the Seas* had taken form through the painstaking craft of her creator; now the time had come for her to leave the security of McKay's shipyard. A large crowd started to gather. City dignitaries, friends of McKay, yard employees and their families began climbing up the building ramp on her starboard side. On reaching the top of the ramp, just under the fore channels, they mounted a ladder that connected the ramp and ship's bulwark and were aboard.

Shortly before noon, Mary McKay came out of their home, Eagle Hill, at 80 White Street, with five of her six children, all especially well-dressed for the occasion. The youngest child, one-year-old Wallace, made the trip to the shipyard via baby carriage, while three-year-old Guy and five-year-old Anna walked by their mother down the hill to Border Street. Al-

Donald McKay. Daguerreotype by Southworth and Hawes, ca. 1864. Courtesy the Metropolitan Museum of Art, gift of I.N. Phelps Stokes, Edward S. Hawes, Alice Mary Hawes, Marion Augusta Hawes, 1937.

though Frances, fifteen, and her brother Lawrence, nine, should have been in school, their mother had obtained permission for them to forgo lessons and attend this family event.

At noon, the tide in Boston Harbor was at its highest. To Frances fell the honors of the day. She stood on the building ramp alongside the ship. Her father gave a command, and the remaining shores and spurs were knocked out. The harsh sounds of hammer blows and splintering wood were replaced by gentle squeaks and squeals as the stately ship slowly began to move. Clutching the traditional bottle, Frances swung it saying, "I christen thee *Glory of the Seas.*" Loud applause and shouts from hundreds of people echoed over the water. Gathering momentum, *Glory* majestically slid down the ways into Boston Harbor, all her flags and streamers snapping proudly in the wind. It was a most successful launch.

At this point the future held desperate hopes for Donald McKay. As he watched his *Glory of the Seas* out in the harbor channel being towed toward a fitting-out dock, he saw her as the reversal of his fortunes — as his means to recoup his losses, pay his creditors, and re-establish his reputation as the greatest and mostly widely respected Boston shipbuilder of his time. Indeed, many triumphs lay ahead for the ship, but tragedy and heartbreak lay ahead for the man.

The name Donald McKay is so well associated with the fast clipper ships of the 1850's that when one thinks of a Yankee clipper, this great master shipwright and naval architect naturally comes to mind. At East Boston during the period of 1845 to 1869, McKay built some of the fastest wooden sailing ships that ever plowed through the seas of the world. Glorious vessels like *Flying Cloud, Great Republic, Romance of the Seas,* and *Flying Fish* made records that have never since been surpassed by any sailing craft. With their sleek, black clipper hulls, towering masts, billowing expanses of white canvas, and large complements of "iron" men, these ships, as a class, made an indelible mark on American history.

Glory of the Seas was the last medium clipper ever built by the brilliant McKay. During her life-span of fifty-four years she brought more long-standing honor and respect to her creator than any other vessel sliding down his shipbuilding ways at East Boston. To follow her history and meet the many colorful people, great and small, who shared in her career, from record-breaking days to declining years, gives us a portrait of the golden age of sail that will never be seen again.

The life of *Glory of the Seas* actually begins about the year 1867. The war between the Union and the Confederacy had been over for more than two years. The restored Union was struggling to regain what it had lost in four years of bloody conflict. During this postwar era Donald McKay was trying to regain his reputation as the foremost clipper-ship builder in the world. He had indeed built great ships, but he was not a good businessman. He often did not give consideration to worldwide economic conditions when deciding what to build, and when; he took gambles, and sometimes he lost heavily. Ten years previously, he had gone bankrupt for this very reason, and during the time since then had constructed few ships.[2] His fame, of course, had dimmed; and now, at fifty-seven, he was just an aging businessman. The year before, in 1866, he had built two 170-foot wooden steamers, the *George B. Upton* and the *Theodore D. Wagner*, for the Boston and Charleston Line of Steam Packets — his first financially successful attempt to construct large vessels in seven years.

By 1867, Donald McKay's business activities were quite diversified. His firm was listed in an advertisement as the "McKay and Aldus Iron Works, East Boston, manufacture locomotive engines and tenders, marine engines, iron and wooden steam ships, sugar mills, machinery, etc."[3] McKay, who had constructed the fastest clipper ships in history, now built railroad engines primarily and ships secondarily. His younger brother, Nathaniel, and George Aldus of East Boston were the principals of this venture;[4] however, over a quarter of the McKay yard property at 406 Border Street was being used as an engine works in addition to a small plant under lease at the corner of Border and Maverick. McKay and Aldus Iron Works had an excellent reputation as locomotive builders. Up until 1867, they had built many locomotives and tenders for the old Eastern Railroad, the Fitchburg Railroad,[5] and heavy mountain engines for the Central Pacific Railroad in California — engines with such piquant names as *Peoquop, Gold Run,* and *Favorite.*[6]

Competition during Reconstruction was brutal for Boston shipbuilders. Maine had become the center of shipbuilding by this time and had the distinct advantage of lower prices — labor, chandler supplies, wood, copper, iron all cost less in Maine than in Boston.[7] Although ship repair trade still remained centered in Boston and New York, Donald McKay's repair facilities were limited.[8] His yard lay just off West Eagle and fronted the west margin of Border Street for approximately 500 feet. It was directly north of Paul Curtis's yard, the building site of such full-rigged ships as the *Akbar* and *Belvidere,* and on the north and west sides was bordered by water. He had no drydock, but fairly large ships could lie alongside his wharf while under repair, and he kept his shipyard as active as possible within its limitations.

Meanwhile, his mind allowed him access to his first love, the wooden full-rigged ships, and in particular, the lady who would become *Glory of the Seas.* McKay was an innovator and time had not slowed his imagination nor made him content with his past successes. Drawing on nearly forty years' experience as a shipwright and naval architect, he pictured her as unique in many ways: a medium or half clipper approximately 250 feet long; of about 2,100 gross tons, relatively fast, fairly economical, and able to haul large cargoes. As he had written several years before in the Boston *Daily Advertiser:* "I never yet built a vessel that came up to my own ideal; I saw something in each ship which I desired to improve."[9] He saw *Glory* as his apotheosis. She would be 500 to 1,000 tons larger than the average American deep-water full-rigger of that era. Only three square-rigged vessels in the entire United States merchant marine measured over 2,000 tons, and none of these had any pretension to speed but had been built full-bodied for large cargo capacity.[10] The full-rigger *Norway,* for example, built in the year 1857, was 2,107 tons, had three decks, but was only 210 feet in length. Obviously, McKay's design for this new medium clipper was a break away from the generally accepted deep-water ship. But even though he felt that she could be highly successful as an ocean trader, no one wanted to finance her, and *Glory of the Seas* remained in the dream stage.

During 1867 the McKay and Aldus Iron Works continued steadily to turn out railroad locomotives. Moreover, McKay himself built a 120-foot brig, the *North Star,* of 410 tons. Late that fall, he started constructing a full-rigged ship, his first since the *General Putnam,* built 1861. Though he called his new vessel medium built, she was closer to a full-model ship than any of his medium clippers of the late 1850's.[11] In February, 1868, he mentioned this vessel, subsequently to be named *Helen Morris,* in a letter he had published in the *Boston Post,* decrying the rapid decline of Boston as a major shipbuilding port:

For myself I have constructed some years 12 ships, while at present I am engaged in building a ship of 1,285 tons, having already spent two months on her, and I cannot find a merchant who will buy her at actual cost, not including therein my own services. Within a circuit of five miles, I can count twenty shipbuilding firms which are now idle and have been since the war and most of them built from two to four ships annually before the war.[12]

Fortunately, the *Helen Morris* was sold to New York buyers, while she was on the stocks, for about $97,000.[13] However, even though he completed her sale in March, 1868, Donald McKay's financial position and that of McKay and Aldus were precarious. They had heavy mortgages on their entire operation and depended on net profits which were evidently not high.[14] Later in the summer, McKay began building a 1,503-ton full-bodied ship for Lawrence Giles and Company of New York, owners of the outstanding medium clippers *David Crockett* and *Seminole*. This firm planned to use the new vessel in the Californian grain trade, a rapidly growing business where over 175 vessels were being chartered annually at average freight rates of 15 dollars per long ton.[15] Though steamers had already taken the cream of the cargo and passenger trades across the Atlantic and were soon to control the Far East trade with the completion of the Suez Canal, square-rig sail still remained queen over the long-haul voyages via Cape Horn.

Over a period of months Donald McKay came to imagine *Glory of the Seas* as a prototype of a large grain carrier, bigger than any vessel then sailing in the California grain fleet. As the Giles ship slowly grew on his stocks at 406 Border Street, so did his plans for the future. Drawing upon his designs for thirteen other medium clippers, he finally decided to use the half-model of a 185-foot ship, modifying it for his purpose. He had previously built a wood lift model about 4 feet in length. Its short entrance with full lines in the upper body gave it a look of power and strength. The midship body was full, flowing back to a slightly concave lower body, and it had a transom stern. But when McKay disassembled the half-model and made the lines full-size on his mold loft floor, it was a completely different design.[16] The finished patterns measured 250 feet, and the transom stern on the half-model had become elliptical. He had even modified the stem to conform more to the one once gracing the *Staghound,* his first clipper. McKay was convinced that this *Glory of the Seas,* though still in the design stage, could be the acme of medium clipper construction. Late that summer, purely upon speculation and the unquenchable desire to realize his dream, he ordered the wood for her frame from a Boston ship timber merchant. McKay was now committed to build her even though he was bearing the entire expense himself.

In November, 1868, he launched his 1,503-ton full-bodied ship and began outfitting her for sea.[17] McKay felt that a brilliant future lay before this new Cape Horner so he took his wife's suggestion and named her *Sovereign of the Seas*. In the meantime the serious financial plight of the McKay and Aldus Iron Works worsened, finally culminating in the closure of their plant on December 5, 1868. Several days later, the *Boston Post* reported:

> The rumors which have been current in the street for several days, that the firm of McKay and Aldus at East Boston were in financial difficulty received confirmation by the stoppage of the works on Saturday, thereby throwing a large number of men out of employment. The journal understands that during the past week the officers of the firm have been investigated, and it is reported that the assets are considerably in excess of its list, if they could be disposed of at their real value. But the situation of affairs is such that certain creditors, in order to test the validity of mortgages which have been given, will force the firm into bankruptcy at once. There is a general feeling of regret expressed that a firm doing so large a business and with such an excellent reputation for the machinery they make, should be obliged to suspend operations. It will be hard for the hundreds of machinists and laborers who are thrown out of employment at this inclement season by the stoppage of the works, and we hope for their sakes that some arrangements may soon be made to resume operations.[18]

The next day a letter appeared in the *Post* from McKay and Aldus saying that the report was not completely correct but admitting they would have to go to court to settle a large amount of money owed to one creditor.[19]

Following the turn of the year McKay and Aldus Iron Works permanently closed their doors, and each of the principals was left desperately fending for himself. Nathaniel McKay unsuccessfully attempted to reactivate another locomotive works,[20] while George Aldus eventually contracted with the United States Navy to make signal lamps.[21] Donald McKay completed the sale of *Sovereign of the Seas* on January 11, 1869, for $113,375,[22] but the bulk of his profits went toward past-due bills. He then saw *Glory* as a way to recoup his losses, but his primary problem remained the same: no one offered to share in the costs of construction. Few investors in those postwar years were willing to risk a large amount of money on a ship that might very well turn out to be a white elephant. Fortunately, Donald McKay, for all his financial blunders, still had a reputation for honesty and integrity and could purchase much of the wood,

Above. McKay's East Boston shipyard. Daguerreotype by Southworth and Hawes, 1855. Courtesy Peabody Museum of Salem. Below. Builder's model, *Glory of the Seas.* Courtesy the Mariners Museum, Newport News, Virginia.

fastenings, and equipment for her on credit. In April, 1869, he signed a note to help finance the initial work on her, putting up "all the engine laths and other machinery and tools" of the defunct iron works as security.[23] *Glory of the Seas* was going to be a very costly venture.

McKay's heavy work load and worries during that summer of 1869 were shared by his devoted wife Mary, seventeen years his junior. She got her husband off to work in the morning, assisted him in secretarial duties, and, of course, managed their family and the large two-story home that accommodated them. The McKays normal routine began about sunrise when the shipbuilder awoke and prepared to go to work. By 6:30 A.M. he was on his way down the hill three blocks to his shipyard. His appearance on that daily walk gave some pertinent clues to his personality. Though he was strongly built, his powerful shoulders were now noticeably stooped. He wore the uniform of a master carpenter, neat work clothes that enabled him to supervise any aspect of the construction of *Glory of the Seas*. His dark wavy hair was combed carelessly back from his high forehead in the manner of a man overly impatient to get personal chores out of the way and get down to the real work at hand.

In a short time, the keel of *Glory* was laid, and then, as her oak frames were assembled on a framing stage, his workmen raised them one by one on her staunch backbone. Six days a week, his carpenters, blacksmiths, joiners, laborers, and other tradesmen put in about fifty-four hours at straight wages, a customary stint a century ago in the Boston area shipyards.[24] McKay had the unusual ability to command the loyalty and respect of all the men working for him and, if the occasion arose, many of them would go out of their way to help him. Their employer's own work day lasted from dawn until dark and many times that summer went on into the long hours of the night. Every hour had to be carefully planned out. His money was limited, chance of failure always lay before him. He supervised every aspect of her construction as she steadily grew on his shipbuilding ways, even carefully selecting his ship timber to make sure it met all his specifications for strength and durability.

On June 11, 1869, the arrival of *Sovereign of the Seas* at San Francisco added further to the strain McKay was under. His newest ship had anchored at the Golden Gate, not in clipper time, but a laggardly 147 days out from New York — a long passage that could not be blamed on uncooperative seas. *Sovereign of the Seas* was just plain slow.[25] McKay had advertised her as being an "improved *Seminole*," a vessel that could at least come close to the ninety-eight-day maiden voyage the smart full-rigger had made in 1865.[26] He couldn't have been more mistaken. To make matters worse the *Helen Morris* had already proved herself to be just as slow as the *Sovereign of the Seas*. At that very moment she was lazing her way on a voyage from Rangoon, Burma, to Liverpool which would ultimately take 205 days. To the shipping fraternity Donald McKay had lost his touch as a naval architect. Two failures in a row added no luster to his already tarnished reputation, and he had to face the fact that it would now be harder than ever to sell *Glory of the Seas* either on the stocks or upon completion.

Ignoring his frustrations, McKay remained determined to put his best into her construction. Her planking and ceiling, or inner, planking meanwhile were slowly bolted and tree-nailed together. He carefully trussed her X-like between the great oak vertical knees in her between decks to give the ship added strength. The personal interest of her creator was in evidence everywhere. She was by far the largest square-rigged vessel on the Boston waterfront and had the distinction of being the biggest full-rigged sailing ship tonnagewise in the American merchant marine, with the exception of the *Norway*.[27] Not one shipbuilder had attempted a square-rigger this large in Boston for the past ten years,[28] and she even outranked all but five of McKay's own famous clippers in tonnage and length.[29] Truly, she was meant to be his greatest medium clipper.

Even though the shipyards in Maine could generally undersell those in Boston, McKay was able to compete to a degree because he had automated his yard. He made use of every mechanical contrivance possible not only to speed up his ship construction and to cut work time loss, but also to save labor expenses, which were excessive in the Boston area. He had a fully equipped steam sawmill set up at his yard which he used to size ship timber. A unique steam-operated bevel saw was hung so that frames could be cut to the proper bevel in less than a third the time required by the use of a broad axe and adze. Though several shipyards in East Boston sized their ship timber by steam power, not one bevel saw was to be found in any down-east yard at this time. In fact, most of the small country yards were still using two-man saws in saw pits. Teams of oxen and horses were also present in McKay's shipyard, dragging heavy timbers to the likewise unique wooden derricks that he had erected next to the shipbuilding ways in order to lift heavy timbers into position on *Glory of the Seas*.[30]

Late that summer, McKay also built an 88-foot, 107-ton coasting schooner on contract. In the matter of a month, the two-masted vessel the *Frank Atwood* was launched and nearly equipped for sea.[31]

Meanwhile, construction on *Glory of the Seas* continued well. McKay arranged for the finishing touches to be provided by Herbert Gleason, shipcarver with the firm of McIntyre and Gleason at 21 Commercial Street. McKay wisely recognized that an elegant, eye-catching figurehead gracing the prow of his new craft could do much to publicize her in the shipping world. Nearly all of McKay's ships had figureheads, some of which had been carved by Gleason's father, but the classical Greek goddess that was to adorn her bow would one day be termed the swan song of the shipcarver's craft.[32] Gleason subsequently had his scantily clad model stand, head uplifted, eyes looking up, so that when her likeness was installed at a 45-degree angle on the ship, the goddess's eyes would seem to be scanning the vast seas ahead. Behind her head her right hand held flowing Grecian draperies, while her left held her robe between her breasts. The finished project was magnificent, a credit to the shipcarvers' art. In addition to the figurehead and decorative trailboards for her pedestal, McKay also had four 14-foot nameboards carved out of cedar with the name *Glory of the Seas* on them, and other elaborate carvings for her cabin and stern.

Although the ship's name had been chosen for months, it had not been officially released to the general public. Mary McKay had named *Glory,* just as she had her husband's famous clippers of the 1850's.[33] Though all her choices tended toward the sensational, she showed merchandising skills to describe them as such. Nearly everyone in the seaports of the world had heard of the McKay ships *Flying Cloud* and *Great Republic.* The sailing records of these vessels had faded into the past, but their elaborate names remained in the minds of the maritime world and continued to bring honor to their creator. So it was that the name *Glory of the Seas* as well as the sheer bulk of the ship on the East Boston waterfront publicized McKay's creative genius. But to make sure that the right people knew of her sound construction and capabilities, he continued to follow another shrewd publicity practice that his wife had instigated early in their marriage — that of elaborately describing a new ship in detail in the local newspapers. A big vessel made good newspaper copy even though sailing ships had been generally eclipsed by steamers, and once again Donald McKay and his wife collaborated with the marine reporter of the *Boston Traveler,* this time to tell how outstanding *Glory* was.[34] The urgency of the message was undisguisable — the more people knew about *Glory,* the faster McKay could sell her and get out of debt. The following appeared several days prior to her launching:

> This is a magnificent vessel of 2,102 tons register, with capacity to carry double that amount of California freight. She has three decks, with all her accommodations on the upper deck, and is of a splendid model to carry and sail. Her bow has a bold, dashy rake, with lightly concave lines below, but convex above, and terminates in a full female classical figure, with flowing drapery. The stern is curvilinear, finely formed, and the run is long and clean, and sets gracefully into the fullness of the hull. The stern is tastefully ornamented with gilded carved work on a black ground. . . . She is 250 feet long, on the line of the wales, between perpendiculars, and 265 feet from the knightheads to the taffrail; has 44 feet breadth of beam, 28 feet, six inches depth of hold, with three full decks, including eight feet, two inches height between each deck; has eight and one-half inches dead rise at half floor, and seven feet sheer, which is graduated her whole length. . . . In all the details of her construction and equipment she is as nearly perfect as a ship need be.[35]

Since the McKay shipyard was open to the public and had neither gates nor forbidding fences, it was a common thing for young children of the neighborhood to play around the unfinished hull of *Glory of the Seas.* One of these children, Frederick Pease Harlow, was to have his life shaped by *Glory.* He was from a seagoing family, and the McKay ship became a further factor inspiring him to ship out from Boston on a deep-water vessel. His subsequent adventures in the 906-ton full-rigger *Akbar* were the basis for his book *Making of a Sailor.* But even apart from this, he would live to be the only person in the world to have known *Glory of the Seas* before her launching and also to witness her end, fifty-four years later.[36]

Launching day for *Glory*. Donald McKay, in top hat, stands beside the building ramp, back to the camera. Photo by J. W. Black. Courtesy Peabody Museum of Salem.

CHAPTER II

McKay's Last Ship

Following her launch, *Glory of the Seas* lay by the old Grand Junction Wharf at the foot of Marginal Street in East Boston. There, Albert Low, one of the chief ship riggers in the district, rigged McKay's new medium clipper during the next three weeks. Low and his gang methodically stepped her lower masts one by one, starting with the mizzen and then sending up her topgallant, royal, and skysail masts. In turn, Manila hemp shrouds, backstays, and forestays were set up taut with deadeyes and lanyards. Miles of running rigging were rove off and sixteen Southern pine yards were sent aloft. By the middle of the second week, most of the great piles of running rigging, blocks, and miscellaneous gear that had been lying on the wharf had dwindled as they became part of the new ship. *Glory* rapidly neared completion.[1]

By the end of Saturday, November 13, 1869, she was fully rigged. Her lofty masts towered above the waterfront. From keel to truck her massive mainmast alone measured 188 feet, more than 20 feet higher than that of the average American full-rigger. Although her spars were not particularly heavy except on her lower masts, McKay had proportioned them staunch enough for her to set studding sails on her fore and mainmasts as high as t'gallants.[2] A second coat of black paint had recently been applied to her shapely hull. Her masts and yards were bright and shiny with varnish. The 5-inch-wide iron hoops on her lower masts with their bright red lead color stood out in contrast to the rest of her color scheme. All deckhouses were painted a flat white with varnished upper decks. On the main deck of *Glory* the hatch coamings and waterways were blue, the common shade for a Boston vessel, and they contrasted with her holystoned decks and freshly painted bulwarks.

Donald McKay had built her in accordance with the "A-1 in red" standards of the American *Record*.[3] During her construction, the marine surveyor of this classification society had periodically inspected her to insure that she fitted the special insurance standards for a ship "fit for safe conveyance of dry and perishable goods to and from all parts of the world."[4] The week following her completion, the surveyor made one final inspection and granted her the A-1 rating for a ten-year period. This entitled her to special insurance rates, but the initial costs for McKay were not inexpensive by any means, and his bill for this certification was 451 dollars.[5]

Glory of the Seas was a beautiful ship and McKay was obviously proud of her, but pride and beauty are not enough to sell a vessel. For months McKay had counted on selling her at a substantial profit to satisfy his debts, but he could not find any firm willing to meet his price of nearly 190,000 dollars.[6] The plodding records of *Helen Morris* and *Sovereign of the Seas* were still fresh in people's minds. Following the completion of *Glory*, McKay was beset by his impatient creditors who naturally needed full payment to meet their own obligations. He was fortunate his debtors could not know that only the shipyard workmen's wages had been paid. Everything else depended upon her sale. Otherwise immediate bankruptcy would have faced McKay again.

Only one way remained open for her owner to prove that *Glory of the Seas* was not a slowpoke — to sail her at his own expense to California. A fast voyage would both re-establish McKay as a good naval architect and prove that the big medium-built ship could sail moderately fast and make a profitable voyage in the Cape Horn trade. McKay, therefore, chartered her to Sutton and Company of New York to load a general cargo of merchandise for San Francisco.

Meanwhile, to satisfy his creditors, McKay had to mortgage *Glory* for 100,000 dollars at 9 percent per annum. The mortgagee was Daniel R. Sortwell, a prominent distiller from Cambridge, who had helped him out financially in the past. On November 25, 1869, McKay and his lawyers went to the Boston Customhouse to complete the enrolling of the ship

and the recording of his mortgage.[7] Shortly before her launching, several
United States Customs marine surveyors had measured her hull to com-
pute her gross tonnage; their figures formed much of her maritime legal
description:

> Donald McKay of Boston . . . having sworn that he is a citizen of the United
> States and sole owner of the ship or vessel called the *Glory of the Seas* of
> Boston, whereas Rodney Baxter is at present master . . . and A. B. Under-
> wood, surveyor for this district, having certified that the said ship or vessel
> has three decks, and three masts, and that her length is 240.2 feet, her
> breadth 44.1 feet, her depth 20 feet, her height 8.3 feet; and that she meas-
> ures 2102.57 tons . . . that she is a ship, has a round stern, and a figure-
> head.[8]

Glory of the Seas was now official.

The next morning, one of McKay's earlier creations, the steamer
George B. Upton, took her in tow at his shipyard. A northerly wind blew
as the *Upton* towed *Glory* out past Boston Light. In addition to the American flag aft, from her mainmast head flew a large white flag bearing a
blue bald eagle with outstretched wings completely enclosed in a large
circle. Though few people realized it, this was Donald McKay's house flag
and *Glory of the Seas* had the distinction of being the only ship in the
world flying it. As the *Upton* towed her toward New York, her loading
port, the colors flying over her were a source of pride to at least two men
who were aboard her that day — Captain Rodney Baxter and Donald
McKay. Once the ships passed Cape Cod to leeward, they continued down
the coast. Early Sunday morning, November 28, as they sailed southwesterly through Nantucket Sound, thick fog enshrouded them. Trying to
pass northward of Martha's Vineyard, the captain of the *Upton* evidently
lost his bearings. Suddenly, the harsh grinding of sheathing against a sand
shoal vibrated through the medium clipper. She was hard aground at
Squash Meadow Shoals, northeast of the Vineyard and about 2 miles east
of the East Chop Lighthouse. Luckily, it was low tide and all they had to
do was wait patiently for high water. Later that day, after the tide had
floated her clear, *Glory* and the *Upton* resumed the tow to New York, and
arrived there on Monday.[9]

At New York, *Glory* was berthed alongside Pier 19 on the west bank
of the East River at the foot of Fletcher Street. To advertise the sterling

qualities of his new A-1 clipper ship, Donald McKay had ship cards printed up telling of her impending voyage, and that she was loading for Sutton's Dispatch Line of California Clippers. Though it was common practice to have these cards distributed among the shipping fraternity, McKay's prime reason for doing so was to interest someone in buying her. But even without printed advertisement, she would have attracted attention, not only because of her size, but because of her beauty, the magnificent Greek goddess at her prow, and the exquisite gilded scrollwork on her bow and stern. Comparing her to the dozens of square-riggers fronting South Street, even skeptical onlookers had to admit that Donald McKay hadn't skimped on craftsmanship.

Shortly following her arrival, Captain Baxter quit the ship and McKay was obliged to find a suitable replacement to take *Glory* out to California. His choice was Captain John Giet, a driver of the clipper-era school. In the late 1850's Giet had been master of the 960-ton extreme clipper *Whirlwind*. He had spent over five years in her and had made a seventy-two-day passage, the second best on record, from New York to Melbourne, Australia, in the year 1858.[10]

All did not proceed smoothly from there. Financial problems had followed Donald McKay to New York. Without a buyer to meet his terms, he was forced to mortgage *Glory* further. On January 24, 1870, Daniel Sortwell turned over an additional 70,000 dollars, asking as a condition of the second mortgage that the freight money for the coming voyage be assigned to him. The only money excepted from the hauling profits was a reserve of 12,000 dollars for ship's use at San Francisco besides 2,500 dollars in freight money on 510 tons of coal that McKay had already collected.[11]

Two weeks later in Boston, McKay's creditors forced him to put up additional security for his debts. He granted Sortwell a power of attorney to dispose of all his real estate holdings and even granted him a bill of sale as collateral for another loan. This further tied up his personal property, his yard, his lumber, and his tools. His business life had never before been in such peril.[12]

The tremendous mental and physical strains of the past year had left McKay ill and weary, and he decided to make the maiden voyage to California himself. He knew that it would greatly publicize *Glory* if he were listed in official command of her, and perhaps an even more valuable outcome would be his return to health. Four days later, on February 11, Mc-

Kay enrolled her at the New York Customhouse for her intercoastal voyage to San Francisco. He was named as master on this document.[13] In actuality, of course, John Giet was to be in command, and McKay would be just a passenger.[14]

Glory of the Seas sailed from New York on February 13. A steamer towed her out past Sandy Hook, and after the pilot had been dropped, Captain Giet gave the command to "make all sail." He, his afterguard, and the foremast hands on board looked forward to a voyage where a fast time was uppermost, and Giet emphasized this fact to all the crew at the onset of the voyage. *Glory,* per McKay's instructions, was to be driven like a gold rush clipper. Stuns'ls and other light weather canvas would be set whenever feasible. The performance of *Glory of the Seas* was to be so impressive that the serious engineering blunders of *Sovereign of the Seas* would be forgiven.

Giet's general east-southeast course for the first 2,500 miles took him far out into the mid-Atlantic. To most modern steamer captains, who lay their course in as direct a line as possible, heading in the direction Giet chose would seem strange. But sailing ships like *Glory* were completely dependent on favorable winds and currents, and many times to them the shortest distance between two points was not a straight line.

On picking up the northeast tradewinds in mid-Atlantic, John Giet set a southerly course. *Glory* crossed the equator March 8 at longitude 30°15′W, twenty-four days out, after averaging 161 miles a day from port to the line. This was a fair run considering that she had encountered light winds.[15] During the next thirty days, she caught light southeast trades which lasted until she crossed latitude 50°S in the South Atlantic Ocean. Her time to date, April 9, 1870, was fifty-four days, twelve hours from Sandy Hook. Two days later, she was within ten miles north-northeast of Le Maire Straits, near the tip of the South American continent. Then a strong westerly began to blow and she could not pass through the narrow straits but instead had to sail around the eastern end of Staten Island off Tierra del Fuego.[16]

On April 13, 1870, she was off Cape Horn still fighting what had turned into a long series of westerly gales. Running under shortened sail, the ship was prepared for what lay before her. Her main deck was often awash with long, sweeping waves sometimes 40 to 50 feet high and completely engulfing her bulwarks. The staunch vessel seemed to be heading into a seething cauldron. Wave crests all around her were blown into a white froth by the awesome winds. The next day, amidst the gale, as she fought to make headway, an especially long, heavy sea loomed ominously on her quarter. With tremendous force it smashed against her hull, twisting the rudder head over so far that it broke short both arms of her patent steering screw.

As quickly as possible, the crew jury-rigged the preventer tiller to keep her from broaching to, and the tragedy was averted.

Slowly but surely *Glory* progressed until she completed her first rounding the Horn on April 24, when she crossed latitude 50°S, longitude 78°30'W in the Pacific Ocean. This segment of the voyage had taken a painful fifteen days and twelve hours. Then, continuing on a northerly course, she eventually caught the southeast trades which carried her up to the equator. On May 17, 1870, her ninety-third day out from New York, she crossed the line in the Pacific. *Glory*'s luck changed for the better when she picked up moderate southerly winds in the doldrums. These carried her up to latitude 14°15'N, longitude 112°W where she reached the extremities of the northeast tradewinds. Beset by light winds and calms, her captain and crew struggled to keep her sails filled. Finally, on June 13, 1870, twenty-seven days up from the equator, she dropped anchor in San Francisco Bay, 120 days out from New York. Though her maiden voyage was not considered clipper time by some, she had made the fastest run of any vessel that month.[17]

Glory had beaten the voyage time of the 975-ton extreme clipper *Sea Serpent* by fifteen days. This vessel, built back in 1850, was a survivor of the California gold rush boom years. She was still considered a smart ship in 1870, and generally made relatively fast passages between East Coast ports and San Francisco. However, *Glory of the Seas* had sailed three and a half days after her, and by the time she had reached latitude 50°S in the Atlantic, *Glory* had already forged into the lead. *Sea Serpent* did not anchor at San Francisco until June 25, eleven and a half days after *Glory*.[18]

On her arrival *Glory* attracted much attention along the waterfront. Again McKay made sure that shipping people knew of her great size, carrying capacity, and thorough construction. The descriptive account that he had helped compose back in Boston was soon published in the San Francisco *Bulletin* along with a fitting introduction which read as follows:

Cowell's Wharf, San Francisco, 1868. Courtesy San Francisco Maritime Museum.

THE GLORY OF THE SEAS
A SPLENDID SHIP IN PORT

On Monday last the clipper ship the *Glory of the Seas* — one of the finest specimens of naval architecture afloat — entered this port under command of Donald McKay, the well-known shipbuilder of East Boston, Mass. The name of this gentlemen is familiar as a household word in nearly every American and English port of commerce — the vessels launched from his shipyard plow the seas wherever the white wing of commerce is known, and have earned a brilliant reputation among nautical men. . . . She is lying at Cowell's Wharf where her cargo will be discharged.[19]

Cowell's Wharf was a small pier jutting out north from the rapidly growing waterfront. During the latter weeks of June, 1870, stevedores busily discharged the general cargo from *Glory,* spreading it over a large area until it could be hauled away by the many horse-drawn freight wagons. Her cargo was valued at $31,019, an above-average freight list from New York during 1870, one year after the completion of the transcontinental railroad.[20]

Despite Donald McKay's efforts to publicize *Glory of the Seas,* the day following her arrival brought attorneys to inform him that *Glory* was no longer his ship. Daniel Sortwell, acting under his power of attorney, had conveyed the ship along with McKay's real estate holdings to Charles E. Brigham on May 18, 1870, while *Glory* had still been twenty-five days from the Golden Gate.[21] Brigham was a partner in Gay, Manson and Company, a small iron and steel firm in Boston that had previously supplied a major part of the iron work for *Glory of the Seas.* On May 12, while McKay had been walking *Glory's* decks with some renewed strength and hopes, Brigham had been made trustee of his assets in behalf of his creditors.[22] A bankruptcy suit with him as principal had been in process for three weeks without his even knowing about it. The object of his creditors was to force McKay to liquidate all his assets. He owed forty-seven men close to a quarter of a million dollars, Sortwell's liability being the greatest at 134,452 dollars. The legal instruments which had been drawn up by attorneys for Sortwell and Brigham on May 18 had finally disclosed that the construction of *Glory of the Seas* had not been fully paid for even though McKay had mortgaged her for 170,000 dollars. He still owed Palmer Brothers and Lathrop who made her sails; George Young, who had made her spars; Albert Low, his rigger; J. F. Baker Company, his chandler and ship grocer; Brigham's firm, Gay Manson; and

Glory on San Francisco Bay, 1870. Courtesy Peabody Museum of Salem.

even Herbert Gleason, who had carved the Greek goddess for *Glory* and was due his $362.35. McKay was ruined.[23]

But in his heartbreak and despair McKay was not forgotten in San Francisco. With sympathy and understanding, his former shipyard employees who now lived on the Pacific Coast held a special banquet in his honor. Many of them no longer engaged in any form of the shipbuilding trade; but William A. McCurdy, a noted master shipwright from Puget Sound, Washington Territory, was one man present who could stand and say he was putting to use all that the great Donald McKay had taught him.[24] These men knew how McKay felt at losing *Glory,* and realized that his career seemed at a disgraceful end; however, the genuine respect they showed him that night stirred emotions in McKay that were to touch him the rest of his life.

Also on the day following the ship's arrival at San Francisco, John Giet was informed that he was no longer captain of *Glory.* Several weeks before, Brigham and the other McKay creditors had placed the management of the ship in the hands of Osborne Howes, senior partner in Howes and Crowell, one of the most highly respected shipping firms in Boston.[25] In turn, Howes had appointed William Chatfield, former master of the ship *Mayflower,* to command her.

In the weeks following the Brigham take-over, Howes and Crowell chartered *Glory* for grain at the rate of 65 shillings ($15.80) per long ton to sail for Queenstown (Cork) Ireland for orders.[26] After taking official command on June 15, Captain Chatfield was immediately occupied in preparing the ship for her cargo.[27]

Before grain could be loaded on board her, an insurance company requirement had to be met, that of laying dunnage boards in her hold to protect the perishable cargo. A wooden ship was expected to leak and work somewhat on the long, 14,000-mile voyage to England, especially as she aged; however, by laying dunnage, the sacks of grain stood a far better chance of not being damaged by salt water. Soon, in the lower hold of *Glory,* men were laying and overlapping two thicknesses of inch board supported by scantling to keep the cargo from direct contact with her ceiling; the sides of her hold were clapboarded so that grain couldn't seep through; and, to protect her cargo from shifting in a storm, the amidship stanchions were boarded up to make a staunch fore and aft bulkhead. Four athwartship bulkheads were built: one forward, one aft, and two between. Even the pump wells were cased up so that a man could go below if necessary to clear the bilge pumps, another insurance requirement. Her masts and water tanks were likewise cased up. Preparing *Glory of the Seas* for a grain cargo was no mean work.[28]

Once her dunnage was laid, stevedores started loading cargo on board. First, she received 84 tons of manganese ore primarily for stiffening purposes while she awaited the bulk of her cargo. By July 28, *Glory of the Seas,* the smart down-easter *Frolic,* and the ship *Bell Hill* had nearly completed their cargoes. In the coming week they all expected to be racing for England.

On Saturday, July 30, *Glory* lay down to her 24-foot draft mark with a cargo of 64,070 centals of grain on board. Contrary to what McKay had advertised in Boston and San Francisco, she was not a 4,000-ton cargo ship; on her sailing date, her full cargo amounted to 2,944 long tons.[29] In addition to laying dunnage, the insurance companies tried to make sure that ships carrying grain were not overladen. *Glory* had been originally insured by McKay for 170,000 dollars, and coupled with her grain cargo valuation of 125,780 dollars, insurance underwriters could not afford to be careless.[30]

On that day, Captain William Chatfield shipped his foremast hands, among them his own eighteen-year-old son William, who signed the shipping articles as an ordinary seaman. A few hours later *Glory* sailed from San Francisco with a total complement of thirty-eight on board. On her arrival in Queenstown, 112 days later, Chatfield found that she had made the fastest run of any ship sailing from California in the entire month of July. She had beaten the medium clipper *Black Hawk* by one day, the medium clipper *Charger* by two days, and several other vessels by nearly a month and more. Following her arrival in November, Captain Chatfield received orders from the grain consignee to proceed to London to discharge her cargo. This done, he sailed her across the Atlantic in ballast to America. She made an uneventful thirty-seven-day passage, arriving at Boston on March 9, 1871.

Following her arrival, Charles Brigham as trustee of McKay's assets endeavored to bring the bankruptcy proceedings to a conclusion but with difficulties. For nearly nine months *Glory* had been the object of a counteraction by Donald McKay. After his return to the East Coast in August, McKay had consulted his lawyer, who had advised him that Sortwell had exceeded his power of attorney. On August 19 McKay protested the Brig-

ham trusteeship in a two-page legal instrument. He wrote in part that
Sortwell had been granted the authority

> ... to sell all real estate lands and tenements owned by me or standing in
> my name either in fee or for any lessor estate absolutely or on condition for
> such consideration or price as he may think most for my interest....
> And whereas said Sortwell assuming and pretending to act as attorney
> in fact for me executed in my name an indenture dated the twelfth day of
> May in the year one thousand eight hundred and seventy purporting to be
> made by and between me ... Charles Brigham ... and the several ... cred-
> itors ... and also on the eighteenth day of said May assuming and pretend-
> ing to act as my attorney in fact executed in my name a bill of sale of said
> ship *Glory of the Seas* to said Brigham in trust.... I do hereby declare and
> make known unto all persons whomsoever that said Sortwell in acting as
> my attorney as aforesaid exceeded the authority granted to him by my
> power of attorney to him and his said acts are not within the scope of said
> power of attorney and are in violation of its interest and in contravention
> of its purpose and said indenture and said power of attorney are not exe-
> cuted by me, are not my deeds, and are absolutely void and of no force or
> effect whatsoever.[31]

Actually, this was a minute technicality that Donald McKay had
grasped in his desperation but, at any rate, the ship could not be resold
until he and Sortwell had settled it. The last two weeks of March, 1871,
often found McKay in lawyers' offices endeavoring to reach an agreement with his creditors in the insolvency suit. He still had the tentative
bargaining point that *Glory* was legally his ship. But at last, on March
24, both he and his wife Mary signed an assignment for benefit of creditors which quitclaimed any interest in *Glory of the Seas*. Moreover, he
disclaimed any interest in his Border Street shipyard as follows:

> All the engine laths and other machinery and tools upon said wharf and
> land. ... Also all the lumber, timber, steel standards, blocking, sliding
> ways, setways, iron, coal, tools, implements, grindstones, office furniture,
> pictures, and other personal property belonging to said McKay situated on
> the said land and wharf or in and about the buildings thereon....[32]

The debts were met. All McKay was left with was his large loving
family and the roof over their heads. Had it not been for the first, the
creditors would undoubtedly have swept the second away also.[33] McKay's
yard was partially dismantled following the consummation of the bank-

ruptcy action, and at last the state of Maine had a chance to use the modern methods of Massachusetts — the steam bevel saw went to a down-east shipyard.[34] Even the builder's model for *Glory of the Seas* was not left to its creator, but went to George Young who had made her spars.[35]

To be expected, McKay was a shattered man, now visibly aged. Yet with his responsibilities he had no choice but to attempt a fresh start. By 1874, with a spirit rising from his own talent tempered by desperation, he was serving as constructor for the United States Navy in building two wooden 615-ton screw steamers with auxiliary sail. One of these, the *U.S.S. Adams,* was built at the Boston Navy Yard; while the other, the *U.S.S. Essex,* was constructed at the Portsmouth Navy Yard at Kittery, Maine. McKay's last piece of marine repair work was on the great schooner yacht *America* in 1875. Following this, he retired to a farm in Hamilton, Massachusetts, where he died peacefully five years later.[36]

Although he had lost *Glory of the Seas* forever, she was to bring him great honor in his lifetime and after, and in her prime she would live up to the name Mary McKay had given her. Donald McKay's last merchant ship was to be a fine testimony to his genius.

CHAPTER III

A Great Captain Takes the Helm

I N March and April, 1871, *Glory of the Seas* lay idle, the victim of a legal storm. The technicalities arising from her conveyance to Charles Brigham as trustee had to be fully settled before she could be conveyed to permanent owners. McKay had been cleared of all his debts including Sortwell's two mortgages when he agreed to confirm Brigham's legal title to the ship on March 25, the day after he and his wife had assigned all their assets to their creditors.[1] This freed Brigham legally to reassign the balance of the 100,000-dollar mortgage to the purchasers and cancel the 70,000-dollar mortgage as being fully paid,[2] and also erased McKay's final large debt of 83,507 dollars.[3]

Meanwhile, *Glory of the Seas* had made no money for anyone for three months. Although she had grossed 45,188 dollars alone from her first grain voyage, Brigham had no wish to pay her operating expenses, and put her up for sale immediately.

Twelve of McKay's creditors offered to buy her in an attempt to salvage the 43,000 dollars they had invested in her outfitting and construction just seventeen months before.[4] Isaac Pratt, president of the Atlantic National Bank, an old friend of McKay's who had been a trustee of the shipyard following McKay's insolvency in 1856, offered to buy a 24/64 interest in the ship.[5] Sailing vessels in the past century were often divided into sixty-four individual shares so that if a man bought a 10/64 interest in a 64,000 dollar ship, his investment was 10,000 dollars. Also, J. Baker and Company, chandlers and grocers at 79 Commercial Street, saw that

DUPLICATE REGISTER.

No. 206

Form B. — Permanent.

№ 85065 — JHLa
JHLC.

In Pursuance of an Act of the Congress of the United States of America entitled "An Act concerning the registering
and recording of Ships or Vessels," approved December 31, 1792, and of "An Act to regulate the
admeasurement of Tonnage of Ships and Vessels of the United States," approved May 6, 1864.

J. Henry Sears of Boston,
State of Mass

having taken or subscribed the _____ oath _____ required by the said Act, and
having _____ sworn _____ that he together with Geo Briggs Andrew
Nickerson Copt & for Isaac Pratt Jr for Joshua Baker John W. Baker, Nelson L. Baker
Joshua Baker Jr Copt for David Whiton Thos E. Whiton Lewis C. Whiton Copts 6.
Cumbroke & Huckins John B. Huckins Copt ⅔ for Geo B Young ⅔ of said Lewis &c &c for ¼ ¾
of Nashua State of New Hampshire in the;
only owners of the Ship or Vessel called the **GLORY** OF THE **SEAS.**
of _____ Boston, _____ whereof _____ Elisha F Sears
is at present Master, and as he hath _____ sworn _____ is a citizen of the United States
and that the said Ship or Vessel was built at Boston State of Massachusetts
in the year 1869, as appears by Register № 75 issued at New
York Feby 9/70 Now Cancelled. Property changed.

And Said Register.

having certified that the said Ship or
Vessel has **Three** Decks and **Three** Masts, and that
her length is Two Hundred forty. _____ 5/10 feet,
her breadth Forty four. _____ 10 feet,
her depth Twenty. _____ 10/10 feet,
her height Eight. _____ 5/10 feet,
and that she measures Twenty one Hundred and Two _____ Tons
and Fifty seven hundredths, viz.:

	TONS.	100THS.
Capacity under tonnage deck	1897	14
Capacity between decks above tonnage deck	65	56
Capacity of inclosures on upper deck, viz.:	153	87
TOTAL TONNAGE	2102	57

that she is a Ship has a round Stern
and a Figure head.
And the said J. Henry Sears having agreed to the description
and admeasurement above specified, and sufficient security having been given, according to the
said Acts, the said Ship, has been duly
registered at the Port of Boston.

Given under our hand and seal at the Port of Boston.
this 18th day of April, in the year one thousand eight hundred
and Seventy one

Horace Bryant
Ep. Naval Officer.

Thomas Russell
Collector.

J. A. Graham
asst Register

Duplicate register, *Glory*, Port of Boston, 1871. Courtesy National Archives.

buying into *Glory* was a good way to recoup part of the loss (over 15,000 dollars) they had suffered. The four principals in this firm owned shares in nearly ninety vessels, which gave them an easy outlet for their products.[6] They arranged to purchase a 16/64 interest. Whiton Brothers, a chandlery firm; Pembroke S. and John B. Huckins, dealers in ship stock; George Young, spar maker for *Glory;* and Luther Roby of Nashua, New Hampshire, all bought into her, not only as an investment but also as a means of silently settling their accounts.[7] Charles Brigham's terms were generous — a total of 90,000 dollars, which included the balance of McKay's mortgage to Sortwell, was the conveyance price agreed upon.[8]

The syndicate arranged to have a managing owner to look after their interests, and the J. Henry Sears Company of Boston was selected. Joseph Henry Sears was an excellent choice, a highly respected, distinguished shipping merchant with a wide background in maritime affairs. Sears had trod the quarter deck of full-rigged ships as master for more than ten years. At the age of thirty four, he and his brother-in-law Andrew Nickerson had begun a modest shipping business in Boston. Even though the war between the Union and the Confederacy had been raging, and the general shipping market had become greatly depleted, the partnership had prospered. By 1871, they and a third partner, George Briggs,[9] had offices on Commercial Street, fronting the waterfront, and managed the affairs of half a dozen deep-water square-riggers ranging from the downeast full-rigger *Gold Hunter* of 1,258 gross tons to the wood ship *Kentuckian* of 1,234 tons. The newcomer, *Glory of the Seas,* was to become the Sears Company flagship, because she would be their largest vessel by tonnage and cargo capacity.[10]

During the second week of April, final arrangements were made with Charles Brigham and the syndicate, which had now grown to fifteen with the addition of Sears, Nickerson, and Briggs. Brigham transferred the mortgage balance over to them and conveyed the ship to the syndicate for a token 10,000 dollars. *Glory of the Seas* was now a Sears Company ship.[11]

During the final negotiations J. Henry Sears had chartered her for a cargo from St. Johns, New Brunswick, to Liverpool and had placed his younger brother Elisha Freeman Sears temporarily in command of *Glory*.[12] Like J. Henry, Elisha Sears was a thoroughly experienced shipmaster who had ably commanded half a dozen full-riggers including the clipper *Wild Ranger*. But Sears, Nickerson, and Briggs had another master in mind for *Glory*. A cable had been sent to the noted Captain Josiah

Knowles in Liverpool, and his reply had been affirmative. He would take command when the new ship reached England.

Glory sailed from Boston April 18 and arrived at St. Johns two days later. There she loaded cargo for nearly three weeks and finally sailed from the Canadian port on May 13, 1871, destined for yet another piece of hard luck — that same day she went aground on a sandbar. She was easily pulled off with little damage, but the tug owners claimed 5,000 dollars as salvage. There went a large part of her voyage net profits without her even getting far out to sea. *Glory* sailed at 10:00 A.M. the following morning and arrived without further mishap at Liverpool twenty-one days later.

Shortly after *Glory* anchored at Liverpool, a tall, middle-aged be-whiskered gentleman came aboard. Once he had stepped on her deck, the curtain fell on her unhappy past. With Captain Josiah Nickerson Knowles in command, *Glory* could begin to realize the dreams of Donald McKay.

Josiah Knowles was the son of Captain Winslow Knowles of Cape Cod. He was the youngest of five brothers, four of whom were shipmasters. Because of his adventures following a shipwreck in 1858, he had an almost storied reputation. At that time he had been master of the full-rigged ship *Wild Wave* of 1,547 tons. In January of that year he had berthed her at San Francisco, 140 days out from New York, discharged his cargo, and sailed for Valparaiso, Chile, on February 9. Twenty-four days later at 1:00 A.M. in the black of night, the lookout frantically cried out, "Breakers!" With the ship going at 13 knots it was impossible under the weather circumstances to bring her about in time. The *Wild Wave* smashed helplessly into a jagged coral reef, and was disemboweled as her dead weight carried her forward. She was a complete wreck in a matter of minutes. Miraculously, all hands including ten passengers took to the boats and landed safely on a deserted island 2 miles away. There Captain Knowles tried to figure out why and where the *Wild Wave* had gone aground. Checking his chart, which was salvaged from the wreck, he found both the island, called Oeno on the map, and the reef incorrectly located 20 miles off their true position. Later, thinking of the mistake a government hydrographer had made, Knowles wrote in his diary, "What a host of troubles that blunder of 'somebody's' had made for me."

With any kind of signal for help being out of the question, he made plans to go to Pitcairn Island, lying about 95 miles to the southeast, in an

Glory as painted by C. J. Waldron, 1872. Courtesy Harry K. Chase.

open boat. Naturally Knowles knew that since 1790 the island had been the home of crew members from the infamous *H.M.S. Bounty* and their descendants; however, he did not know that the British Government just two years before had transported all the inhabitants 3,800 miles west to Norfolk, a larger island in the South Pacific, because of overcrowded conditions on Pitcairn.

While Knowles waited for the weather to moderate, he wrote of his frustrations in his diary, "I cannot divert my mind from the one subject — home and friends." Once the surf had flattened out, he set out for Pitcairn in a longboat with his first mate and five seamen. The rest of the crew and the ten passengers were well provided for at Oeno since there was more than enough fresh water and food readily available to them. Ninety-five miles was a long distance to row in an open boat, especially for Knowles, who for years as shipmaster had not been accustomed to this kind of manual labor. In a matter of hours, his hands became blistered and raw from rowing, but turning back was unthinkable. Two days later, they arrived at Pitcairn, beached the boat, and, with sinking hearts, found themselves alone on the island. All the houses still stood, but their only inhabitants were livestock and chickens. Before trying to cope with the problem, the captain and his crew sank down to an exhausted sleep, their first in fifty-six hours. The following day they searched the entire island, and on their return were faced by yet another disaster — an unusually high surf had smashed their longboat beyond repair.

A week and a half later, on April first, Knowles set the crew to building a boat from the keel up, a schooner-rigged vessel seaworthy enough to carry them to Tahiti, 1,500 miles away. The men's first job was to scavenge the 2-mile-long by 1-mile-wide island for any tools the Pitcairners might have left behind. Their search yielded six axes, two hatchets, two chisels, three planes, a hammer, and a spike gimlet, but no saw. This meant that every timber cut for the vessel would have to be roughly hewn by hand to the required thickness and then planed.

The work began in earnest, and Knowles had to suffer stoically for two weeks before his badly blistered hands hardened. Within those first weeks all the necessary large pieces of wood were cut, dragged to the construction site, and properly sized to meet their requirements. The men burned down some houses to salvage nails, but in the main they resorted to treenails to hold the growing hull together.

On May 26, Josiah Knowles echoed what his family and friends at home were feeling when he wrote, "My 28th birthday. . . . My friends . . . [have] given up all idea of ever hearing from me again." Most of his longing centered on his wife, Ellen Sears Knowles, the younger sister of Joseph Henry Sears, who had been expecting their first child when he had left on this voyage. Indeed, there was cause for both joy and concern. At home he had a three-month-old baby daughter, but his wife was gravely ill.

On June 4 the boat hull was complete except for the caulking. The little vessel was 30 feet long, 8 feet wide, and 4 feet deep. Knowles and his six men had accomplished a masterful feat. The captain rigged her to set three sails, which were made of a multihued patchwork of silk, cotton, wool, and any other fabric they could find. Knowles decided to name the craft *John Adams* in honor of the *H.M.S. Bounty* ex-mutineer who had settled on Pitcairn and had lived a peaceful existence until his death in 1829. The men provisioned their schooner with salted pork, goat meat, and the various kinds of fruit which grew abundantly on the island. When it came to making a suitable flag for the *John Adams,* they faced a great scarcity of material, but Josiah was determined that their boat would fly an American flag. One last search finally turned up a suitable red cloth from the pulpit of the deserted church; the white stripes were the remains of a shirt; and the blue field came from a pair of overalls. The banner was so thoroughly makeshift that it had only twelve stars, but the "faded, worn, but gallant little ensign," as Knowles called it, was a source of morale to the shipwrecked mariners.

On July 23 the *John Adams* weighed anchor (an old anvil) and sailed for the Marquesas Islands instead of Tahiti because of strong head winds. The little schooner sailed 1,150 miles, reaching the island group on August 3. The following day, as they entered Nookakeeva Bay, Nukuhiva Island, the exhausted men saw a sight glorious to their eyes. In the distance lay the American sloop-of-war *Vandalia* at anchor. Knowles and his crew brought the *John Adams* alongside the Navy ship and went aboard. They told the captain what had happened to the *Wild Wave* five months before, and orders were given directly to set sail the next morning and rescue the rest of the crew and passengers at Oeno Island and the few sailors left behind at Pitcairn. Meanwhile, Knowles, with great New England thrift, sold the *John Adams* to a missionary for 250 dollars, but he carefully wrapped up the "gallant little ensign" to keep as a relic of the adventure. Knowles then sailed via Tahiti and Honolulu for San Francisco. His reception there was that of one returned from the dead. He wrote: "September 29, arrived in San Francisco. . . . My old boatman . . . looked at me in perfect amazement and exclaimed, 'My God! Is that you, Captain Knowles?' " After several days, he sailed for home via the Isthmus of Panama, arriving at Brewster on October 31. In his diary he noted with emotion, "Found my wife in a feeble state of health, but the baby well and hearty. . . . The meeting with my family was quite affecting. Such a meeting seldom takes place. Everyone had long since given me up as lost. I was indeed glad to be at home and at rest."[13]

Shortly following his return, his beloved young wife died. All the fame, glory, and excitement of the past six months dwindled next to his loss. He arranged to have his daughter Nellie cared for by her uncle and aunt, Andrew and Olivia Sears Nickerson, and, in 1859, the captain took his grief to sea at the helm of the 1,176-ton full-rigger *Expounder* of Boston. With the coming of the American Civil War he consistently kept his vessel in the general trades, braving the threat of capture and destruction by Confederate commerce raiders. In 1863 he was appointed to the command of the 1,169-ton medium clipper *Charger*.

Four years after his wife's death he began courting one of his cousins, Mary Eaton of New Bedford. The young woman was comely, slim in stature, dark-haired, with fine features and large expressive eyes. On December 6, 1864, they were wed. Because they both came from seafaring families, their interests were similar, and Mary was to share many voyages with her husband. They sailed in the *Charger* in the California trade until 1866 and then went ashore for nearly a year. In September, 1867, J. Henry Sears Company made Knowles temporary master of their 184-foot, full-rigged ship *Kentuckian*, which he sailed from New York to Leghorn, Italy.[14] On November 3, 1868, at New Bedford, Mary Knowles gave birth to twins, a boy and a girl, who were named Henry J. (Harry) and Mattie. Two years later, she bore another daughter who became her namesake. In April, 1871, the three small children and their mother were staying in New Bedford with relatives while Josiah, again temporarily in command of the *Kentuckian*, was completing a passage from New Orleans to Liverpool.[15] By this time fate was working in Boston to give the Knowles family a seagoing home, the beautiful *Glory of the Seas*.

When Josiah Knowles received the cable from Joseph Henry Sears, he was tantalized by the contrast between *Glory* and the *Kentuckian*. *Glory* was 56 feet longer and 863 tons larger, a definite challenge to any experienced shipmaster. When he first set foot on her, Knowles had just turned forty-one, and his 6-foot, strongly built frame gave seamen the impression that he was no man to trifle with. Befitting the style of the times, he sported a full beard, reddish-brown with specks of gray. He was every inch the two-fisted Yankee skipper, but he maintained a composed dignity, impressive to anyone who met him. His means of ship management differed from those of his brethren who chose to make the lives of their crews a living hell, treating them as just so much scum on a voyage. His grandson, Josiah Knowles III, offered an interesting view on his grandfather's character:

> I understand that he was a very strict disciplinarian especially as regards a clean and taut ship. He was not known to use cruel means as punishment such as use of rope's end. His punishment consisted of extra work or duty, deprivation of food, etc. He was also a man of very clean language. He never swore or used unseemly "adjectives," but his orders were sharp and to the point and were expected to be executed promptly. As I said before he was a stickler for a clean and taut ship. On his inspections he would wear a pair of white gloves and if any dirt appeared on them, somebody caught hell and was disciplined.[16]

A sailor who had shipped out with Knowles on *Glory of the Seas* added another sidelight many years later: "He could carry sail when other ships were ready to strike sail. It was drive, drive, drive all the time. It seems that there wasn't a moment's time but drive."[17] Knowles was no old woman kind of captain who snugged a ship down for the night. He was not reckless, but knew just how much sail he could carry and for how long in given circumstances, and both ship and men under his command realized their potential.

Still, being master of a square-rigged Cape Horner did not mean twenty-four hours of work a day. In his spare time, especially when he sailed without his family, Josiah Knowles kept himself busy with hobbies. On whalers it was scrimshaw, but on many other sailing ships it was needlework. Over the years Knowles made many pillows and even did tapestry. But his favorite pastime was carpentry. On Pitcairn he had learned the tools and satisfactions of woodworking, and since that time had hand built many fine pieces of furniture for his home and friends. On one voyage he constructed a four-poster bed. When in command of the *Charger,* he built a doll house for his little daughter Nellie, a scaled-down replica of his home on Cape Cod in the 1850's. He furnished it meticulously with miniature chairs, tables, beds, and the like that he purchased in England on a Cape Horn passage. He built a beautiful writing desk for himself, and for little Harry Knowles, he carved and doweled together a small cathedral-type chair. Since there were times when he and his wife had to be separated, he kept a cherished picture of her with him on board ship, and by hand contrived a 6- by 8-inch carved frame for it.[18]

Captain Knowles moved on board *Glory of the Seas* while Elisha Sears was still technically in command and was finishing the affairs of his voyage to Liverpool. At the time, Sears was also managing a bit of extracurricular business in which he took lively interest: the commissioning of a maritime artist, C. J. Waldron of Liverpool, to portray the ship in oils for his older brother in Boston. With photography still in its infancy, artists like Waldron were much sought after by ship owners and captains to show off a vessel's best qualities. And, on the other hand, a full-rigger under sail was a beautiful subject for a painter. Waldron depicted *Glory* scudding along in an action setting, close-hauled on her starboard tack in choppy seas. To show the growing intensity of heavy weather, he drew her knifing gracefully and almost effortlessly through short but steep waves, her fore and mizzen royals and main skys'l furled, while the main royal was clewed up ready to hand, in customary working order. The finished product was a masterful 3- by 5-foot painting, fittingly framed. The cost to Sears was nearly 150 dollars.[19]

Meanwhile, Knowles was arranging for a California cargo. In those days shipmasters had the authority to procure charters for vessels, especially in foreign ports. On June 12, 1871, he completed negotiations for taking a shipload of railroad iron from Cardiff, Wales, to the Central Pacific Railroad in Oakland, California. The prospective profits for this voyage were excellent, amounting to nearly 28,000 dollars in gross revenues.[20] Eleven days later Knowles displayed his commitment to *Glory of the Seas* by purchasing a 1/16 interest in her for 5,625 dollars.[21] He had definitely decided that he and *Glory* had a future together.

When he took command, Knowles kept Sears's after guard but shipped a crew of runners for his fo'c's'le, on the short run down to Cardiff, where they arrived the second week of July, 1871. Here *Glory* loaded 15,703 bars of railroad iron, an expensive cargo for an American deepwater ship sailing out of a British port. Despite the profitability, it had its drawbacks because all of its 2,811 long-ton bulk was concentrated in her lower hold and she would be stiff on the coming voyage.[22]

On August 15, Captain Knowles collected all the vouchers, notes, and disbursement receipts for ship supplies and services during the months of July and August in Cardiff. His accounts for this interval well illustrate the expenses of operating a full-rigged Cape Horner while in port. All entries were figured in pounds, shillings, and pence (one pound equaling $4.84); his total outlay was 1,409 pounds (approximately 6,820 dollars). Loading her cargo cost 143 pounds (692 dollars), and shipping the crew was another costly item. Although there was generally no shanghaiing of seamen carried on at Cardiff, Captain Knowles still had to pay out 139 pounds (673 dollars), a month's advance wage or "dead horse," for his foremast hands to a boardinghouse master, the notorious deep-sea employment agent.[23]

Glory of the Seas began her first deep-water passage under Josiah Knowles on August 19, 1871. One hundred and twenty days later, she anchored at San Francisco Bay. On his arrival Knowles wasted no words in writing a résumé of his voyage for the local shipping pages. His no-nonsense, Yankee approach is evident in his memoranda, which appeared in the San Francisco *Commercial Herald:*

> December 16 — from Cardiff. On September 6 lat. 18°N. long. 26°40′W. signalized ship *Congress* from New York to Melbourne; was 33 days to the equator in the Atlantic and 57 days to Cape Horn. Off Cape Horn spoke British ship *Warwickshire* from Cardiff; November 8 off Island of Messafuera, spoke whaler *John Coron* of New Bedford. Crossed the equator in the Pacific in 97 days; had light weather the entire passage; have been within 200 miles of this port for the last ten days with light airs and calms.[24]

Though his passage had not been exceptionally fast, he had proved, as had his predecessor John Giet, that *Glory of the Seas* was definitely no sluggard. In comparison to other ships arriving at San Francisco that month, she had made a good showing. The 1,328-ton Boston ship *Pharos* anchored at San Francisco 171 days from Wales. Even the moderately fast, iron British ship *Montgomery Castle* had taken 166 days from Liverpool. Obviously, *Glory* was in capable hands.

She unloaded her cargo at Oakland at the new Central Pacific Railroad Wharf, which had been completed earlier in the year. This 2-mile-long combination wharf and trestle had been built out from the Alameda County mainland to reach deep water so that heavily laden ocean-going

ships, many of which drew over 20 feet of water, could easily unload.
There stevedores carefully discharged the railroad iron from *Glory,* using her cock-billed lower yards as cargo booms.

Mary Knowles and her three small children welcomed Josiah when
Glory anchored off Oakland in December, 1871. The family had recently
moved from New Bedford to the San Francisco Bay region. With *Glory* in
the grain trade between California and Europe, the port of San Francisco
had technically become home base for them all. Indeed, although the
name Boston was painted on the stern of *Glory of the Seas,* the great New
England port was destined never to see her again.

CHAPTER IV

The Second Voyage

D URING the nearly two months it took to ready a grain cargo at San Francisco, Josiah Knowles made wise use of the time by hiring local shipwrights to modify *Glory of the Seas*. The improvements to be made were based on his personal preferences and on the lessons he had learned from years of practical experience at sea. One of the most evident additions was a 16-foot-square house abaft the mainmast and forward of the mizzen hatch, which was built specifically to house deck boys and miscellaneous gear. Knowles generally shipped four deck boys; it was his method of training apprentice sailors and officers. There was a reason for the precise location of the new boys' deckhouse: In keeping with an unwritten rule of the sea, anything forward of the mainmast was sailor country; anything aft of the mainmast was officer territory. Housing the boys in this manner kept them apart from the sailors and at the same time out of the officers' way. Changes were also made aft. The shipwrights extended *Glory*'s wheelhouse 12 feet forward to include not only her wheel, brass binnacle, and the helmsman's tobacco juice spittoon, but also the after cabin companionway. The wheelhouse was snugly proportioned with four windows forward, and two doors were added for access on either side. No longer would the driving winds and snow off Cape Horn (or Cape "Stiff" to those who had experienced it) freeze the helmsman in foul weather. Knowles's changes came to nearly 800 dollars, but he knew *Glory* would make up the difference by her more comfortable and safe passages.[1]

In mid-January, 1872, *Glory of the Seas* was towed to a San Francisco wharf to load her cargo from grain barges. Grain freight rates had dropped below the average for the 1871–1872 fiscal year, even though a shortage of tonnage existed on the Bay at the turn of the year. J. Henry Sears Company had to rest content with a rate of 52 shillings, 6 pence ($12.71) per long ton for this voyage.[2] Also receiving wheat were the beautiful British iron ship *La Escocesa,* the 871-ton *Montgomery Castle,* and the Sears down-easter *Titan.* By January 31, *Glory* was loaded with 64,415 centals of grain valued at 158,900 dollars. To illustrate the common fluctuation of rates in the grain market, Sears had obtained a slightly better price by 1 shilling 3 pence (31 cents) than had the owners of the *Montgomery Castle* (cargo valuation — 49,000 dollars), but the rate per ton of the main skys'l yarder *La Escocesa* (72,000 dollars) was five shillings ($1.21) higher. No matter what the rate, Knowles had a decided advantage over both of these small lime-juicers, as British ships were called in seamen's slang, in that *Glory* could carry over twice as much cargo and thereby make much higher gross profits. Her prospects were indeed promising, especially with Knowles in command.

A wooden square-rigger the size of *Glory of the Seas* required more operating capital than the British iron ships and the average Yankee square-rigger. *Glory* was one of the largest ships in the American merchant marine and not even a half dozen sailing ships had been built since 1870 to equal or even exceed her tonnage. Knowles's port expenses for *Glory* in San Francisco from December 16, 1871, through February 5, 1872, amounted to over 14,500 dollars. At the same time, Sears Company also sent a bank draft for 4,076 dollars to Captain Benjamin Berry to cover the port expenses of the 189-foot *Titan* via Knowles. This 1,288-ton vessel required less than a third of the operating capital of *Glory of the Seas* during this particular stay in port.[3]

Glory sailed for Liverpool February 7, 1872, with *La Escocesa* following her five days later. On February 22, the old extreme clipper *Young America* also sailed for England. Built by William H. Webb, this well-known ship was in her nineteenth year in the Cape Horn trade. Of sterling construction, she had outlasted most of her California gold rush contemporaries and at the same time continued to maintain a superb reputation for reliability and speed.

On this passage Josiah Knowles shaped the course of his ship so that on March 7, 1872, she lay off Pitcairn Island. No longer was it deserted. In fact, several months after Knowles sailed from Pitcairn in the *John Adams* in 1858, sixteen former inhabitants resettled the island and found a letter Knowles had left there. During the ensuing years ships that called at Pitcairn filled in details of his building the *John Adams* and his voyage to the Marquesas, so that Josiah Knowles had become a hero to the Pitcairners.

Knowles wrote the following account of his reunion many years later:

> At 12 [noon] could distinguish the homes and the English flag flying from the staff. At two P.M. we lay becalmed under the land and being about giving up seeing any of the people sighted a boat coming off. In it was a party of men, seven or eight in number. They soon hailed us and came on aboard bringing with them a large quantity of fruit.
>
> The captain of the party who was the chief magistrate of the island introduced himself to me. I made myself known to him, at which he seemed to have lost his senses. He yelled to his party, "Captain Knowles of the *WILD WAVE!*" "Are you really Captain Knowles?" and "But they said he was dead." "Are you Captain Knowles of Cape Cod?" They seemed to doubt my word until I described my hen house to them and gave them other details of my life on the island, at which they were satisfied.
>
> They insisted on my going ashore with them which I declined to do. At four P.M. they left us taking with them quite a load of books, paper, etc., promising to come back again in an hour or two. At six P.M. they came back bringing a heavy cargo of fruit, etc., live fowls, and a gift of some sort from nearly everybody on the island. My arrival had created no little stir ashore, and the whole population regretted I had not paid them a visit longer. At nine P.M. they left us with their boat well loaded with a variety of useful things including a pig. At 9:50 P.M. we took a fine breeze from the east and in two hours Pitcairn Island was far out of sight. The wind seemed to order for us this day, dying away calm on our arrival and springing up strong at dark, as the boat was leaving us.
>
> The supply of fruit was a very large cargo and we enjoyed watermelons and bananas off Cape Horn and oranges nearly all the way to Liverpool, where we arrived May 28, 1872.[4]

Glory of the Seas anchored in the River Mersey the same day as the *Montgomery Castle*, *Glory* having made the run in 112 days; whereas the lime-juicer had taken 119 days. *Glory* also beat the 1,001-ton *La Escocesa*, which finally arrived at Liverpool on June 12, 1872, 122 days from San Francisco. The *Young America*, sailing two weeks after *Glory*, had actually made a much better elapsed passage time of 104 days to Liverpool. Although better weather may have been a factor, it still probably could not have accounted for a full eight-day difference in voyage time. This aging 1,439-gross-ton vessel could still more than compete both speed- and cargo-wise with the ships of the 1870's. She and *Glory* were nearly the same length, breadth, and depth of hold, but *Glory of the Seas* was 664 gross tons larger, 2,103 tons compared to 1,439 tons. The extreme clipper lines of *Young America* and 20-inch deadrise at half floor, in comparison to *Glory*'s medium build and 8½ inch deadrise, obviously explained the difference in their sailing characteristics; moreover, the heavily sparred Webb vessel spread three skysails. In light weather she could easily run away from *Glory,* but in heavy weather the McKay vessel would normally have proved to be the more weatherly.

At the port of Liverpool *Glory* was first towed to the Birkenhead docks to unload some of her cargo into the grain sheds there. She was then berthed across the river at the Waterloo Dock to discharge the rest. While in port, Captain Knowles once again supervised routine duties: a return charter for *Glory;* painting; replenishing sea stores; laundering the ship's linen on shore. As in San Francisco, Knowles continued to make minor modifications in *Glory.* At an English port, where labor was cheaper than at home, American shipmasters were inclined to do as many of their repairs as possible. Knowles made a few more changes on *Glory*'s main deck, having a donkey boiler and engine installed in her forward house. Although this piece of machinery was not yet in general use on American ships, its diversified merits intrigued Knowles. It could be used for pumping ship in an emergency, discharging and taking on cargo, and even, for example, hauling upper topsail yards aloft when few hands remained on board in port. Knowles also had the boats relocated abaft the mainmast. Two of her 26-foot longboats were placed upside-down on wooden boat gallows built out from both sides of the new deckhouse. In addition, a small 16-foot dinghy, a recent acquisition, rested rightside-up on chocks on the deck boys' cabin top. A flying gangway, or "alley-way," a rarity on an American ship, was built to span the 17-foot distance from her after cabin top to the boat gallows. By hinges on its forward end, it could be hoisted to clear the mizzen hatchway when cargo was being discharged.[5]

Many people today harbor a mistaken, overly sentimental attitude toward the full-rigged sailing ships of the clipper and down-east eras.

The clipper ship *Young America,* by deserved reputation the fastest all-around vessel of her generation. Courtesy San Francisco Maritime Museum, Fireman's Fund Collection.

These vessels were workhorses of the seas, the deep-water freighters of yesteryear, designed to haul cargoes to all ports of the world. Lumber, sugar, bulk coal, iron, grain, case oil — any cargo within reason — these merchantmen carried as long as they could make a reasonable profit. For example, the 23,000-dollar cargo *Glory of the Seas* loaded for San Francisco was termed general because it consisted of many items. Two thousand tons of it were steam coal and pig iron, but 1,000 tons of perishable merchandise ranged from hogsheads of beer and cases of olive oil to cases of mustard.[6]

Final preparations for *Glory* to sail included hiring new fo'c's'le hands to replace the twenty-three men who had deserted upon arrival in England,[7] which was a common occurrence. All shore bills, which amounted to 3,903 pounds, 2 shillings, and 6 pence, had to be paid before she left port.[8] By Friday afternoon, everything looked shipshape on board. *Glory* lay at a wet dock with sails all bent. Her hull was down to the 24-foot draft mark, while above the waterline, a fresh coat of black paint enhanced her sides. All spars were scraped and coated with varnish; all her standing rigging was smartly set up taut; and her yards were nicely squared. She was every inch a first-rate Yankee deep-water ship, one of the most admirable breed.

Saturday morning she cast off. This was the last time she would be in contact with land for three and one-half months. Josiah Knowles recorded this day and the next two in his abstract log:

Commence Sea Account, Saturday, July 27, 1872
    At one o'clock passed the Waterloo pierhead in tow of steamer *Resolute*. At three P.M. pilot and tug left us at Bell Buoy. Ship in charge of Channel pilot Mr. Toavaskas. Made all sail. Light breezes from SW to SE. Through the night light airs and calms. Morning off Holyhead. Light breezes from SW. Stood over to Irish coast. At noon close in, tacked off.

Sunday, July 28, 1872
    First part — very light breezes from SW. Middle part — much the same. Made several tacks at midnight. Bardsey Island light bore east distance 15 miles. Morning — fresh breezes from south, misty and raining. At nine A.M. passed two miles to windward of Tuskar Rock. Wind increasing and a very heavy sea on. Took in all light sails. At noon the Smalls Lightship bore NW distance four miles from which we take our departure. Intended landing Channel pilot here but blowing so could not and proceeded out on course trusting to fall in with some inward bound vessels.

Monday, July 29, 1872, One day at sea

Commences with fresh gales from SSE Thick and rainy. Heavy swells. Under easy sail. Middle — more moderate. Made all sail. Ran down Dutch brig and put our pilot on board, she bound in to Queenstown. Latter — light breezes from east and north, cloudy. Made 120 miles.

Lat. obs. 50º 34'N
Long. DR (dead reckoning)
8º23'W[9]

In this modern age of electronic navigational aids, some readers may find it hard to visualize the seamanship required for Josiah Knowles to guide his big square-rigger. Celestial navigation — that is, sailing by the position of sun, moon, and stars — largely depended upon good visibility. If the sky was overcast, or the horizon could not be clearly discerned, Knowles would not take a fix. While today, of course, the shipmaster of an ocean-going vessel can pinpoint his position accurately by instrument despite fog or cloudy weather.

For determining latitude, Captain Knowles "shot the sun" by using his then modern sextant to measure the altitude of celestial bodies above the horizon. By proper manipulation he arrived at his latitude after checking his calculations with special navigational tables. His longitude was determined by the chronometer, a compact clock of the highest accuracy, carefully set for the time of day at Greenwich, England; with it he computed the ship's longitude by determining the difference in time at his new position from that at Greenwich.

For example, at about eight a.m., on a typical day, August 2, 1872, Josiah Knowles stood aft on the half poop of the *Glory* as she sailed majestically through the waters of the North Atlantic on her starboard tack. He prepared to shoot the sun to arrive at her longitude, 17 degrees, 18 minutes west. Meanwhile, his chief mate was below in the after cabin getting an accurate reading of the ship's chronometer. As Knowles yelled "Time," the mate wrote down the exact hour, minute and second. At the same instant, Captain Knowles took a reading of his sextant.

Four hours later, Captain Knowles took a noon sight to establish the ship's latitude, 40 degrees, 57 minutes north. Then, going below, he used the three readings along with special navigational tables to plot the *Glory*'s correct position.* The following is that day's position, which he computed by using logarithms:

---

* This paragraph and the one preceding it have been corrected in this edition thanks to Capt. Allan Villiers and Capt. Adrian F. Raynaud.

Friday, August 2, 1872, Five days at sea

10°03'	42°45'	.12354	17°38'21"	5'57"
19"	10'	.02094	40"	8°48'40"
10°03'19"	42°55'	9.30947	17°39'	8°54'37"
29"	41°12'	9.76200	90°	89°50'
10°03'48"	72°21'	19.21595	72°21'	66°31'
8°54'37"	156°28'	9.60797		23°19'
1°09'11"	78°14'			17°38'
	12°55'		Lat.	40°57'N
Long. 17°18'	35°19'			
noon				

Made 110 miles   104-36=110 miles

WSW¼W*

Throughout this day light breezes from NW to west. Fine, pleasant weather, smooth sea

On overcast days, Knowles determined his position by dead reckoning, as on August 11, 1872, when clouds and fog cancelled the visibility. In the chartroom immediately forward of his cabin on the starboard side, he laid out his course taken from his last known position. He checked the angle of this course with a meridian to establish his true compass error because the earth's magnetic pole is different from the North Pole. To find his position accurately, he prudently took into consideration that prevailing winds and currents might blow *Glory* off course. Knowles was a careful navigator. His margin of error in dead reckoning was normally slight — no mean skill considering the limited navigational equipment at his disposal. With years at sea behind him and sixteen of those as master, Knowles had earned an ability to read or interpret the winds and ocean currents that the deep-water sailor of today, with his heavy dependence upon electronic aids, might consider uncanny.

Glory of the Seas crossed the equator in the Atlantic on August 23, twenty-six days from Liverpool, passing, as Knowles' log said, "close to Island of St. Paul. At noon it bore south ten miles." Continuing southerly, on her fifty-fifth day out, "Cape Horn bore northwest and north distance 40 miles." In those southern latitudes, especially near the tip of South America, Knowles needed a barometer. This instrument, by measuring the weight of pressure of the atmosphere, indicates changes in

---

* The calculations for August 2, 1872 have been corrected in this edition thanks to Capt. Stanley R. Haight.

Captain Josiah Nickerson Knowles as he appeared ca. 1895. Courtesy Mrs.
Alice Knowles Roberts.

weather. Many times, disaster at sea has been averted by following its advice. For example, a sudden fall in *Glory*'s barometer from 28.60 down to 27.80 off Cape Horn on September 29, 1872, foretold that a storm was imminent. The barometer was correct, as Knowles's terse log entry the following day disclosed: "Lightning and heavy squall . . . squally and heavy sea running. Carried away steering gear. Fixed ropes."[11]

Squalls among men were also plaguing Knowles at this time. The main problem was the lazy and unruly boatswain, or fourth mate, Jonathan Lee. The captain wrote the following in the back of his abstract log book:

September 25, [1872] In tacking the ship this morning I spoke to the boatswain Jonathan Lee for having the braces fouled and not attending to them properly, to which he gave me insolence. I told him that if he ever gave me anymore, I would put him in the forecastle as he was a useless officer avoiding all work and incompetent to take charge of men, [signed] J.N.K.

Again, a week later, as *Glory* fought against the westerlies in rounding the Horn, he wrote:

October 2 — Mr. Shield and boatswain had some trouble, the latter grossly insulting Mr. Shield. I then told him if he ever used any name to any of the officers he would go forward.

October 7 — At 11 A.M. wore ship. Boatswain out as usual, no appearance of being stiff or anything the matter. At one P.M. in tacking about, saw all the watch about but the boatswain. Asked Mr. Shield whose watch was on deck. When he [Lee] said he was laid up, sent for him to come aft. He came and appeared to be very stiff. I asked him what was the matter. Said he was stiff and had pains all over him. I told him he was moving about limber enough two hours ago and it was very singular that he should be drawn up in that shape so suddenly. How, he would not be much missed if he was laid up. He was of little use. He then cursed abusive language. I told him he was the most miserable scoundrel and that he could pack up and go in the forecastle, that he was no longer an officer for he was not competent to go officer in anything that floated the ocean. If he wanted any medicine to get it from the steward. He went forward to the boys' room where he has been sleeping for a few days and took his things to the boys' forecastle.

November 4 — Went to the forecastle and called the boatswain out. It was a pleasant day for him to come out and sun himself. That would do

him more good than anything. Have had him come aft several times to
see how he was but said he was not much better and sent the steward frequently to see if he wanted any medicines. At noon I went forward to take
the sun. Found boatswain lying on the deck in the shade reading. Took his
pipe from him and told him I thought he was making mast if not all and
was as able to work as any man in the ship, as he could scarcely move when
any man was looking at him and not a half hour before he ran up in the
forecastle as quick and limber as any one could, not knowing anyone was
looking at him. Mr. Pearson saw him to which he personally signs his
name as acknowledging it. [J.P.P.] He, boatswain, was very much enraged
at this and said if he had two of his "tipperance boys" here he would fix me
and Pearson out. He also used very insulting language. Mr. Pearson asked
him then if he was not able to work in sails, he was not able to do anything.

November 5 — Fitted up a place under the alleyway for "b" where I
could see to his medical treatment as I find he has been going out evenings
forward, which I think is very injurious. I don't think that he is a safe man
to be among sailors. As to his health, looks as well as can be. Says he is in
good bodily health except he is stiff. Says he had a fall some two months
ago which he never reported until lately. I told him I thought he would
improve alone faster than in the forecastle. Has a good, comfortable place.
Comes out when he wants to.

November 6 — Called in "b" this morning and inquired after his health,
to which he is much better and thinks he can work some on sails if I would
like for him to. I told him I thought he was getting well much too fast and
had better wait where he is for a few days longer. Been out all he wanted
to today.

November 6 — "b" still better today and thinks he can do some work but
told him he had better wait a few days longer and get strong. Out walking
decks most of the forenoon and out in the P.M. as much as he chose to.

November 9 — Boatswain came and wished to go to work. Would do all
he could which is all I ask of any man. Says his back is much improved but
that he feels weak. At one P.M. Sea. At nine o'clock called on J. Lee to see
how he was. Says he is very weak. There is not air enough in his room. So
took 2nd mate's room, he taking the place Lee had been occupying. At first,
there was too much for him and had canvas nailed up all, and was out on
deck six hours yesterday, and same today. When in his room kept it
locked as I wish to know how much he is out and when.[12]

So ended the rebellion of the ship's malingering boatswain. Knowles
did not record what discipline, if any, had been meted out to Lee, other
than isolating and disgracing him in the eyes of afterguard and fo'c's'le
crowd alike, but it evidently had the desired effect. He had finally almost
begged Knowles to give him some duty. On a true "hell" ship, of which

there were many, Lee could not have gotten away so easily with his insub-
ordination. One black night, or during a storm, he would have been silently and swiftly knifed by one of the officers and thrown overboard to be
food for sharks with no one the wiser. A man of Knowles's principles and
patience wasn't found on most deep-water vessels.

The last five days of this passage, *Glory* caught strong north and northeast winds enabling her to make port in 119 days. On anchoring in San
Francisco Bay on November 25, 1872, a familiar vessel passed her. Being
towed out to the Heads was the slowpoke *Sovereign of the Seas* on her way
to England with a 2,250-ton cargo of wheat.[13] In spar plan the two ships
were almost identical in arrangement including stuns'ls on fore and
main except that *Glory*'s spars were all proportionally larger than her
1,503-gross-ton sister. At this point these ships and the *Helen Morris* were
the only Donald McKay–built full-rigged ships left under the American
flag, and soon even that number was reduced when the *Helen Morris* was
destroyed by fire at sea off the coast of Chile.[14]

Mary Eaton Knowles and her three children moved on board *Glory*
while she lay at San Francisco. The children were now three and five, old
enough to make the next voyage with their father. Knowles's first child
Nellie would not be traveling with the family. By this time she was of
school age, and her aunt and uncle looked upon her as their own daughter. They would continue to care lovingly for her and would provide her
with an uninterrupted education impossible for a child at sea.[15] Sometimes frustrating but always lively times lay ahead for Mrs. Knowles and
her husband in trying to raise three vivacious children in a space 24 feet
by 45 feet (the ship's afterhouse), shared by as many as six other people.

About the only change Knowles had to make for his family was the
addition of a specially made bed for little Mary and Mattie. Under his
own bed he built a little trundle bed. At night it could be pulled out like
a drawer and during the day pushed back into place out of the way.[16]

In the course of a year in the California grain trade many commonplace but action-filled events took place on a typical full-rigged ship.
Everyday maintenance and repairs on the vessel meant never-ending,
back-breaking work for the iron men in the crew. Occasional discipline
problems and quarrels were part of the life. For those men who went
down to the sea in ships excitement was often the bitter experience of
fighting different weather extremes. But no matter whether gales had
blown off the English coast or the ship had lain becalmed in the dol-

drums; whether the passage had been under the torrid sun of the tropics, or on the frigid, ice-choked seas around Cape "Stiff," at the completion of a round passage hardly a man existed who would not say with pride that he had shipped aboard *Glory of the Seas* under Josiah Nickerson Knowles.

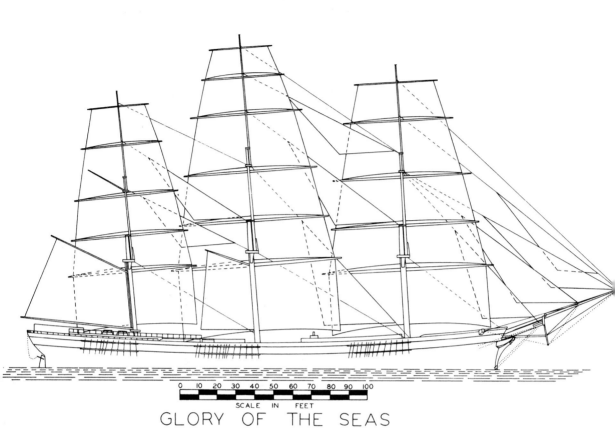

GLORY OF THE SEAS

SCALE IN FEET
0 10 20 30 40 50 60 70 80 90 100

Sail plan, *Glory,* as of 1875. Drawing by the author.

CHAPTER V

"A Very Tedious Passage" Is Redeemed

As the grain year of 1872–1873 (July 1, 1872, to June 30, 1873) progressed, 136 American vessels including *Glory* and *Sovereign of the Seas* were chartered for grain from San Francisco Bay.[1] When *Glory* made port in November, 1872, many British iron ships had already received charters 2 shillings higher per ton than those of the wooden-hulled ships. Even so, American shipowners had no reason to complain about the discrepancy, because grain rates were extremely high, running 4 pounds or more per ton (approximately 20 dollars).[2]

On January 15, 1873, *Glory of the Seas* sailed for Liverpool. She was followed three days later by the 196-foot *John Duthie*, a British wool clipper with a reputation as a flyer. Her composite-type hull had a decided advantage over the average American down-easter, not only in receiving better insurance rates, but also in having a longer life expectancy. A composite ship had iron frames and keel with hardwood planking and decking, a sounder construction than the all-wood vessels that were susceptible to dryrot and the starting of fastenings as they aged, and, therefore, called for more upkeep. The 190-foot, iron-hulled *Montgomery Castle,* in shipbuilding techniques one step beyond a composite vessel, sailed three days after the *John Duthie.*

On February 19, 1873, *Glory of the Seas* again neared Pitcairn Island. She was now a familiar sight to the islanders, easily distinguished close up by her main skys'l, beautiful figurehead, and long black hull. Knowles wrote at noon this day and the next:

> Wednesday, February 19th, 1873, 35 days at sea
> Throughout, light breezes from east. Pitcairn Island bearing south by west distant ten miles. Chronometer right. At 11 A.M. hove off Pitcairn Island and was boarded by two boats. Sent me on shore for things for us. Ends — light breezes from east and pleasant. English bark *Santiago* hove to here waiting for fresh supplies.
> Made 115 miles. Long. 30°11'noon Lat. 25°01'
>
> Thursday, February 20th, 1873, 36 days from San Francisco
> Throughout this day light breezes from east, pleasant weather. At 12:30 P.M. went on shore at Pitcairn for an hour and got a lot of fruit and proceeded on our way. Left the English bark *Santiago* off the island, the captain on shore.[3]

Some weeks later, Knowles wrote a much more detailed account of this visit to Pitcairn Island, in the following letter to a friend in San Francisco:

> SHIP "GLORY OF THE SEAS,"
> AT SEA, Wednesday, May 7, 1873.
> Dear Sir,
> I have not forgotten that I promised to write on my way to Liverpool, and if I fulfill my promise, it is about time to commence. . . . I am now 112 days at sea, and some distance from my port yet. Was in hopes to have been there before this, but have had nothing but light winds and calms. . . . Thirty-five days out I made Pitcairn's Island and was soon up with it. It was a pleasant day and a little breeze. Some time before I got up to the island the boats were off alongside, and were very glad to see me, or at least pretended to be, and I guess they were. They were very anxious for me to go on shore, so I went, and was well paid for going. On the rocks at the landing stood about twenty-five or thirty women and children, all of them barefooted and a great many were inclosed in rather scanty wardrobe. As soon as the boat came in they rushed out to me and would have taken me on shore in their arms; but I took the hand of one buxom lass and sprang on the rocks dry-shod, and on the very rock which I built my boat on. They gathered around me as thick as flies. "And is this really Captain Knowles?" I expect they would have kissed me if I had made an advance, but, you know, I am a diffident youth in the presence of ladies. Miss Rosa Young, the belle of the island, presented me with a huge boquet, which took several men to carry. After greeting them there, we started up the hill. After a hard climb, we arrived at the top rather fatigued. There another group —

an old woman looking as if she went there in the *Bounty,* and a dozen or so almost naked children. I asked her if all those children were hers. No, she said, they were her grandchildren. Then we took some refreshments — cocoanut milk and oranges. Then we went on to the settlement. Everything looked very natural to me, other than seeing so many about there and the houses occupied. Went into all the houses. They did not look as if they had many luxuries, nor as if they were very industrious; but it had been a dry season and they were short of most everything. Went into my house. It looked as natural as could be. Everything just as I left it — the table I ate off all the time I was there, was in the same place as I left it. It is occupied by Mr. Moses Young, who had twin daughters fifteen years old and as pretty as pinks, and if dressed as our young ladies are, they would take the shine from a great many who pass for belles. After walking about for an hour, looking at my old resorts, we started for the landing. You ought to have seen our escorts. Not every king has had such a one. Webb (a young gentleman who is with me) and I headed. Then in order came followers: Mary Young, one of the twins, with a bottle of cocoanut oil; her sister with a bottle of syrup; Mrs. Young with two hens under her arms; Alphonso Young with figs; Moses with a large bunch of bananas; women with a lot of ducks; man with a sheep; woman with a pumpkin; and so it went, every man, woman, and child having something — enough to load the boat. It looked good to me to see my ship lying off there to take me away, and it brought to mind the many hours and days I spent there, always looking off, hoping to see some ship coming to take us off, but no such good sight did we see. Then we had to leave them, after an affecting parting, and the last I saw of them they were waving their hats, or anything they could find to wave at us. I shall long remember the day spent there. Got lots of fruit, of which we have a lot now. So ended my visit. I gave them lots of things, and promised to call again when I passed there. Wish you could have been with us.

Yours, etc.,
Josiah N. Knowles.[4]

By that time, *Glory of the Seas* was thousands of miles away from Pitcairn Island nearing the final leg of this voyage. Captain Knowles recorded her last two days at sea in his abstract log as follows:

Thursday, May 22nd, 1873, 127 days at sea
  First part — light breezes from NW. Pleasant. At five P.M. spoke Cork pilot. At nine o'clock spoke and boarded by another pilot. Latter — moderate from NNW. Ends — pleasant. Exchanged signals with English ship *Ganick.* Mine Head bearing by compass 20 miles NE.
Long. 7°00' noon   Lat. 50°58'   132 miles

Friday, May 23rd, 1873, 128 days at sea
Throughout this day moderate from SW. Passed Tuskar at four o'clock. At nine A.M. we passed Holy Head. At two o'clock took pilot. At nine o'clock anchored in River Mersey.[5]

Meanwhile, the *John Duthie* arrived at Liverpool five days before her, having made a passage of 122 days. *Montgomery Castle* also beat *Glory*, arriving the same day at Liverpool but 122 days from San Francisco. Still, none of the three masters could boast of having broken any records on their passages.

As stevedores unloaded the cargo from *Glory* into the grain sheds at Liverpool, Knowles received orders from Joseph Henry Sears to proceed to New York, as soon as discharging and repairs were completed. There she was to load once again for Sutton's Dispatch Line. Five weeks following her arrival at Liverpool, she cleared for New York, and the first five days, as taken from Knowles's abstract log, were merely a preview of the misfortune that would dog her all the way to New York:

Ship *Glory of the Seas* from Liverpool to New York, July 1st, 1873
Sea Account, Wednesday, July 2nd, 1873
At noon left the River Mersey in tow of tug *Retriever*.
At three P.M. tug left us off Holy Head. Made sail with wind SW.
Ends — thick and rainy.

Thursday, July 3rd, 1873
Throughout, thick and rainy with a head wind, moderate. At 12 midnight Bardsey Light bore NE distant six miles. Ends — thick. Judge ourselves halfway between Bardsey and Tuskar.

Friday, July 4th, 1873
Throughout this day headwind. Making short tacks. At six o'clock close into Tuskar. Squall from WNW. At noon Smalls Lighthouse bore distant four miles.

Saturday, July 5th, 1873
First part — moderate from west, pleasant. At seven P.M. put pilot on board Dutch bark bound to Liverpool. At nine o'clock lightship bore west five miles. At one A.M. it bore north eight miles. Middle — from SE. Thick. Ends — fresh from S to SW. At 11, Ring Sail bore NW ten miles.

Sunday, July 6th, 1873, Five days from Liverpool
Commences strong breezes from south. Thick and rainy. At four P.M.

blowing heavy, took in light sails. At five p.m. wind shifted to NW and blowed a gale for four hours. Split crossjack, lower main topsail, upper fore topsail, main top staysail, and inner jib. Middle — moderate. Made all sail. Reefed all sails lost. Ends — light from WSW, pleasant. Several ships in sight all with loss of sails.
Long. DR 7°57'W Long. by obs. 8°00'W Lat. obs. 50°07'N"[6]

Those five split sails meant several days' steady work for *Glory*'s sailmaker. Every square-rigger carried a sailmaker, just as every steamer carried a chief engineer — an experienced professional whose duty was to keep the ship's motive power in working order. In a case like this one, the split sails were unbent and lowered to the deck, while replacements from the sail locker were sent aloft and bent on one by one. Then, with new canvas for patching and with sailmaker's palm and needle, the damaged sails were repaired. Finally, they were either rebent or stored in the sail locker, depending on the over-all condition of the sails that had been sent aloft to replace them.

In July of 1873, a steamer captain would have plotted his course southwesterly from England on a great circle to a point in about lat. 42°N to long. 49°W, and then piloted his vessel toward New York. Today, a large ocean liner such as the *S.S. United States* makes the run from England to New York in about four and one-half days, whereas sailing ships in the nineteenth century often beat against the westerlies in the North Atlantic for thirty to forty days.

With winds blowing from south and southwest, Captain Knowles set a northwesterly course up to lat. 53°15'N once he was clear of St. George's Channel. On her ninth day at sea the wind hauled around to west, allowing *Glory* to head south-southwest. Both this day and the next, with fair winds blowing, she reeled off 213 miles each twenty-four hours. Knowles's account in his log for Friday, July 11, was: "Throughout this day fresh breezes from WNW. Cloudy most of the time. All sail set by the wind. Made 213 miles." She continued on this general course down to latitude 40°47'N, longitude 25°38'W, where the wind shifted again to southwest. After several more days of "pleasant weather" the wind began blowing from NW, so he steered her on a generally southwesterly course, making a fair run of 221 miles on July 20, his nineteenth day from Liverpool.

It was about this time that the captain sat down one day in the after cabin and wrote a medical report in the back of his abstract log book. It concerned a foremast hand suffering from one of the venereal diseases common among deep-water sailors. At sea, isolated from women and cooped up in cold cramped quarters, sailors found little to do in the way of recreation except for fancy rope work or building ship models. While off duty, to break the monotony, they could either walk around the decks or up aloft, hardly an inspiring way to pass leisure time. After four, five, or six months of this at a stretch, the crew upon hitting the beach was ready to cut loose in a big way. The results were often what Josiah Knowles now set down:

> About two weeks before leaving Liverpool Russell informed the mate that he had the venereal disease. I gave orders for him to go to the hospital for treatment to which I supposed he went, but after getting at sea, find he only went there twice. After being at sea a few weeks he came aft for medicine. I told steward medicine to give him which he took for a few times and stopped. He then took some medicine for the officers which he said had cured him. This was about the middle of July. [He] Told me the medicine the officers gave him had cured him. Told him he had better look out or it would come out on him again.
>
> About the middle of July I saw him walking rather stiff and on inquiring found it had come out on him again. Ordered him medicine which I find he does not take as ordered and requires much persuasion to keep himself clean and attend to himself. Have no doubt he would have been well long ago if he had taken his medicine or if he had gone to the hospital in Liverpool as he was told to do. It is through his own neglect that he is not well now. [Signed] — J. N. Knowles.[7]

Off the Grand Banks of Newfoundland, *Glory of the Seas* sailed into thick foggy weather which meant Knowles had to calculate his course by dead reckoning. Then, heading westerly near latitude 40° for four days, she caught a strong breeze from southwest which carried her up to lat. 44°07′N.

The most exasperating day for him this voyage was August 1st, when the ship lay becalmed. Knowles wrote:

> Friday, August 1, 1873, 31 days at sea
>   Throughout this day light baffling airs and calms. Mostly calm and hot. Made nothing but drifted for 30 miles east Long. 55°40′ Lat. 40° Lost 30 miles[8]

The most annoying thing about that day was that *Glory of the Seas* was supposed to be heading toward New York, not back to Liverpool.

Glory off the Welsh coast, as painted by Samuel Walters. Courtesy San Francisco Maritime Museum.

Knowles recorded the last six days of this frustrating voyage as follows:

Wednesday, August 6th, 1873, 36 days at sea
First part — fresh breezes from NE, pleasant. Middle — moderate from NNE. Latter — light airs from north, pleasant. Passed many fishing vessels. At six A.M. New York pilot spoke with us, but would not pay him offshore pilotage so did not come on board.
Long. 68°15′ noon Lat. 40°56′ Lat. DR 41°10′N
Long. 68°15′W DR Made 175 miles

Thursday, August 7th, 1873, 37 days at sea
First part — light baffling airs and calms from north. Middle — light airs from S to SW. Latter — moderate from SSW, pleasant. *Young America* in company. Passed through tide rips. At noon [old] South Shoal Lightship bore by compass NW by N.
Lat. by DR 40°50′N Long. DR 69°50′W. Chronometer about right by DR. Distance eight miles.

Friday, August 8th, 1873, 38 days at sea
At one P.M. South Shoal Lightship bore north five miles distant. Fresh breezes from SSW. First part — fresh breezes from SW to WSW. Cloudy. At eight P.M. Gay Head Light bore by compass NE 15 miles. Through the night moderate from SW to west, thick and heavy rain. Latter — light from SW to WSW, cloudy. No sight at noon. Made 94 miles. Long. 71°18′ DR Lat. — no sight at noon

Saturday, August 9th, 1873, 39 days at sea
Throughout this day light winds from westward. At five A.M. made Montauk Point. Light being NNW distant eight miles. Ends — light airs from NNW. Made nothing and wore, then nothing.
Long. 71°38′ noon Lat. 39°16′

Sunday, August 10th, 1873, 40 days at sea
Throughout this day light baffling airs and calms from north to SE Pleasant. Long. 72°50′ noon Lat. 39°57′ Made 70 miles

Monday, August 11th, 1873, 41 days at sea
At four P.M. took New York pilot. At eight P.M. up to lightship. Lay to until steamer towed us in and anchored at Battery at nine o'clock. So ends a very tedious passage. [signed] J.N.K.[9]

Knowles's final remark mirrored his opinion of the entire voyage. It had been indeed a passage where the winds, in mariner slang, were "antitrades" and most certainly anti-*Glory of the Seas*. The captain had further reason for disgust after learning that *Young America* had arrived three days before her, but only twenty-three days from Liverpool.[10]

After making port, Knowles made arrangements to have *Glory* docked and resheathed with yellow metal, an alloy of copper and zinc. Almost four years had passed since she had been sheathed by Donald McKay's workmen at East Boston. Even though her old suit was not badly corroded by sea action or in other ways damaged, it was time for a renewal in keeping with American merchant marine standards. Once she lay high and dry, laborers quickly stripped off her old sheathing. Her hull was thoroughly inspected and caulked before tar and sheets of felt were applied up to her 22-foot draft mark. After several days of this intensive work she was ready to receive the first of the thin yellow metal plates. Over 3,500 individual sheets, each weighing six and one-half pounds and measuring 14 by 48 inches, were necessary for the job. According to general custom in the New York repair yards, Knowles had purchased the sheathing earlier in the name of J. H. Sears Company. He had then arranged to have the $12\frac{1}{2}$ tons of metal taken to a concern on South Street where nail holes had been punched by a special machine in the outer edges of each sheet, and then delivered back to the dockyard for application to the waiting hull of *Glory of the Seas*.[11]

By the beginning of October, all repair work had been completed. She was undocked and towed to Sutton's pier on the East River, just below where the Brooklyn Bridge was already three years along in its construction. There New York longshoremen carefully loaded her 47,303-dollar cargo, which was consigned to the George Howes Company in San Francisco.[12]

Mrs. Knowles and the children were "down" at New Bedford visiting her family much of the time *Glory* lay in port, and the Captain had joined them as often as he could get away from the ship. They were a well-liked couple with hosts of friends glad to see them after a year's absence. Two months in port gave them a chance not only to take in a few sights for the sake of the children, but also to see relatives on both sides of the family. When their shore leave was over, they held a bon voyage party on board ship and prepared to sail for San Francisco on a most propitious voyage. With rough but cooperative winds ahead all the way, *Glory of the Seas* was about to join the ranks of record breakers.

The following excerpts from Knowles's abstract log best tell the story:

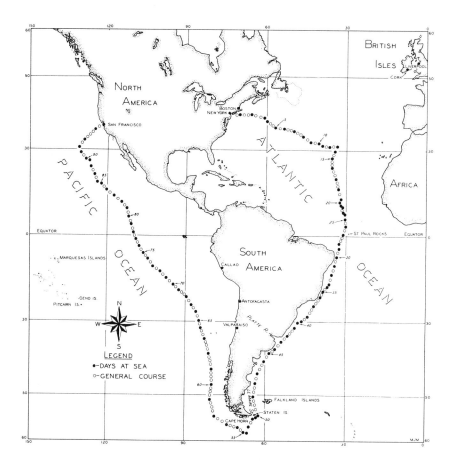

Glory's passage from New York to San Francisco, October 13, 1873, to January 16, 1874. Map by the author.

Monday, October 13, 1873, Sea Account
At eight o'clock took tug *C. F. Walcott* at Pier 18.[13] Went on board with quite a party of friends. At ten o'clock started for San Francisco. At 12 o'clock noon off Sandy Hook.

Tuesday, October 14, 1873, One day at sea
At one P.M. tug left us outside the Bar. Pilot and friends left in her. Throughout this day light breezes from west-northwest to west-southwest. Clear and pleasant with smooth sea. All sail set before the wind. Long. 70° 40′ noon, Lat. 39°55′ Made 157 miles

    . . . October 16, 1873 . . . children and all a little seasick. . . . October 20 . . . ship rolling badly . . . October 21 . . . ship rolling badly throughout. . . . October 24, 1873, Eleven days at sea . . . fresh gales from south-southwest, thick and rainy, heavy sea from southeast. Ship pitching heavily . . . made per log 72 miles.[14]

The passage had started poorly for Mattie, Harry, and little Mary Knowles, but by November 3rd the weather had moderated considerably. During that day a small festivity was held aft for the twins, for their father wrote in his log, "Children's fifth birthday." Captain Knowles made no further mention of the children the rest of the voyage. Apparently they had achieved their sea legs and were relegated somewhat to the background of their father's chief concerns.

The last two days of the passage appear in the log as follows:

Thursday, January 15, 1874, Ninety-four days at sea
    Throughout this day strong winds from southeast, thick and rainy. No observations.
Long. DR 125°02′W Lat. DR 36°14′N Made pr. log 300 miles

Friday, January 16, 1784, Ninety-five days at sea
    First part — fresh gales from southeast, thick and rainy. At six P.M. took in all sail we had not blown away, but lower topsails, and hove to judging ourselves near land. At daylight made the land off Pigeon Point 15 miles south of San Francisco having drifted to southard some during the night. At noon 15 miles from Golden Gate. At two P.M. up to the Bar. Pilots all inside and Bar breaking heavy. Stood off and on all night. Morning — stood in. Bar smooth. Went over and took a pilot and came in to anchor making my passage 95 days. Beat all I sailed with. Good, good, and satisfied.[15]

Glory of the Seas had experienced favorable weather the entire passage, and had passed many a sailing vessel during her fine run. Among these was the bark *Martha Davis* which had arrived the day after Knowles's ship, 122 days from Boston. Another ship to suffer from comparison was *Sovereign of the Seas*. She had arrived on January 14, three days before *Glory*, but it had taken her 162 days to sail from New York, more than two months longer than her "big" sister. In brief, *Sovereign* had made the passage from latitude 50° south in the Pacific to the equator in twenty-nine days. The final segment of her voyage was twenty-six days from the Line to port, a total of fifty-five days from latitude 50° south. *Glory of the Seas* had been only thirty-five days on the same course. In summary of *Glory*'s feat she had sailed from Sandy Hook to the equator in twenty-seven days; then down to latitude 50° south in the Atlantic in twenty-two days. She had rounded the Horn in eleven days. From latitude 50° south in the Pacific to the Line, the excellent time of eighteen days was made; from there to port took seventeen days. Although there were no remarkable day's runs except for the one 300-mile day off the California coast, her steady sailing proved that she was a smart and "lucky" ship with an outstanding master. In making passage in ninety-five days, *Glory* became the ninth fastest wooden sailing ship to ever make the westward voyage to San Francisco via Cape Horn. After the year 1874, no American sailing vessel would ever beat her record. Of the eight previous ships to make the passage in less than ninety-five days, four of them — *Flying Cloud, Flying Fish, Great Republic,* and *Romance of the Seas* — had been built by Donald McKay.[16]

Glory of the Seas' reputation as a good ship was now firmly established, and Captain Josiah Knowles could take comfort from the fact that he had more than made up for his tedious forty-one-day passage from Liverpool to New York.

CHAPTER VI

A Typical Round Voyage

DURING the grain year running from July 1, 1873, to June 30, 1874, there were to be only 247 vessels in the California cereal trade, quite a drop compared to the preceding year when 339 ships had been chartered.[1] However, the eventual slight shortage of tonnage to move the grain resulted in continuing high freight rates for the ships involved. *Glory,* the smart *Young America,* the British iron ship *Wasdale,* and the ex-caloric steamer *Ericsson,* for example, all received rates of four pounds (approximately $19.44 per long ton) when they were chartered in January and February, 1874. They were bound to make profit-making voyages.

The masters of these four crack full-riggers were looking forward to the time when their cargoes could be completed and they could race to England. Each vessel was known to be fast, and bets were made in San Francisco on who would win, since all four were sailing within three weeks of each other.

The *Ericsson* sailed first on February 19. She was a former transatlantic sidewheel steamer of clipper hull design. Her wooden, iron-strapped hull had been built in 1852, but after partial rebuilding and major conversion to a three-masted sailing ship in 1868 in New York, she was judged sound by the insurance surveyors and insured to carry perishable cargoes.[2] Managed by Howes and Crowell, the vessel was 248 feet in length, 40.4 feet in breadth (4 feet narrower than *Glory*), and had a registered 27.6-foot depth of hold, but her gross tonnage was only 1,645, more than 450 tons less than *Glory of the Seas.* Her fine lines forward and aft put her in the category of an A-1 extreme clipper, while aloft she spread single tops'ls and also flew a main skys'l. In 1873, the down-easter *St. Nicholas* had beaten her to Liverpool via Cape Horn by six days, but this year, it was generally thought in shipping circles that she would make a fine, fast run to the British Isles.

Glory sailed on February 26, followed by the *Wasdale* the next day. The *Wasdale* was two years old and owned by the J. D. Newton Company of Liverpool. The smartly kept vessel was 227 feet in length, had two decks, and grossed 1,220 tons. Crossing a main skys'l and having double tops'ls, she was sufficiently large and lofty enough to put up a good fight against her three larger competitors.

This passage would mark the thirty-fourth rounding the Horn for *Young America.* Her new master, John L. Manson, formerly ten years in the smart *Valparaiso,* was determined to continue his outstanding reputation as a driver. In his first voyage in *Young America* (he arrived at San Francisco February 13, 1874, 107 days from New York), he had definitely proved that he was no slouch at driving the old clipper. Even though she was not to sail until March 12, bets were made that she would nonetheless catch up with the other ships.[3]

On the day *Glory of the Seas* sailed from San Francisco, Josiah Knowles once again started his daily record. His first two days at sea were as follows:

Sea Account, Thursday, February 26, 1874
     At ten o'clock A.M. took steam tug *Rescue* and went off to ship with a large party of friends. Hove up anchor and proceeded to sea. At 12 noon passed out of the Golden Gate.

Friday, February 27, 1874, one day at sea
     At 12:30 P.M. tug left us just inside the Bar. Light airs from NE to north, clear and pleasant. At 1:30 P.M. pilot left us at the seven fathom buoy, nearly calm. At three took a light breeze from WNW. At eight P.M. Farallone Light bore north by west 20 miles distant from which we take our departure. Remainder of this day light airs, pleasant weather. Ends from northwest, very light.[4]

Running down through the northeast trade region, she crossed the equator nineteen days out at longitude 124°W. Again, her captain had shaped his course to take him to Pitcairn Island. Knowles wrote in his log on Tuesday, March 24, 1874; twenty-six days at sea:

Throughout this day fresh trades from east to ESE. Occasional squalls. At nine A.M. sighted Pitcairn Island bearing south by compass distance 35 miles. At 12 hove to a mile from the island. Boat come off with a lot of fruit and all glad to see us. . . . Boat alongside from shore took what they had from us. Gave them a lot of things such as we could find. At one P.M. they went on shore for another load of fruit. Came off at five o'clock with a good load of oranges, bananas, limes, cocoanuts, pineapple, sweet potatoes, pumpkins, and watermelons. At 5:30 P.M. boat left us and we proceeded on our way after a pleasant call. It was quite rough at the landing which caused some detention to the boat in getting off.[5]

In this age when refrigeration on ocean-going craft is taken for granted, it is strange to imagine what it was like to live and work aboard a sailing ship in the past century. The crew of *Glory of the Seas* considered fresh fruits and vegetables a rarity. They were normally eaten the first few weeks at sea and were primarily reserved for the afterguard and passengers. After a couple of months at sea, what had not been consumed had perished in the moist salt air. The unrefrigerated forepeak and pantry, where stores were stowed, did not keep food fresh for long. The general fare for fo'c's'le hands on American deep-water ships was salted meats, dried vegetables, "weevily" bread (hardtack), plus the sailor's grade of coffee. As could be expected on a four-month voyage, this became monotonous, day after day. Considering the varied menu on the average modern freighter, what is served to fo'c's'le hands today on American ships is better than the best cabin fare eighty-five years ago. One can appreciate how the entire crew of *Glory* felt on seeing a boat heavily laden with luscious fruits and vegetables come alongside their ship off Pitcairn.

All of Josiah Knowles's family and the ship's officers took their meals in the dining saloon, the forward part of the after deckhouse. Though their food was always cooked forward in the galley, deck boys customarily carried it aft to the pantry, where the ship's steward and stewardess arranged it before serving. That these two people served an important function is evidenced by the fact that Knowles paid them almost as much as the chief mate.[6] On a typical evening at suppertime the captain sat in his special chair at the after end of the table in the dining saloon while his wife, the three children, and several officers each sat in their respective chairs eating their hot meal. Their dining table was uniquely crafted with horizontal wood separators between the individual dish settings. Donald McKay had designed it for *Glory* so that rollicking weather could not

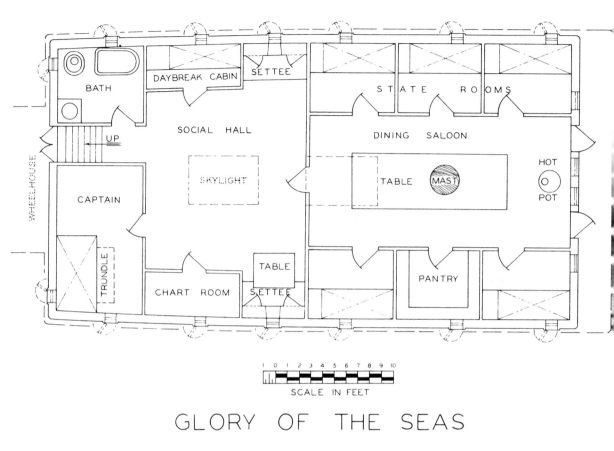

BATH

DAYBREAK CABIN

SETTEE

STATE ROOMS

WHEELHOUSE

UP

SOCIAL HALL

DINING SALOON

HOT

SKYLIGHT

TABLE

MAST

POT

CAPTAIN

TRUNDLE

TABLE

CHART ROOM

SETTEE

PANTRY

SCALE IN FEET

1 0 1 2 3 4 5 6 7 8 9 10

GLORY OF THE SEAS

After cabin plan, *Glory*. Drawing by the author.

cause the food dishes to slide all over it.[7] The table was directly below a
6-foot skylight which provided enough illumination for daytime meals.
At night a whale-oil lamp was lit and swung from the cabin overhead. The
swinging lamp had also been especially designed for shipboard use. No
matter what direction *Glory* rolled in a heavy sea, it remained amazingly
upright.[8] Though this dining saloon would appear cramped and antiquated next to the first-class eating accommodations of a modern ocean
liner, in the year 1874 *Glory of the Seas* was considered a comfortable
seagoing home.

On her thirtieth day out from San Francisco, Knowles wrote of out-
sailing a lime-juicer: "At ten A.M. exchanged signals with English ship
Lady Driffin 39 days from San Francisco. Ends — five miles astern." *Glory*
sailed 250 miles this day, which was evidently quite a bit better than the
Britisher.

As she neared Cape "Stiff," a heavy gale struck her on April 8, 1874,
during which she experienced the terror of every Jack Tar, shifting cargo.
Knowles's abstract log for the next three days told of the crew's fight to
save the ship from disaster.

Wednesday, April 8, 1874, forty-one days at sea
First part — light baffling airs. Cloudy, misty weather and a falling barometer. Midnight — it commenced blowing heavy and increased to a
heavy gale from SSE. Violent squalls — took in everything but fore and
main topsails. At 11 A.M. shifted cargo. Wore ship to westward and
trimmed ship. Made 40 miles.

Thursday, April 9, 1874, forty-two days at sea
First part — heavy gales from SSE and violent squalls. Middle — moderating but very heavy sea. Latter — moderate gales from south, rain
squalls. Bad sea on. Ran the ship six hours northeast before the wind to get
pumped out.
Long. 97°04′ noon. Lat. 44°07′S

Friday, April 10, 1874, forty-three days at sea
First part — moderate gale from south and moderating. Sea running
causing ship to roll heavily. Middle — light from SW to west, cloudy and
rainy — 3/4 SE. Latter — stormy from WNW, thick and rainy. Made per
log 126 miles.
Lat. DR 45°13′S Long. DR 94°41′W.[9]

After rounding the Horn, she proceeded into the South Atlantic. It
took her thirty-one days to sail from latitude 50°S in the Atlantic up to the

equator. Because she encountered mostly light winds, she made slow progress, but not as snaillike as one bark she caught up with.

> Thursday, April 30, 1874, 63 days at sea
>   Throughout this day light baffling airs from southeast to SSW. Pleasant weather, smooth sea. Boarded by boat from English bark *Longoy* 98 days from Portland, Oregon. Short of coal. Supplied them.
>   Long. 36°32' noon. Lat. 35°39'S Made 67 miles. Made week 889 miles.[10]

After losing the northeast trades, Josiah Knowles shaped his course once again for St. George's Channel between England and Ireland. The progress of *Glory* was still slow, but on her 105th day out, her captain proudly wrote in his log: "Several sail in company going same way. Beating all of them." On the final day of this voyage, Knowles recorded, simply, the closing events:

> Tuesday, June 23, 1874, 117 days at sea
>   First part — light breezes from southwest. Cloudy. At 10:30 made Smalls Light. At 7:30 Bardsey bore east distant six miles. At 12 passed Holyhead. At 1:30 took pilot. At four took tug. At eight o'clock came to anchor in the River Mersey. So ends this passage.[11]

Young America had been the bettors' favorite to reach Liverpool first, but *Ericsson* won, making the passage to port in 103 days. *Glory* had been out of the race for over a week, ever since June 16, 300 miles southwest of Ireland's Cape Clear, when *Young America* had gradually surpassed her in the unpredictable weather. Knowles was 111 days out while *Young America* was only ninety-eight days from San Francisco. *Glory* had been close-hauled on her starboard tack much of this day and had made only 124 miles. The lofty Webb-built ship's ability to sail in moderate weather was too much for the McKay-designed vessel. The old clipper came up and passed her. *Young America* also overhauled the *Wasdale* on this stretch. She made the Liverpool Bar twelve hours ahead of *Glory* and nearly a full day before the *Wasdale,* completing a voyage of 103 days, which was two weeks faster time than the medium clipper and the iron ship.[12]

During the latter part of July, stevedores loaded *Glory* with her homeward cargo. This was her first experience with an entire cargo of bulk coal from the great mines in Lancashire. Since the early 1850's, coal exportation from the British Isles had increased at a rapid rate each year; this year alone over 13 million tons of coal were to be exported from England to ports all around the globe.[13] Liverpool's large dock facilities and close proximity to the coal mines had made it one of the principal "black diamond" ports in the British Isles. Long railroad spurs ran down to quays on the River Mersey to facilitate loading the many outward-bound vessels. Once *Glory* had her cargo of 2,100 tons of coal, Captain Knowles made final preparations to sail for California.[14] Although she was carrying a relatively small cargo, it was to be one of the factors that would save the ship from destruction in the coming months at sea.

The new Liverpool-based ship *Langdale* sailed the same day as *Glory of the Seas,* August 13. Just completed the past June, she was a trim 1,237-ton vessel with an iron hull. In command of Captain Jenkinson, this new addition to J. D. Newton's Dale Liner fleet had been built approximately the same size and rig as the *Wasdale,* and was expected to be just as fast. Captain Jenkinson was out to make her reputation as a flyer on the maiden voyage. He would have his chance in pitting *Langdale* against Captain Knowles in *Glory of the Seas.* Since both vessels sailed from Liverpool the same day, almost identical weather conditions prevailed for both ships initially. In fact, at the end of the four-month voyage, their logs would be amazingly alike.[15] Captain Knowles began writing his abstract log as follows:

August 13, 1874, Thursday, Sea Account
At nine A.M. steam tug *Enterprise* took us in tow and proceeded down river. At 12 o'clock at Bell Buoy. Liverpool river pilot and tug left us.

Friday, August 14
Commences first from southwest. Pleasant and clear. At 12 made all sail at Bell Buoy and proceeded on our way down channel. From eight P.M. to two A.M. light baffling airs and calms. At two A.M. Man Light bore by compass east 14 miles distant. Wind came out in a squall from NNE and blowed. First took in the light sails. At eight A.M. made coast of Ireland. Ship *Baltic* and several others in company. At 11 A.M. past Tuskar. At 12 Point Carnsore bore north distant ten miles from which I take my departure.
Ends — strong winds from northwest.
Lat. 52°05′ Long. 6°22′

Saturday, August 15

Commences strong winds from NW to WNW, pleasant. *Baltic* about ten miles astern. Middle — fresh breezes from WNW, pleasant. All sail set. At six A.M. hove to and put Channel pilot on board American bark *John Bunyan* from New York for Havre which detained us for about an hour. Latter — fresh from west, pleasant.
Lat. DR 49°02′ Long. DR 8°24′[16]

Shortly after sailing, one of the crew saw wisps of smoke rising from the cargo hatches. It could only be one of the most dreaded horrors on any wooden vessel — fire in her combustible cargo. Knowles quickly gave the order to rig the force pump forward so that water could be pumped on board. Meanwhile, the crew removed the cargo hatches to clear the dense smoke so they could go below. Then, spraying a stream of water as they climbed over her bulk cargo in the 'tween decks, they sought to find the center of the blaze. Billowing clouds of steam accompanied by ominous hissing rose as the sailors played water on the burning coals and dug down with large scoop shovels to reach the central fire area. All indications were that the blaze had started by spontaneous combustion. Hours passed quickly as the crew continued hosing down the small fire area. Finally, by round-the-clock vigilance, the blaze seemed under control. However, danger still lurked, because days later, steam was observed rising from the hold. Throughout the rest of this passage, Knowles wisely kept the hatches off whenever possible for ventilation. Even so, the cargo remained in a heated state until *Glory* reached California.[17]

On her fifty-seventh day out from Liverpool, as *Glory of the Seas* neared Le Maire Straits, a sail was sighted far astern. As it came up in company, the ship was made out to be a full-rigged lime-juicer. Signals were soon exchanged and she was identified as the *Langdale*. The two vessels entered the Straits, the 17-mile neck of water separating Tierra del Fuego and Staten Island, and sailed together this day and the next; but gradually, *Langdale* pulled ahead until *Glory* was far astern. After passing Cape Horn, *Glory of the Seas* continued her rounding the Horn (sailing from latitude 50° south in the Atlantic to latitude 50° south in the Pacific), not having sighted the Britisher for nearly two weeks. On October 20 *Langdale* was once again sighted astern. This time, as Jenkinson's command came up to join *Glory*, they sailed in sight of each other for three days. Finally, the iron ship took the lead again as both vessels doggedly fought strong westerlies in their efforts to head northerly into the Pacific. Nevertheless, *Glory of the Seas* rounded the Horn one day faster than *Langdale*.

Captain Knowles now shaped his course to take her into the southeast trades, but to no avail. *Glory* did not pick them up until she reached latitude 16° south. She continued making very slow progress, already having taken almost a month to come up from latitude 50° south.

Glory of the Seas and *Langdale* crossed the equator the same day, though neither sighted the other. Continuing northerly, strong trades carried *Glory* up to within 600 miles of San Francisco. Then, for the following thirteen days, baffling airs and calms plagued her, so that she did not arrive at port until December 22, 1874. On entering the bay, Knowles gave the command to drop anchor off Point Diablo on the northern shore of the Golden Gate at 7:00 P.M., completing a long passage of 131 days.

Knowles was surprised to find that the *Langdale* had not arrived. However, the next day she too dropped anchor. Subsequently, both he and Captain Jenkinson published general memoranda of their passages in the San Francisco newspapers on December 24. Such a poor maiden trip was damaging to the new ship's reputation. To save face, Jenkinson publicly objected to Knowles's memorandum references to *Langdale.* In turn, Josiah Knowles, gentleman that he was, sent a reply which in part read:

> If it will satisfy the captain of the *Langdale,* I will say that whenever I raised his ship, she was astern of the *Glory,* but came up and passed her. When I got to 'Frisco, there was no *Langdale,* but as the passages of the ships were 131 and 132 days respectively, I think that is sufficiently long to prevent any discussion as the great speed of either.[18]

Among the shipping fraternity, there was complete agreement, and even higher respect for Josiah Knowles.

In comparison, the *Young America,* which arrived December 25, 1874, at San Francisco, 117 days from Liverpool, had sailed from Liverpool more than two weeks after *Glory* and *Langdale.* Captain Manson's memorandum indicated that he had experienced generally more favorable winds his entire passage. For example, the two latter ships had taken thirty-five and thirty-four days, respectively, to come up from latitude 50° south in the Pacific to the Line, while *Young America* was only twenty days on this segment.

Once the cargo of *Glory of the Seas* was discharged, the extent of her fire damage could better be seen. She was indeed fortunate not to have been damaged structurally, although minor repairs were in order in her 'tween decks.[19]

During this year fire had struck another J. Henry Sears Company ship, the 1,365-ton *Mogul*. She too had been carrying coal from Liverpool for San Francisco and after a long and hard fight, her captain, William Freeman, had realized that nothing could be done to quell the tenacious blaze in her hold. She was abandoned in the South Pacific on August 7. To replace the *Mogul*, Sears Company in October bought a 49/64 interest in the new down-east four-mast bark *Ocean King*, the first of this rig to be constructed in the United States since the ill-fated McKay clipper *Great Republic* in 1853. This three-skys'l yarder was surprisingly short for a bark at 250.6 registered length, only 10 feet longer than *Glory*. *Ocean King* was destined to be slow and a poor investment for Sears and Company.[20]

To comprehend a round voyage in a deep-water square-rigger, a reader of today must visualize a slower paced world than the one he lives in. A modern freighter, via the Panama Canal, can make the same general run as *Glory*'s in less than a quarter of the time she took. The freighter's crew are at sea less than a month; *Glory*'s men expected to be out from three to five months on a Cape Horn passage. The freighter's sailors take for granted the propulsion of a powerful engine; the square-rigger demanded pure muscle to work her sails through the different climates of the world. The motive power was God's wind which filled her great, billowing expanses of canvas and pushed her along at an average of 5 to 7 knots on the voyage, depending on the winds and seas. If the challenge to race another ship arose, it was accepted with gusto, the crew working as a team to make *Glory* the winner. Lying at a foreign port for several months, the ship awaited her turn to take on a return cargo, then shipped a crew, and proceeded to set sail for home. On the return passage, the same backbreaking work continued for another four and a-half months or so until the proud sailing ship anchored once again in San Francisco Bay.

✳✳

CHAPTER VII

Success and Tragedy

As the year 1875 began, shipping was especially poor for American full-riggers engaging in California grain commerce. Not only had freight rates dropped down to an average of 55 shillings 4 pence ($13.44) per long ton, but also, what limited charters existed were falling mainly to the British iron ships.[1] By the time the grain year was to end, only sixty-two American square-riggers would be chartered, whereas 203 foreign vessels were to sail from the Golden Gate laden with wheat.[2]

Josiah Knowles, on seeing that *Glory* would not be chartered, decided to speculate. He prepared her for a voyage to New South Wales, Australia, where he planned to purchase a cargo of coal on the ship's account. On her return to California he had high hopes of selling his cargo to a Bay business firm. As the day came closer for her to sail, Knowles arranged with a boarding house master to supply him with foremast hands. He ended up paying 60 dollars "dead horse" per able-bodied seaman, which was the highest Captain Knowles ever paid out for a crew. Moreover, his mate, Pearson, had quit at the end of December, so another chief "kicker" had to be shipped. The new mate was William Craig, from down east, a man as large as Captain Knowles, and sufficiently adept at keeping men in line.[3]

Glory of the Seas sailed from San Francisco March 14, 1875, bound for Sydney. From the first day at sea Knowles found her much too crank. For a ship her size, a very minimum of 500 tons of ballast was needed to hold her up properly on an offshore passage, and she had quite a bit less than

77

that on board.[4] With a beam wind she was almost on her beam ends, exposing a large part of her yellow metal on the windward side. *Glory* drew only about 14 feet of water fore and aft, which meant that Knowles wasn't able to carry as much sail as he wanted. In fact, the stuns'l booms, royal yards, and main skys'l yard were sent down on deck after several days at sea to offset her tender condition. Nevertheless, this was her finest passage, in which she broke the record for a sailing ship from San Francisco to Sydney. With more ballast Knowles would have been able to carry more sail, meaning that she could have been even faster on the passage.[5]

Mary Eaton Knowles had more than her hands full at the onset of this voyage. Besides having the care of Mattie, Harry, and little Mary, she herself was eight months pregnant and would undoubtedly give birth during the passage to Australia. Fortunately, a trusty, middle-aged steward and stewardess were part of the afterguard, and the woman was to prove a great help to Mrs. Knowles and a welcome assistant in handling the children.

The captain recorded his first two days at sea as follows:

Sunday, March 14, 1875, Sea Account
   At six A.M. tug *Rescue* took us in tow and proceeded to sea with a strong northwest wind. At 8:30 cast off tug and made sail. At 9:30 pilot left just outside bar. At 12 midnight South Farallones bore north 24 miles from which we take our departure. Strong northwest wind. Going 12 knots. Made 50 miles from anchorage. Sailed 50 miles.

Monday, March 15, 1875, One Day at Sea
   Strong winds from northwest, cloudy. Ship very crank. Cannot carry as much sail as otherwise would.... sailed 278 miles.[6]

During her sixth day at sea *Glory* lost a spar, an exception to the rule as far as Josiah Knowles was concerned. He wrote, "carried away foretopmast stunsail boom." As a matter of fact, his logs for 1871–1876 mention only one other instance of such an occurrence. Few square-rig skippers of the driver breed could match this record. *Glory* sailed 1,606 miles that first week at sea, her best day being 278 miles. During her second week, tradewinds from northeast to southeast pushed her 1,436 miles at an average speed of 8½ knots. However, during her third week she sailed only 1,231 miles. She more than made this up by making 1,801 miles during her fourth week at sea, which was nearly an 11-knot-per-hour average.

On April 18, two days out from Sydney, Knowles jotted, "Sunday, April 18, 1875, Thirty-four Days at Sea, First and Middle — Strong breezes from southeast, squally. Latter — Moderate from east-southeast, pleasant, made 78 miles, sailed 149 miles." What he did not mention was the arrival aft of a baby boy, Thomas. The event was not in the log probably because it was somewhat overshadowed by the superb run *Glory of the Seas* had made to date, one which would never be equaled by any sailing ship. The satisfied captain recorded his final two days as follows:

> Monday, April 19, 1875, Thirty-five Days at Sea
> First part — moderate from east-southeast to east, cloudy and frequent rain squalls. At 12 midnight Port Stephens Light bore west-northwest 20 miles distant. At five A.M. Newcastle Light bore northwest distant 20 miles. At eight A.M. made North Head and at nine A.M. took Sydney pilot. At 11:30 A.M. anchored in Sydney harbor, making our passage in 35 days. Made past week 770 miles. Sailed 952 miles.
> Average eight and 1/8 miles per hour. Total — made 6,844 miles.
> Passage — anchor to anchor, 35 days, 11 hours, 15 minutes.
> Passage — pilot to pilot, 35 days, 5 hours, 15 minutes.[6]

On her arrival at Sydney, Captain Knowles made arrangements to load *Glory* at Newcastle, the great coat port north of Sydney. Shortly afterwards, a steamer towed her to Newcastle Bay where her meager ballast was soon discharged. Before receiving the greater part of her cargo, laborers stiffened her with a barge load of coal while she lay out in the roadstead. Then, several days later, she was towed to King's Wharf, a large, 700-foot quay where stevedores loaded the rest of her 2,970 long ton bulk cargo. With its completion, *Glory* was towed back to Sydney.

While anchored out in Sydney harbor, *Glory* received two passengers for her return trip, a Mrs. Hendreth and her small daughter Alice, who were planning to settle in California. After ascending the tall ship's quarter gangway aft, they were introduced to their quarters, one of the staterooms off the dining saloon. Sixty-two years later in San Mateo, California, the little girl's daughter, Mrs. Katherine Ludlow Roach, would meet the Knowles's grandson, Josiah Knowles, III, and reminisce about the voyage, the majestic ship, and the captain and his family — matters that both of them had heard told when they were young children. Although Alice Hendreth had been on board *Glory of the Seas* for less than two months, the passage had made a deep impression on her young mind.[7]

On Friday, June 4, *Glory* sailed from Sydney harbor. Knowles recorded the events for this day: "At six A.M. pilot and tugboat came off, hove up anchor, and 7:30 proceeded from harbor. At 9:30 passed the Heads. At ten o'clock pilot and tug left us. Light winds from SSW to SSE, cloudy. At 12, South Head bore west 26 miles from which we take our departure. Two hours at sea.[8]

The first day at sea was her best distance covered that week, 184 miles. Then steering an easterly course, Knowles ran into some heavy seas and swells that impeded his progress. The first week of this homeward trip, *Glory of the Seas* made only 766 miles.

On June 12, her eighth day at sea, she exchanged signals with a downeaster that had left Sydney the same day. Evidently Knowles made a mistake in reading the other vessel's identification flags. He thought she was the *St. John*, a ship which was actually lying in New York at this time. *Glory* made a run of 204 miles this day, in a matter of hours leaving the other vessel hull down on the horizon, as both ships passed off the northerly coast of New Zealand. *Glory of the Seas* made 1,084 miles this second week, after having caught westerly winds mixed with many rain squalls.

During her third week at sea, *Glory* sailed over 200 miles every day. At the beginning, the winds were strong from north to northwest. On June 19, strong gales blew from north-northwest with an extremely heavy sea causing the vessel to roll uncontrollably. Knowles wrote, "ship rolling and shipping much water." One can believe that there were seasick sailors and passengers on board (especially little Alice Hendreth). This heavy gale lasted for two days, *Glory of the Seas* making 219 miles the first day and 263 miles the second. The last day of the week, she caught the southwest tradewinds, making a run of 252 miles as she now steered northeast. For that entire week, *Glory* sailed 1,630 miles, one of the best seven-day runs she ever made in her deep-water days, heavily laden.

As the lofty medium clipper steered north with winds from east to northeast, she passed through many of the South Sea island groups, the Tubuaï Islands, the Society Islands with their romantic isle of Tahiti, and others. On June 26, a beautiful clear day, far off in the distance the high mountainous peaks of Tahiti were sighted bearing west-northwest 44 miles. At 8:00 A.M. the next day, Matahiva, another South Sea island, was passed to westward as *Glory* on her starboard tack with all sail set, regally reeled off ten knots.

The ship crossed the equator July 1, twenty-eight days from Sydney, and continued up to latitude 4° North where she lost the southeast trades, but luckily caught the northeast tradewinds the very next day.

Easterly winds forced Knowles to steer her north on longitude 150° west, or thereabouts, up to latitude 38° north. Here, winds were caught from south to southeast, enabling the captain to lay an easterly course for San Francisco. During this final week at sea off the California coast, the ship logged a 256-mile day. Knowles's log for that day illustrates how intense a Pacific coast northwester could be in the summer: "First — strong winds from north, cloudy. Middle and latter — fresh gales from north to northwest, stormy, heavy sea, shipping much water."

On July 26, the final day of his voyage from Sydney, counting from noon to noon, he wrote:

> Conclusion — light airs. Sailed 54 miles. Made 54 miles. Calms from north to west. Thick and cloudy. At seven P.M. passed South Farallones Light. Point Reyes bearing northeast. Through the night light airs and calms. At 5 A.M. passed inside Farallones. At seven A.M. took San Francisco pilot. Find our passage of 53 days the best made lately.[9] Total we made, 8,613 miles. Total we sailed, 8,897 miles.[10]

Knowles's gamble had paid off. Shortly after arrival, he sold his coal cargo to C. L. Taylor and Company. The shipmaster of the ex-steamer *Ericsson* had also speculated and carried coal from Australia on the ship's account, since Howes and Crowell had been unable to charter her for grain at a profitable rate.

The shipping trend in the California trade continued downward in the 1875–1876 grain fiscal year. Only 174 vessels, both foreign and American, eventually loaded wheat before June 30, 1876. At least the number of American ships employed had increased to eighty-two, twenty more than the year before.[11] *Glory of the Seas* and *Ericsson* were two of these, but both vessels loaded on their owner's accounts, hoping that their cargoes would be sold before the ships reached England.

Knowles prepared *Glory* for sea, and again, with his family, planned to sail for Liverpool, Thursday, October 7, 1875. By now, Henry and Mattie, the twins, were seven years old; Mary was almost six; and little Tommie was five months old — and extremely frail. Mrs. Knowles and her husband hoped he would improve in health on the coming voyage.[12]

Once the ship was at sea, the Captain decided that Henry was at an age where he should have duties to teach him responsibility. Years later,

Henry told his son, Josiah Knowles, III, of his job, and he, in turn, wrote the following:

> [Captain Knowles] . . . believed, outside of paying passengers, no one aboard should be without a duty and a job to be done. There should be no idleness and everyone should be kept busy. This accounts for my father who was too young and too small to go aloft having the job of maintaining a lifeboat. This consisted of scraping all the paint off and then repainting the boat and its equipment. He was required to remove everything from the boat, oars, lines, water breakers, hatches [sic], knives, etc., paint, change the water. This was then restowed in the boat in its proper place and secured. Upon his completing this job and it having passed satisfactory inspection, he started all over again and repeated the work. This he did all the way to Liverpool, England, and [during the] return to San Francisco.[13]

Young Henry had two ways of gaining access to this lifeboat: by way of the flying gangway from the break of the poop to the boat gallows, or by a ladder on the side of the boys' house. The job was a rugged responsibility for a seven-year-old, but it helped him appreciate that there was more to operating a big square-rigger than just watching her sail. Chipping, cleaning, and painting was never ending on a wooden deep-water vessel such as *Glory of the Seas*. The salty, humid air played havoc with the paint work and Henry, by necessity, completely painted the boat several times on the round voyage.

Mutiny occurred on this trip. With a generally unreliable, uneducated, superstitious lot of men in the fo'c's'le, anything was liable to spark an uprising on a long deep-water voyage. Harry Knowles, years later, went on to relate to his son what had happened:

> The crew were planning to kill the captain, his wife, and the first mate. The plot was discovered and the men assembled on deck where the ringleader attacked the captain with a knife. The captain shot him with the revolver that is in the [San Francisco] Maritime Museum's display on Josiah Knowles. At that point the mutiny was squelched and the crew returned to normalcy.[14]

Labor relations, dangerous as they were, were not the worst part of this passage. Little Tommie Knowles's health was steadily growing worse. He began coughing continually and symptoms of tuberculosis were evident. These were the days when the majority of merchant vessels carried no ship's doctor. The captain attended to all medical problems as best he could with his one-volume medical encyclopedia;[15] but because Knowles did not know exactly what to do to help his son, Tommie gradually grew weaker until he died January 8, 1876. This took the heart out of the Knowles family and affected the morale of the entire ship's company. Death was always something of a blow on a sailing ship, but particularly in this case, for the victim was only nine months old.

Captain and Mrs. Knowles did not want to bury their son's body at sea, so the carpenter was asked to build a small box that could be sealed tightly and filled with preservative. The child's remains were stowed below until the ship reached England. *Glory* finally arrived at Liverpool February 17, 1876, completing a long, tragic passage of 133 days that had brought mutiny and death on board her. The sorry events had sapped the incentive of the crew and captain, causing the slow voyage. While lying at the British port, Tommie's little body was shipped to New Bedford and buried there by Mrs. Knowles's family.[16]

About the same time the three-skys'l-yarder *Triumphant* had made a run from San Francisco to Liverpool in 108 days, beating both *Glory* and *Ericsson*. However, since this was the best eastward Cape Horn voyage *Triumphant* ever made in her thirteen-year career, she could reap no titles as an exceptionally fast vessel.[17]

One can well see when viewing the happenstances on *Glory of the Seas* in 1875 and 1876 that the everyday lives of about forty people had been deeply involved. Some of them, the foremast hands, were on board the ship for only a few months; the captain, his family, and many of the afterguard expected to stay on for years. But for all of them, whether fo'c's'le crowd or officer, their destiny was to sail in the deep-water windships, and the events on shipboard were the events of their life.

While in England, Captain Knowles commissioned Samuel Walters, a member of the British Royal Academy and one of England's most prominent maritime artists, to picture his ship in oils. Under the direction of the captain's unerring eye for nautical detail, the artist was to depict the final day of a voyage to Liverpool. As time passed, a previously uninteresting piece of artist's canvas began to live in Walters' studio once the outline of the ship was drawn. For correct proportions, he visited her frequently as she lay at Liverpool.

He showed *Glory* on canvas to her best advantage — abeam and close-hauled on her starboard tack heading on a generally northerly course off the Welsh coast as she made ready to pick up the pilot. The time of day depicted was early afternoon when the fog, which is prevalent in this region especially during the summer months, had sufficiently dispersed to show the white, round tower of a lighthouse to the east. Further eastward, the tall heights of a mountain on the Welsh mainland could likewise be glimpsed through the haze in the distance. The picture contained much of the striking action of the final day of a voyage. A launch from a pilot boat lying off the lighthouse was making for *Glory*. On board the clipper, activity was particularly visible on her main deck. Captain Knowles, his wife, and a daughter stood on the after cabin top viewing part of the crew clewing up the mains'l preparatory to hauling around the mainyards so as to "heave-to" to pick up the pilot. As the painting neared completion, it was as nearly accurate as a photograph, but more romantically beautiful.

With her image caught in oils, *Glory of the Seas* sailed from Liverpool laden with 12,000 dollars worth of coal on Tuesday, May 2, 1876, about to be plagued twice again by death. In the matter-of-fact tone of the abstract log, Knowles recorded the dramatic events:

Thursday, May 4th, 1876
First part — light winds from the south. At four P.M. Kinsale Lighthouse bore west distance ten miles. Middle — light airs and calms, barely steerage-way. At nine A.M. G. E. Lundberg, seaman, shot himself through the head, killing himself instantly. Was in his berth at the time. No known cause for doing so. Committed his body to the deep. Latter part — light from SSE, pleasant. At 11 A.M. Kinsale Lighthouse bore NNE distant 11 miles.

Friday, May 5th, 1876, four days at sea
First part — moderate from SSW, pleasant. At five P.M. Fastnet Lighthouse bore NNE distant eight miles. Middle part — strong winds from south, pleasant. Took in light sails. At five A.M. carried away head gear. In getting the back ropes up, Osborne Bell fell overboard. Every exertion made to save him but could not find him. Latter — fresh gales from south, cloudy, heavy sea on.

(In Knowles's published memoranda at the end of this voyage he stated: "Osborne Bell was washed off the jibboom, the ship going 12 knots at the time and a heavy sea on. It was impossible to save him.")[18]

On clearing St. George's Channel, Knowles made his customary westing on latitude 50° north, longitude 19° west to avoid sailing into the Bay of Biscay because of the westerly winds off there. Then, continuing on a southerly course, the captain steered her to westward of the Madeira Islands.

On May 17, off Cape Verde at latitude 19°41′ north, longitude 26°42′ west, *Glory* caught the northeast tradewinds. The following day she maintained an excellent speed for a medium clipper of 13 knots for several hours, sailing 262 miles from noon to noon.

May 26, 1876, Josiah Knowles recorded in his journal: "No preceptable comment in this is my 46th birthday." It didn't seem possible that nearly five years had passed since he took command of *Glory of the Seas*. His hair and beard were quite gray now, but he stood tall and erect as ever, still conspicuous as a Cape Cod shipmaster of the old school.

As his stately ship steered southerly off the coast of Brazil, Knowles wrote in his abstract log on May 28 that two California-bound sailing ships had been sighted and "signalized" — the new 2,020-ton down-easter *H. S. Gregory* and the smart 2,046-ton *Triumphant*, which had beaten *Glory* to Liverpool earlier this year. The main skys'l-yarder *H. S. Gregory* had been completed in October, 1875, and was now making her first Cape Horn voyage, having sailed from New York on May 5, 1876. *Triumphant* had crossed the Line in the Atlantic on May 23rd, the same day as *Glory of the Seas,* although she had been twenty-three days to the equator to twenty-two for *Glory.* This passage was to decide the superiority of one ship and crew against the others. On May 28 through May 30, Captain Knowles wrote of these vessels and others heading south for Cape Horn:

Sunday, May 28th, 1876, 27 days at sea
   Throughout this day moderate trades from southeast by east, SE-ESE. Clear, pleasant weather, smooth and hot. At eight A.M. signalized American ship *H. S. Gregory.* At same time made out the ship *Triumphant* which left Liverpool day before us, she a long way to windward of us, but know her. Made 179 miles.

Long. in 34°42′W   Lat. obs. 15°46′S
Long. DR 34°46′W   Lat. DR 15°38′S

Monday, May 29th, 1876, 28 days at sea
   First and middle — light baffling trades from southeast to south to east, pleasant. Latter — stormy and squalls, SSE. Ends — pleasant with strong wind, heavy sea, SSE. *Triumphant* out of sight astern. *H. S. Gregory* six miles astern. Made 169 miles, sailed 175 miles. Made past week 1,414 miles. Sailed, 1,424 miles.

Long. in 36°34′W   Lat. obs. 17°39′S
Long. DR 36°31′W   Lat DR 17°22′S

Tuesday, May 30th, 29 days at sea
   Through out this day strong trades from SSE, cloudy and passing rain squalls. Short, heavy sea. Several ships in company, *H. S. Gregory,* no *Triumphant.* Made 96 miles. Sailed 172 miles.

Long. in 37°30'W   Lat. obs. 19°09'S
Long. DR 38°00'W   Lat. DR 19°05'S.[19]

On May 31, another square-rigger was sighted as *Glory of the Seas* sailed about 150 miles off the east coast of Brazil. Knowles wrote later this day: "Exchanged signals with ship *St. Charles,* 33 days from Liverpool." This sharp-ended, 188-foot down-easter dated back to 1866. A 1,166-ton royal-yarder, she was considered a very well-built vessel by insurance underwriters because of her iron-strapped hull. Although she was ten years old, *St. Charles* still had a fine reputation as a dry vessel in the grain trade. On this voyage she had crossed the equator on her twenty-fifth day out, which was, incidentally, the same day as *Glory* and *Triumphant.* On June 1, Captain Knowles wrote: "*St. Charles* in company about eight miles on weather quarter. Sails nearly as well as we do." On June 2, 1876, he recorded: "*St. Charles* out of sight astern, saw him at ten miles." *Glory* was making her best westward run since her record voyage from New York to San Francisco in 1873–1874.

As she continued sailing off the eastern coastline of South America, she caught moderate winds much of the time until she lost the southeast trades in latitude 28°08' south. On June 16 she lay becalmed for six hours, though her crew was not at a loss for something to do. Knowles wrote, "during which we caught a lot of codfish in about 60 fathoms water."

Latitude 50° south in the Atlantic was crossed on her forty-seventh day at sea, June 17, *Glory* making a run of 238 miles that day. At 8:30 A.M., three days later, she entered Le Maire Straits. *Glory* was through the narrow channel by 11:00 A.M. proceeding toward Cape "Stiff" once again. Five hours later, a three royal-yarder was sighted. Captain Knowles wrote in his journal, "At four P.M. exchanged signals with ship *St. Charles.* In company night, all." Fighting the westerlies, *Glory of the Seas* made her eleventh rounding of the Horn in eleven days, crossing latitude 50° south in the Pacific on June 28, 1876. Neither *St. Charles* nor *Triumphant* experienced moderate weather in these southern latitudes. *St. Charles* finally took twenty-two days to round the Horn, while *Triumphant,* which lost several sails on this segment, eventually sailed from latitude 50° south to 50° south in the Pacific in twenty-one and a half days. Both of these smart windships were now well behind *Glory of the Seas*. As *Glory* headed up the western coast of South America, strong southwesters forced her, as Knowles said in his memorandum at the end of the voyage, "close into the Chile coast, and at 65 days out, we were within a few hours sailing of Valparaiso."

On Friday, August 11, another sail was sighted far ahead. As *Glory* came up and exchanged signals with her the next day, the stranger was identified as the *General McClellan*, a Lawrence Giles vessel bound for San Francisco. On August 12, she was 135 days out from New York compared to 103 days from Liverpool for *Glory of the Seas*. The vessel was quite bluff at both bow and stern, which made her a comfortable but slow vessel. She was a 191-foot down-easter of 1,583 tons, and dated back to 1862. *Glory* steadily pulled ahead of her until at noon the next day she was "about seven miles astern," Knowles wrote. The next day, he noted, "*General McClellan* was just in sight astern." There hadn't been much of an opportunity to race the two ships because *Glory of the Seas* made only 94 miles the first day that the Lawrence Giles vessel was in sight, 78 the second, and 42 the third, but it had been enough to prove that Knowles's ship was far faster even in light weather.

Her final day at sea was logged as follows:

Wednesday, August 23rd, 1876, 114 days at sea
    Throughout this day moderate breezes from WNW. Thick fog at 12 noon. Hove to inside Farallones. 43 fathoms at two P.M. Stood off. At 12:30 cleared up, found ourselves close to Farallones. Tacked and stood in. At 3:30 took San Francisco pilot. So ends my passage — 114 days. At five P.M. passed in the Heads. Made 189 miles. Sailed 215 DR.[20]

Glory beat all four ships she passed this voyage. *St. Charles* and *General McClellan* arrived at San Francisco the day after her with passages of 118 and 147 days respectively. *Triumphant* did not make port until September 7, after a voyage of 130 days, while *H. S. Gregory* completed her passage to the Golden Gate in 119 days.

For United States Customs inspection, Josiah Knowles had to keep an accurate record of what was on board his ship besides the regular cargo. The following is a list of some items on board this trip, not only for the ship's use, but also including imported liquor to keep the captain's friends in good spirits ashore:

In Store Room Starboard Side

3 Boxes of California Wine for Andrew Nickerson
1   ”   ” Cider
9   ”   ” Lime Juice
2   ”   ” Old Rum
3 Chests of Tea
1 box chickery
2 Boxes raisins
10 Bottles Claret
1 Jar Cumets
5 Bottles Gin
6   ”   Sherry
3   ”   Port
3 Cases Brandy to Fosters
2   ”   ”   ”   ”
4 Barrels, 1 Brandy, 1 Port, 1 Ale, 1 Blass
2 Cases
3 Boxes
2 Tool Chests
1 Chair
2 Bundles
1 Bookcase[21]

As *Glory of the Seas* entered the Golden Gate, a young boy, J. H. Tucker, was watching her from shore. In later years he described, in a letter to Frederick C. Matthews, maritime historian, her arrival in 1876 and the subsequent events of discharging the cargo. The letter, dated April 9, 1922, reads in part:

> I saw her in her deep-water days. I can picture her so plainly passing old Alcatraz coming up the channel with Captain J. N. Knowles in command. Oh, God, what a sight! Letting go her hook and swinging to the flood with main topsails flat aback, royals and topgallant sails hanging in clews. . . . Well, she came in and was discharging coal at Pacific Street Wharf. I climbed aboard her mizzen channels and up aloft I go. The mate, a Mr. Colby hailed me.[22] I, without compunction, told him to go to hell. I went from her mizzen royal over her main skysail. Keeping an eye on him all the time, I crossed over the fore royal and down the fore royal stay clean out on her flying jibboom and coming in to the forecastle head, he was laying in wait for me. As I came down the companion-way he got me and say, man, you can tell "um," I got as fine a rope's end as a kid ever got. You talk of "local color," believe me I sure got plenty.[23]

Knowles received two letters from J. Henry Sears and Company in Boston three weeks after he arrived at San Francisco. They asked him to become their agent on the Pacific Coast. To engage as a commission merchant, he would have to leave *Glory*, a thought he didn't relish. Knowles was not too sure about the success of such a business, but late in the evening of September 18 he made up his mind, deciding once again to take a calculated gamble. The following is from his personal files:

San Francisco
September 18, 1876

Messrs. J. Henry Sears & Company
        Boston
Gentlemen:
    Your letters of 7th and 9th inst. reached me today and contents noted.
    The opening for a successful season does not look to me very encouraging as so many of the American vessels heading this way have been chartered to arrive that it leaves a very few on which we can depend to make a commission.
    For some time to come I can conduct the business under very moderate expenses as I shall probably need but desk room somewhere and some stationery and on thinking the matter over have decided to try the business and see what can be made out of it on the conditions you propose by: the gross receipts from the business to be equally divided, and the office expenses not to exceed $2,000 per year to be deducted from your half proportion until my interest amounts to $3,000 per year.
    Should I find the business did not realize our anticipations and I wish to join my ship again on her arrival in Liverpool or in New York I am to be allowed to do so on giving you timely notice of my wish to give up the business.
    Should this meet with your approval you can telegraph me and I will commence at once. Much of the success of the business *for the present season* at *least* will depend on the amount of business you can secure from Eastern Owners and direct to us here.
    I will do my utmost here to make it profitable.[24]

Shortly after writing this letter, Josiah Knowles began making plans to move his family and himself ashore. No longer would *Glory*'s quarterdeck be his domain, but he was destined to be in command of entire merchant fleets.

After several years of renting homes, Knowles bought a stately two-story house in Oakland in 1879 for 8,470 dollars. By this time his family ranks had been joined by a second set of twins, Alice and Thomas, born in 1877. Their spacious new residence was to hold yet another Knowles baby, a daughter who would be born in 1880. In the coming years the gray, beautifully landscaped house on the northeast corner of Fifteenth and Jackson streets would become a landmark of old Oakland, to be pointed out as the home of the distinguished Captain Knowles and his family.[25]

The successful sea captain became a prosperous landsman, acquiring a fine standing as a shipping and commission merchant. His business grew to include agenting for the New Bedford whaling merchant William Lewis. With the formation of the Pacific Steam Whaling Company and Arctic Oil Works in 1883, Knowles was made the general superintendent of both corporations, having under his supervision the main offices, the whaling fleets, and dock facilities at San Francisco.[26]

On leaving *Glory*, Knowles still owned one-sixteenth interest in her. Even though he was to sail with her no longer as captain, she was in many ways to remain identified with him. In her Cape Horn days he had been her finest skipper, with two record runs to his credit, New York to San Francisco in ninety-five days, San Francisco to Sydney in thirty-five days, and his unforgettable final swift, competitive voyage in command of *Glory of the Seas*.

CHAPTER VIII

Three Round Voyages under
a New Captain

THE necessarily fast search for a new master to command *Glory of the Seas* ended when J. Henry Sears and Andrew Nickerson examined the qualifications of one Daniel S. McLaughlin. The fifty-three-year-old captain had stepped down from the helm of *Herald of the Morning* in the summer of 1875 when the ship had been sold at Hamburg, Germany. It was a happy coincidence of availability of capable man and able ship, and the Sears Company was grateful to be able to sign up McLaughlin to command the fastest ship in their fleet.

Daniel McLaughlin's colorful existence began in November of 1823 in Nova Scotia. His father had migrated there and married a Halifax girl after serving gallantly as dispatch carrier in the British Army at the Battle of Waterloo. When Daniel was five years old, the family moved to Grand Manan Island, New Brunswick. At the age of thirteen, young McLaughlin, after a brief education, embarked on a seafaring career, shipping from Eastport, Maine, as a foremast hand on coasters. By the time he was twenty-three he had learned his trade thoroughly and had received an appointment to command the brig *S. G. Bass*. Two years later, in 1850, the new, full-rigged *Grey Feather* of 586 tons was given him off the stocks at Eastport. He made his first deep-water trip from New York to San Francisco in her, via Cape Horn, in 126 days, arriving just before the first San Francisco fire of May 3–4, 1851. The conflagration gutted a great part of

Captain Daniel McLaughlin. Courtesy Lawrence D. McLaughlin.

the gold rush city, leaving it in ashes and in dire need of supplies. Mc-
Laughlin sold his ship's cargo of flour for 50 dollars a barrel and the lumber on board went for an even higher figure. Although Captain Dan's
greatly inflated price did not endear him to his buyers, his name was
golden to his vessel's owners. His excellent profits more than paid for the
138-foot *Grey Feather*'s initial construction cost.

His next command was the 1,400-ton full-rigger *Aetos,* of Eastport,
which he sailed in the far-eastern trades. At the start of the Civil War an
English firm bought the vessel, and McLaughlin was appointed to command the 1,399-ton *Western Empire.* The Union Army subsequently
used her in the transport service during the war to carry horses, ammuni-
tion, and other supplies. In 1865 Captain McLaughlin temporarily quit
sailing ships, taking over the 215-foot screw steamer *Cassandra* of Mystic,
Connecticut. He left her in 1866, after deciding to return to square-riggers. A thorough seaman and navigator had no business wasting his talents
on "steam kettles," even though they did offer more of a future. Shortly
thereafter, he took command of the clipper ship *Swallow.*

The first real tragedy of McLaughlin's life struck in 1867, when
Hanna, his wife of nineteen years, died at Malden, Massachusetts, leaving
behind four children, two boys and two girls. The following year, Mc-
Laughlin was married again, to an Eastport girl, Miss Maggie (Margaret)
Benson. During nearly all his seagoing years, his headquarters were at
Eastport at the home of his sister Julia Ann, which in part explains why
so many activities in his life centered around the small Maine shipping
community. Captain Dan's second wife, like his first, followed the sea,
and sailed with him on the *Swallow.* In 1871, he was granted a coveted
membership in the Boston Marine Society, an old and rich benefit organization that predated the Declaration of Independence. The following
year he took the quarterdeck of the lofty *Herald of the Morning,* fast and
truly beautiful, registering 1,109 tons and crossing three skys'l yards. In
1876, after having rounded the Horn thirty-two times and sailed three
times completely around the world in sailing ships, Daniel S. McLaughlin was offered a further step up to command *Glory of the Seas.* Though
she crossed a skys'l on the main only — in contrast to the three skysails
on the 203-foot-long *Herald of the Morning* — *Glory* was almost double
her gross tonnage, a 994-ton difference. McLaughlin would shortly be
finding out how well the big, McKay-designed medium clipper performed
under canvas, especially in heavy weather, compared to the performances
of his former, smaller commands.[1]

Daniel McLaughlin soon took steps to travel to the West Coast to take over *Glory;* but first he made practical arrangements for his school-age children to stay with relatives. Before long, he and Maggie were on their way to San Francisco. On their arrival, Josiah Knowles introduced them to their new home, *Glory of the Seas.* Captain Knowles could speak with pride about the way she had performed under his command, and undoubtedly told Captain Dan of her sailing characteristics, good and bad, since both men treated their profession as a detailed science. As Maggie started setting up housekeeping aft, the new captain of *Glory* looked for a suitable afterguard, since all the ship's officers had quit when Knowles left her. Within a few days Captain Dan shipped three mates, a boatswain, two carpenters, two stewards, and a cook.[2]

Glory of the Seas, St. Charles, and *Triumphant* loaded grain at an entirely different location this year — the new facilities of the 8,900-ton capacity Grangers' Warehouses at Martinez on Carquinez Strait.[3] Though there had been some loading of ships at the short-lived grain elevator at South Vallejo in the early 1870's, this was the first substantial effort to load deep-water ships on the straits. To facilitate transfer of the sacked grain to the new wharf, a track had recently been laid so that a tramway could shuttle back and forth. In July, 1876, Grangers' Warehousing and Business Association, the corporate name, advertised in the newspapers to show why having vessels load on the straits was advantageous to both shipper and farmer:

> The (ware) houses are connected with deep water by tramway, over a broad, substantial, and eligibly located wharf with all desirable appliances to accommodate the largest seagoing ships. . . . Farmers along the San Joaquin and Sacramento Rivers are respectfully invited to examine our location, which offers the best landing for large vessels. Securing to you the same prices that rule the San Francisco market, also saving time and expense by avoiding the dangerous passage of grain barges through the Straits of Carquinez and the rough waters of the lower Bay.[4]

They had a pretty sound argument.

The first ship to load at these new facilities was the *St. Charles,* which arrived at Martinez under tow at noon, September 18, 1876. To commemorate her arrival, the town dignitaries held a big celebration, for they knew their town's economy was in for a boom. *St. Charles* loaded 1,800 tons of grain during the following two weeks.[5] The first part of October, *Glory,* likewise, was towed up from San Francisco. On October 21, the *Contra Costa Gazette* at Martinez reported:

The ship *Glory of the Seas* of over two thousand tons register, chartered by the Grangers' Business Association, for shipment of wheat to Liverpool on Farmers' account has completed her cargo, which embraces some two or three hundred tons belonging to farmers of our county and district, who are likely, with the advance of the market and prospects of further rise, to do well with their venture.

Glory was one of ninety-four American ships loading cereals in the California trade this year. Although the value of wheat had dropped from the previous fiscal year, J. H. Sears chartered her in September for 57 shillings, 6 pence per long ton ($13.97), about 5 shillings higher than the average vessel's rate for this entire grain year. To illustrate the drop in grain prices, her cargo, 67,996 centals, was valued at only 116,341 dollars, a 32,000-dollar drop from the previous year. The Pacific Coast grain trade was a highly competitive and speculative market where high cereal prices could exist one month with correspondingly high freight rates, and then either drop or rise quickly. For example, during the month of October the smart new English emigrant clipper *Brodick Castle* and the crack Boston ship *Great Admiral* both received charters for 3 pounds ($14.58), while the lime-juicer *Hawkesbury,* chartered later in the same month, received a rate 3 shillings higher.

At San Francisco, Daniel McLaughlin directed his two carpenters and other workmen in making minor modifications in *Glory*'s deck arrangement, besides changing her general color scheme both on deck and aloft. The two longboats abaft the mainmast were placed right-side-up, while the 16-foot dinghy was repositioned so that the line of its bow and stern ran athwartships. Josiah Knowles had painted the main pump wheels a bright orange-red and McLaughlin changed the color of the two capstans to the same shade. Her lower masts also took on a new appearance. Between the red lead-painted hoops, the chappels were painted white, as was the custom of several down-east shipmasters. Her taffrail and alleyway stanchions were no longer varnished as they had been under Knowles, but now were painted a flat white. To emphasize the seven-foot sheer of *Glory,* Captain Dan had his men paint a 6-inch yellow stripe on the line of the plank-sheer the entire length of her hull, and add a 3-foot yellow stripe along her waterline. With these few but noticeable changes, the shipping fraternity could be sure that *Glory of the Seas* was now under command of a new master.

At dawn, Tuesday morning, October 24, 1876, *Glory* lay in Mission Bay prepared to sail for England. A motley bunch of half-drunk sailors had been brought on board earlier by boardinghouse "crimps" to make up the rest of the crew. Nineteen foremasts hands were shipped at the outrageous price of 66 dollars "dead horse" per man, an outright extortion that meant it would take a sailor more than two months at 25 dollars per month before he could make a cent.[6] This gave little incentive for any seaman willingly to go to sea, and was a common example of the cheating methods carried on by boardinghouse masters. *Glory* was in readiness for the tug that would soon tow her to sea. Her sails were prepared so that when the anchor was up, they could be loosed immediately. Before long, the crew made fast a towing hawser from a bay tug on her fo'c's'le head. The time had come for shipboard action. McLaughlin gave the command to the mate, "Man the windlass." Going forward, the mate supervised the big job of weighing anchor. The modern stockless anchor cannot be compared to the old kind of hook on the sailing ships. Today's anchor is not catted; it goes up into a hawsepipe and, except for the stowing of chain, the sailor has very little work to do in the entire operation. In ships like *Glory of the Seas,* heaving in the anchors was done mostly by pure brawn.

Foremast hands, still suffering from the effects of their last drunk, had the windlass lever handles shipped ready to start heaving away. Eight men, four on each side, led by a chantyman soon were working the levers up and down to his rhythmic tune. The initial exertion was to break loose the anchor from the muddy bay bottom. As the men heaved down and then up with all their strength on the lever handles, the great 12-foot-long log windlass directly below slowly turned on a strongly built iron ratchet connected to the geared windlass rim. Though this unique mechanism saved manpower, it still asked a lot of muscle to weigh anchor. The foremast hands were heaving in a 5,700-pound iron-and-wood hook and many fathoms of heavy anchor chain. Once the anchor broke loose from the bottom, McLaughlin was notified, "Anchors aweigh." The men on the fo'c's'le head now heaved to the chantyman's faster song pace and to the further accompaniment of the steady clank, clank, clank of the windlass revolving as the anchor slowly came up from the bottom of San Francisco Bay. Meanwhile, directly below on the main deck, several seamen scrubbed mud from the heavy chain as it came up through the hawsepipe, while others fed the chain back and forth on specially made wood racks adjacent to the forward hatch so that it could run free when going out again. The tug and *Glory,* connected by a long cable, headed out the

Golden Gate. *Glory's* anchor shackle was soon up to the hawsepipe ready to be "fished" and hauled up to the cathead, a job that had to be done quickly so that the great mass of wood and metal wouldn't bang under the bows and scar the yellow metal sheathing.

With a large "fish" hook, one of the crew caught the anchor shackle. The hook was then made fast to the fish tackle, a large temporary tackle used for hoisting anchor. With the aid of her fo'c's'le head capstan, the fish tackle was now used to cat the anchor and haul it inboard over the bows. Once the nearly 3-ton hook was up to the cathead, another tackle was dropped and caught onto a fluke. As sailors heaved around the capstan, the fluke slowly lifted until it swung inboard over the buffalo rail. Then, when the wooden stock was almost vertical, the crew lashed the anchor securely. This operation completed, *Glory of the Seas,* with her tug left far astern and the pilot dropped, began her first passage under a new captain.

On his maiden voyage in *Glory,* Daniel McLaughlin made the fastest eastward Cape Horn passage in her entire deep-water career, 103 days. After she arrived at Liverpool on February 3, 1887, Captain Dan found that she had beaten every ship sailing from San Francisco in October except for the *Young America,* also under a new captain, and boasting a run of ninety-nine days to New York. The latter vessel had sailed from San Francisco four days before *Glory* and arrived at her destination on January 27. The British composite-built *Hawkesbury* also had bettered her by a run of 100 days to Le Havre. Daniel McLaughlin, though, had much to be proud of in his first passage. *Glory of the Seas* had outrun the *Triumphant* again, this time by fifteen days, and also her sister ship, *America,* by twelve days. The *Brodick Castle,* which had made her first homeward trip, was beaten by more than thirty days. Even the J. D. Newton Dale-Liner *Borrowdale,* a reputedly fast ship, had been left behind by McLaughlin this voyage. Captain Dan had lived up to his reputation of being a thorough shipmaster. His initial passage in *Glory* was even faster than his first eastward Cape Horn passage had been in the *Herald of the Morning.*

After unloading her cargo into the grainsheds at Liverpool and Birkenhead, *Glory* took on sufficient coal to stiffen her before she went to the docks to receive the rest of her homeward cargo. The 2,994-long-ton cargo was valued at 20,000 dollars, which allowed for a freighting profit of about 13,000 dollars. Very seldom did a sailing ship of this down-easter period make a profit on her westward Cape Horn passage. The freight rate on coal from England was barely a fourth the average grain rate, but the profits did help to pay ship operating expenses. For the last several years the gross freight profits on grain for *Glory* had averaged 40,000–45,000 dollars per voyage, which well illustrated the fact that she depended on grain charters to make money for her owners.

McLaughlin's good fortune changed on his return passage to San Francisco. Bad weather dogged him from the first day out, April 2. *Glory* took a week just to clear St. George's Channel. Continuing on a southerly course, she ran into the doldrums of the Atlantic, and these slowed her up considerably. She finally crossed the Line thirty-three days out from Liverpool, which, coincidentally, was the same number of days Knowles had taken to the equator in his first passage in *Glory* in 1871.

Two and one-half weeks after *Glory of the Seas* left Liverpool, the nearly new, 1,509-ton down-easter *Samaria* cleared and made a run to the Line in twenty-three days. Her captain, Charles E. Patten, naturally tried to prove his three royal-yarder the superior ship. Both *Glory* and *Samaria* made long runs from the equator of forty and thirty-nine days respectively to latitude 50° south, but by this time Patten was only a week behind McLaughlin. This interval remained almost constant until they both reached the equator in the Pacific. Then, the 217-foot *Samaria* was one day behind her. Both ships arrived at San Francisco the same day, August 23, 1877, *Samaria* in 125 days from Liverpool and *Glory* in 144. McLaughlin was greatly embarrassed to have made such a long passage. To try to explain, especially to his brother shipmasters, he published a lengthy and elaborate memorandum for the newspaper shipping page, a part of which read:

> . . . to lat. 43°S, long 60°W had nothing but bad weather. [head] Wind from southwest to west with strong gales and heavy sea. . . . On June 19, lat. 58°S, long. 75°30′W had a very heavy gale from west-southwest, which only lasted seven hours, barometer in the gale standing at 28.16, which is the lowest Captain McLaughlin ever saw it. . . . The only fast time made from lat. 43° in the Atlantic to lat. 26°S in the Pacific in 25 days. On the whole the passage has been a tedious one, the longest Captain McLaughlin or the *Glory of the Seas* ever made. . . .[7]

Nonetheless, his first passage had redeemed him in advance, and he was judged well able to handle his largest ship in forty years of sailing.

After being discharged of cargo, *Glory of the Seas* was towed off her berth at a San Francisco wharf to be temporarily anchored in Mission Bay. Two months passed before she loaded wheat for England. During this interval the photographer of Fireman's Fund Insurance Company went down to the waterfront to photograph the first-rate sailing ships in the harbor. On a typical foggy day in the fall of 1877, he lined up *Glory* almost broadside in his camera lens. In his picture, the immensity of her underwater body is especially evident because in ballast she drew about 12 feet of water. Also, McLaughlin always fixed it so that nobody could miss his big ship in port. He customarily lashed a long piece of canvas on the port quarter gangway with the name *Glory of the Seas* in black, 2-foot-high letters, and this showed up well in the photograph. In addition, her yards are squared to a "T," showing the pride of the captain in a taut ship.

A poor crop of wheat in the grain belt and a subsequent shipping slump had caused *Glory*'s two-month lay up. By the turn of the year the *Commercial Herald* reported that California's wheat was of an "inferior quality," meaning that few ships would be chartered. Because of its low value, freight rates dropped correspondingly lower. As a result, almost 200 fewer sailing ships than the preceding fiscal year carried cereals from the Golden Gate during 1877–1878. Of the 109 ships loading grain, only fifty were American.[8] In October, 1877, Josiah Knowles, acting as agent for J. Henry Sears Company, chartered *Glory of the Seas* for the then very low rate of 35 shillings per long ton ($8.50). But in many ways she was one of the few fortunate ones; at least she had a cargo. Since such a small number of ships were engaged for England, *Glory* loaded valuable merchandise reminiscent of the clipper days. The following cargo manifest[9] was the most expensive she ever carried:

Assayer Sweeps	sacks	84	Copper ore	tons	80
Borox	centals	1,027	Personal effects	pkg.	6
Canned Beef	cases	1,850	Pearl shells	cases	136
Canned Fruit	do.	420	Silver plates		1
Cotton, Foreign	lbs.	3,319	Salmon, domestic	cases	9,245
Dry Goods	cases	8	Do. foreign	do.	4,056
Mustard Seed	centals	395	Wheat	centals	50,393
Orchilla	bales	649			

Total Value	*$242,665*

McLaughlin made another excellent run to Liverpool, in 107 days, arriving there February 24, 1878. After discharging cargo, *Glory* took on a load of Lancashire coal and sailed from the British port on April 27.

During July, she rounded the Horn once more, proving herself a most seaworthy vessel in this dangerous zone. In that dark, bleary weather, she was caught several times in the teeth of rising gales. With the froth-crested rollers roaring high, she'd time and again climb a long, gray sea and then coast down the front, plunging her bowsprit under as she reached the hollow. Then, with a bone in her teeth, she'd climb another huge wave. This great mass of wood, hemp, and canvas fought gallantly against the elements as she slowly made headway under shortened sail. The majestic vessel, though knocked about, pitching like a cork, and rolling drunkenly in the heavy seas, rarely hove to, proving that she had another driver the caliber of Josiah Knowles who could carry sail until "the moon is blue."

On September 4, 1878, 900 miles west of the California coast, another ship sailed in company with her. She identified herself as the Newton Dale–Liner *Borrowdale,* bound to Astoria, Oregon, with a cargo principally of salt.[10] This fast, ten-year-old lime-juicer had been once credited with a twenty-four-hour run of 360 miles. Furthermore, she had averaged 108 days out to San Francisco from England in three consecutive voyages. But on this passage, neither Captain Kelly of the *Borrowdale* nor Daniel McLaughlin made "decent" passages. *Glory* was already 128 days out from Liverpool and the Britisher 127. Since the two ships sailed in company of each other for half a month, both commanders could carefully compare their general arrangements and sailing characteristics. *Borrowdale* was a two-decked, 1,277-gross-ton, iron-hulled vessel crossing three royals aloft, which made her quite a bit smaller than *Glory.* Her paint scheme was the same as the other Newton-owned ships. She had white lowermasts and doublings. Her black topsides had a white stripe on the line of the sheer strake. Below the black, she was gray to the load-line.[11] Captain Dan saw that this smart Dale-Liner scudded along easily even in the lightest of winds, but neither vessel had a chance to show its heels, because of continuous calms. The two windships parted company on September 19, as *Borrowdale* steered for the Columbia River while McLaughlin shaped his course for the Golden Gate.

Ten days later, *Glory of the Seas* anchored off Oakland, 153 days from Liverpool, by far the longest passage she would ever make. To the newspapers Captain Dan endeavored to explain his snaillike passage, in which *Glory* averaged only 4 knots. Shipmasters generally published detailed accounts of their Cape Horn Passages to San Francisco only in unusual circumstances. They normally gave just the days to the equator in the Atlantic; thence to the Horn, then to the Pacific Line, and to port, plus a brief mention of any mishap. But after *Glory* anchored in the Bay, Mc-Laughlin went below to his cabin to spend many hours composing an elaborate memorandum. He expressed himself exceptionally well on paper, as the following published account shows:

> Per *Glory of the Seas*. September 29, from Liverpool.
> Was one week clearing the channel; light headwinds and fog; then got strong gales from south to southwest, with bad weather which lasted ten days. Had to go east of Madeira in lat. 30°N. Took the wind northeast which took us down to lat. 8°N. and after four days calms got a breeze from north which in time hauled to south-southeast, where it hung so that we had to beat all the way along the Brazil coast. After passing at lat. 42°S., long. 60°W., the wind came up from south-southwest and south where it hung for 13 days blowing a gale with lots of snow and hail. On July 14, wind hauled to northwest and west-northwest; run through Straits of Le-Maire and at ten same evening Cape Horn, bore north distant three miles. Made good westing but could not get north, the wind hanging between northwest and north for 17 days. Stormy bad weather and I may say the darkest and most disagreeable month I ever spent at sea. After the norther broke up got the winds from southwest to northwest until lat. 26°S., long. 90°W., where we took the southeast trades which were brisk for four days; then light until we lost them in lat. 9°N. and after a week's calm got the north wind; also light and variable. On September 22, tacked in lat. 38°-20'N., long. 138°25'W., and after three days calm got a west and southwest breeze which afterward hauled to north. For the last ten days have had rain and winds from southwest to north and northeast. Crossed the equator June 5, 36 days out; rounded Cape Horn July 14, 76½ days out. Crossed the equator in Pacific August 22, long. 113°W., 115 days out and thence to port 38 days. From 50° to 50° 16 days; was in company with British ship *Borrowdale,* from Liverpool for Portland for 15 days. Parted company September 19.[12]

McLaughlin's "bedfellow," Kelly of the *Borrowdale,* had reached his destination three days after *Glory* made San Francisco. His passage had been 155 days, and one captain could have been the alibi for the other.

Shipping continued on a downward trend in the bay port. Although the number of ships employed in grain commerce in 1878–1879 more than doubled, freight rates on the average dropped even lower than the year before. McLaughlin laid *Glory* up east of Goat Island (Yerba Buena) after her arrival because the rates were not high enough to make a profit. By January, 1879, the situation still remained bleak. The *Commercial Herald* that month stated that ". . . no money has been made the past two or three years in the exportation of breadstuffs to Europe."[13] It was generally acknowledged that in addition to another poor crop, too many vessels for the amount of cargo had been built in America and Great Britain up to the year 1877. As a result, many deep-sea vessels were picking up short-term charters for coal from British Columbia and Puget Sound to San Francisco between their grain cargoes so as to make more of a profit for their owners. But so far, McLaughlin had held off putting *Glory* in the coastal coal trade. As the shipping slump continued, many vessels loaded grain on their owner's account, but fortunately for *Glory of the Seas,* five months after her arrival, Knowles chartered her in February, 1879, to load for George McNear of San Francisco. The first weeks in March she lay at a San Francisco wharf taking on sacked grain which had been barged down from up river.

Frank Chappell, McLaughlin's steward since 1876, returned to the ship, having missed her last passage. On this voyage his wife Millie accompanied him and signed as stewardess. Together, they would be staying by *Glory* for the next four years. Captain Dan also shipped a Chinese cook and a mess boy, Ah John and Long Eng.[14] On many deep-water sailing ships in the late 1800's, men of Chinese extraction were often used either to prepare the food or serve it, mainly because of their passive dignity and the courtesy with which they carried out their duties.

Glory of the Seas finally sailed from San Francisco bound to Queenstown for orders. She made another fine passage of 111 days; but on arrival, McLaughlin found that the *St. Stephen,* a Chapman and Flint downeaster, had beaten her by eleven days. The trim 1,392-ton, three-skysail yarder had made the fastest eastward Cape Horn voyage of her ten-year career.[15] However, *Glory* did beat the ship *Frank Pentleton* by five days and the down-easters *Challenger* and *Josephus,* which completed their passages in 126 days each. A few days after his arrival at Queenstown, Captain McLaughlin received orders from the grain consignee to proceed to Le Havre, France, to discharge her cargo. That accomplished, Mc-Laughlin set sail in *Glory* bound for New York where she arrived on October 12, 1879, thirty days out from Le Havre.

During November and early December she took on a general cargo at New York.[16] However, vital to her owners' interests, during the first week in December, a resurvey for her special insurance certification was called for. Ten years had passed since Donald McKay had launched his dream at East Boston, and the time had come for her A-1-in-Red classification to expire. Naturally, all the ship's owners were interested in having this special certification extended because it meant continued high dividends for them. During her stay at Liverpool in 1878 she had been "opened" up for survey according to the classification society rules. Moreover, at that time she had been caulked and resheathed with yellow metal, so that it was not necessary now for her to be opened for her ten-year inspection.[17] However, *Glory* was still thoroughly surveyed without being docked and the result was an extension of her top rating for another two years.

On December 9 at 4:20 P.M. *Glory of the Seas* sailed from New York to begin her ninth eastward Cape Horn passage, and eventually made what proved to be Daniel McLaughlin's best run ever to San Francisco, 118 days. McLaughlin commented on the passage in his memorandum at the end of the voyage: ". . . winds the entire passage were very light with the exception of one gale in lat. 46°S., long. 62°W. Ship has not had topgallant sails off her for 67 days. . . . Had northwest to southwest winds two days which ran us up near the Farallones, where we lay becalmed for 24 hours; took a pilot at midnight, April 4."[18]

The indomitable *Young America* bettered her once more with a run of 102½ days, but Captain Dan had something of which to be proud: *Glory* had taken ten days to round the Horn to sixteen for the *Young America*. The *St. Stephen* also beat *Glory* again, making port the day before her, 113 days from Philadelphia.

In three voyages on the quarterdeck of *Glory of the Seas,* Daniel Mc-Laughlin had been unable to make good time on the westward Cape Horn voyage. His average was 138.3 days. Though an accomplished shipmaster, Captain Dan seemed to be proving that *Glory* was too much for him to handle on the hard westward run, especially in light winds, but strange to say, he did very well on his passages from San Francisco to the British Isles, averaging 107 days. The primary object, though, was not how fast *Glory of the Seas* sailed, what ships she beat, or what ships beat her, but how financially successful she was in carrying cargoes safely and economically to her destination. This she continued to do reasonably well.

CHAPTER IX

Two Close Calls with Disaster

A new grain year began July 1, 1879. As it progressed, more American tonnage was chartered than in the past six years, but the number of ships, American and foreign, eventually sailing out of the Golden Gate laden with cereals, stayed about the same as before.

In mid-April, 1880, several weeks after *Glory* arrived at San Francisco, Sears Company acted on McLaughlin's suggestion to have her rerigged before she went on another deep-water voyage. As wire rope was just starting to become popular with shipowners, Josiah Knowles made a fair deal with a bay rigger to change the ship's original hemp standing rigging. A few weeks later, she was modernized so that her sails clewed up to the yardarms instead of to the quarters, a practice fast supplanting the old method. Just as new and better ideas are presented today and put into practice, so it was on the deep-water ships, even though shipowners often did things at a slower pace. A ten-year-old vessel, such as *Glory,* had to keep up with the times or she would be left behind in more ways than one.

On Friday evening, May 29, *Glory of the Seas* shipped a foremast crew as she lay out in the bay. Along with the half-drunk sailors and wharf bums that had been dredged off the San Francisco waterfront by a boardinghouse master was eighteen-year-old William B. Joseph, who had been shanghaied by a crimp while down near the docks earlier that evening.[1] Although Joseph was the son of a Boston sea captain, he had no real sea experience, and McLaughlin signed him on as ship's boy on the bottom of the maritime social ladder. Joseph, though stocky and big-boned, had

Glory on San Francisco Bay, ca. 1877. Courtesy San Francisco Maritime Museum, Fireman's Fund Collection.

not been able to defend himself handily against the crimps. He was suffering from tuberculosis and, having lost the fight to stay ashore, must now either win or lose the battle with his health on *Glory of the Seas*. The general treatment for tuberculosis today is, of course, complete rest and a careful diet. With the "four on, four off" watch system of *Glory*, Joseph would be fortunate indeed to get even eight hours of sleep in any twenty-four during the entire voyage — no rest cure.

By the time he was a week at sea, his landsman's hands were in rough condition. Unless a sailor had a rope burn, his experienced hands seldom blistered. But Joseph's unusually large palms and fingers were tortured by doing what his seasoned shipmates considered child's play.[2] Besides attending to the endless sweeping down, washing of paint work, and other normal ship's boy duties, Joseph learned the art of working a big square-rigger by hand. Although his hands were still in the process of healing, the mate didn't allow him to take time off. Only by building up heavy calluses would he be able to stand such hard duty as hauling on a rope, which bears no relation to merely pulling on a rope. Not knowing the technique, Joseph with his limited energy hauled his guts out. He quivered with exhaustion until he finally got the hang of it, and learned, like any novice, to haul as one in rhythm with his shipmates. Strange to say, as the weeks and months at sea passed, Joseph began toughening up and filling out. Captain Dan was undoubtedly keeping an eye on the lad, knowing of his disease; but the medicine he gave him, an overabundance of hard work in the fresh ocean air and the common sailor's salt-heavy diet, cured him completely by the end of the four-month passage.[3]

On September 28, 1880, 120 days out from San Francisco, *Glory* anchored at Queenstown, Ireland. The following week, on October 3, after receiving word of his discharge port from the grain consignee, McLaughlin weighed anchor and stood out for Dublin with a St. George's Channel pilot on board. The next day, she was off Kish Bank when a sudden easterly gale sprang up. The pilot sought to cross Dublin Bar, but with it breaking so heavily, *Glory* with her 25-foot draft couldn't hope to cross safely. The channel pilot then gave instructions to Captain Dan to make for Kingstown on the southern part of Dublin Bay, where he had hopes that the ship could be temporarily anchored to ride out the storm. Though she was soon at anchor, the holding ground proved extremely poor. *Glory* began dragging her hooks as the stiff gale continued increasingly to stir up the seas in the bay. All at once, her bower cable went slack — *Glory* had lost an anchor. Now she slowly dragged the remaining hook astern as she made for a lee shore at Kingstown. The inevitable took place; she ran aground with the seas still pounding relentlessly against her. Several agonizing hours passed until the gale gradually died, leaving *Glory* helpless on the beach at low water. The great ship still had a chance to survive. Tugs were soon dispatched to her assistance, and once the tide came in, they made fast their cables on board her and pulled mightily to break her loose from the land's grip. When she was towed clear and brought to a deep-water berth, part of her cargo was lightered out into barges.[4] A few days later, a tug towed her through the Dublin Bay ship channel to a dock where she discharged the rest of her grain. Then McLaughlin had her drydocked and asked a marine surveyor to determine the extent of the hull damage. The repair costs were estimated at 4,000 dollars, and it was decided that she should be partially caulked and resheathed. The owners were relieved that none of her 122,000-dollar cargo had been damaged, and once Andrew Nickerson and J. Henry Sears in Boston had a clear picture of her condition, they decided that since she was already in dock, her hull should be completely overhauled and resheathed, and they stood the rest of the repair expense.[5]

Meanwhile, most of the crew jumped ship, including William Joseph. He was soon shipped on a vessel bound out from Dublin for San Francisco, and about five months later, he entered the Golden Gate, this time to stay far away from crimps. He eventually married and settled down in Oakland, becoming thoroughly and happily landlocked as a stationary engineer at several buildings in the downtown district. He never forgot his fateful sea adventure, though, and in his later years built a detailed model of *Glory of the Seas* as he remembered her. His project took him a full twenty-eight months.[6] He built his model at a scale of 1/8 of an inch equaling 1 foot, and he used his memory to supply rigging and deck details. Though the finished product is not professional, it has the feeling that only a shellback, who had worked an actual ship at sea, could reproduce in wood, metal, and cloth. Joseph was especially accurate in reconstructing deck details, such as the old pumphandle anchor windlass and the ship's brass bell on her fo'c's'le head, a large balsa raft and the ship's fire buckets on her forward cabin top, and, last of all, the boys' house abaft the mainmast, which had been his quarters on the real *Glory of the Seas*. The model resides today encased in glass in the Oakland Public Museum, a testimony, perhaps, to a miracle at sea. William B. Joseph had seemed destined for death at an early age, but in 1942, sixty-two years after being shanghaied, he died at the age of eighty.

After *Glory* was repaired, Captain McLaughlin shipped a crew of runners to sail her to Cardiff, where he chartered *Glory* to load coke and pig iron for San Francisco. Then, several weeks later, on December 27, 1880, she sailed from the Welsh port bound for home.

Two American vessels were competing, unofficially, with *Glory* on the westward Cape Horn run, the down-easter *Tam O'Shanter* and the new Boston product *Emily F. Whitney*. Though these vessels had sailed from the East Coast of the United States, all three cleared their respective ports within the same week. The 1,206-ton *Emily F. Whitney* was on her maiden voyage and would be driven accordingly. The *Tam O'Shanter* already had a fine reputation as a smart sailer in five years in the California trade. The three ships crossed latitude 50° south in the Atlantic almost the same day, but Captain Dan proved the superiority of *Glory* in rough weather in rounding the Horn. He covered this segment in eleven days, whereas his two competitors took nearly a month to do so. At this point *Glory* was only sixty-one days from Cardiff. But she fell behind once she was within a few days' sailing of San Francisco. McLaughlin had to run her up to almost 1,000 miles northwest of the Golden Gate before he could make a slant to carry his ship in. Her passage was 129 days. *Tam O'Shanter* made the best run of the three of 122 days, while the *Emily F. Whitney* bettered McLaughlin's passage by three days; however, Captain Dan did beat several ships. The down-easter *Eliza McNeil* arrived the same day as *Glory*, 142 days from Philadelphia, and the ship *Columbus* was bettered by McLaughlin by five days.[7]

The month following her arrival, Knowles again chartered *Glory* to George W. McNear. Though the market value of wheat continued its slow downward trend, the freight rate Knowles obtained for her was by far the highest she had received for over six years: 72 shillings, 6 pence per long ton ($18.44).[8] There were two excellent reasons for the high rates — a bumper crop in the California grain belt and a scarcity of ships. By the time the grain fiscal year would end, 559 ships, 154 of them American, would have carried 1,128,031 tons of wheat and barley and 919,898 barrels of flour from the bay to Europe. Every available bit of sailing tonnage, including *Glory*, was engaged.[9]

In June, a tug towed her, not to a San Francisco wharf to load, but up the bay more than 25 miles to Port Costa on the south shore of Carquinez

Strait to be berthed alongside the new loading facilities of George Mc-
Near and Associates. Since Captain Dan had made his first voyage in
Glory, after loading at Martinez, many changes had taken place on the
straits. On the Contra Costa County shoreline, a boom in commercial
construction was under way, a small preview of great things to come. Because the Central Pacific Railroad had shortened its track route west from
Sacramento by constructing a giant railroad ferry to traverse Carquinez
Strait, the economic advantages of Contra Costa County had been acknowledged by wheat merchants. The monster 3,549-gross-ton *Solano,*
the largest sidewheeler in the world, had been built in 1879 especially for
the cross-river route, and made her first run on September 24. Later that
year at Benicia, she loaded entire train loads of grain on the four sets of
tracks laid on her 420-foot deck, then chugged across the strait to dock at
a massive wooden slip at Port Costa.[10] From there, the wheat quickly
went to the waiting holds of sailing ships berthed alongside the new grain
facilities.[11] McNear loaded *Glory* in this manner in the year 1881.

While in port, Captain Dan and his wife Maggie took a trip down to
Fresno, California. They were seriously thinking of making this soil-rich
region their home when not at sea. The latter part of May, 1881, they
bought about 60 acres of farmland around the community of Oleander,
about 5 miles outside of Fresno, suitable for raising stock and planting a
vineyard.[12] Just as they were getting settled, the time came due for *Glory*
to sail for Europe; so they joined her while she lay in the bay.

She sailed on July 11, bound for Le Havre with a crew of thirty-one on
board. The voyage was uneventual until she crossed into the frigid "roaring forties." There, at latitude 41°15′ north, longitude 106°30′ west,
Glory of the Seas almost went to a watery grave.[13] Forty-six years later,
William Gribble, an able-bodied seaman, told his story of this voyage to
a British Columbia newspaperman.[14] Though he had colored his yarn
after years and years of retelling it, the essential facts of his near-miss with
death stand out. The following is Gribble's story, with the names of the
crew involved and other data placed in brackets:

> We were rounding the Horn laden with 3,000 [long] tons of wheat. It
> was August 22, 1881. A southerly gale was blowing at the time, and by eight
> A.M. we were running with close-reefed topsails and had stowed the jib and
> mainsail. The seas were breaking over her and about ten o'clock, a tre-
> mendous sea swept over the deck, smashing one boat and drawing the bolts

out of the skids, allowing the cargo to shift. The ship went over on her beam ends.

The strain of 3,000 tons of shifting cargo was so tremendous that the seams in the deck opened and allowed the water to pour down into the hold. The pumps became choked. All hands were called to clear away the wreckage and lower sail, but so dangerous was the position of the ship, with her deck being pounded by tremendous seas, that no person would venture along to carry out the necessary work.

The captain told the mate to go forward and do what had to be done. The mate refused. Then the captain asked, "Have I no one that will go?" I was at the wheel, and I [and several others] answered that I would. He [Captain Dan] told me to slip a rope over my shoulders and they would pay it out as I went forward. I told them that I would prefer not to have any rope about me, and only wanted them to watch the seas and let me know when a big one was coming. Watching my chance, I ran forward. Then came the warning about of "seas" and I jumped to the rail and caught firm hold of a stanchion. The big sea pounded me hard, but I was ready for it and managed to hang on. Before the next sea came, I [and the others] darted forward and carried out the work that I was sent to do and which permitted the ship to be brought about. I was black and blue from being forced against the weight of the seas.

When the *Glory* had been brought about but was still in a dangerous position, the captain called for a volunteer to go below to clear the pump, which had become choked with wheat. There was about four feet of water in the hold, so it meant diving down among the water and grain. No one offered and the captain turned to me. "Jack," he said, "I hate to ask you to do it, but will you? If you do, you won't have to do another tap of work during the whole trip."

I went and it was a pretty tough job. My arms were skinned to the elbows in the effort. It was tremendously hot there too, but I was fortunate in getting the main pump cleaned and started again. Then all hands were put to work trimming the cargo, while we started off to Valparaiso to refit.

The wife [Millie Chappell] of one of the men was stewardess on the ship and she dressed my arms. She told me that he [Frank Chappell] had been watching when I went forward and thought that I would be killed. She told me that I was white as a sheet and asked me if I was not afraid. "Afraid," I exclaimed, "that is why I went. I was afraid not to go, because unless some person did, the ship would turn over and everyone would be drowned. It was better to risk being washed overboard and have a chance for life, then to hang back and meet certain death."

I turned up to do my duty when my watch was called and the captain asked me what I was doing, reminding me that I did not have to do any work. I told him that I did not want any reward for saving my own life.[15]

Although his story is interesting, there is a certain tone missing in the yarn when he makes his remarks about Daniel McLaughlin. With his ship lying nearly on her side and broached to, in such a helpless condition that one extremely heavy sea could stave in a hatch in short order and quickly sink her, McLaughlin, with forty-five years experience at sea was not going to plead with a fo'c's'le hand to attend to his duty. Perhaps the mate did shrink back, but Captain Dan's question "Have I no one that will go?" was most likely said in great disgust at the cowardice of the man in the face of danger. Gribble had to have erred when he said he alone saved *Glory* from capsizing. It was an impossibility for one sailor to clear away the wreckage and shorten whatever sail that wasn't torn to ribbons, especially while the ship lay on her beam ends. Though Gribble undoubtedly volunteered for this dangerous duty, it took at the minimum half a dozen men to carry out the job. As the official "casualty report" and Captain Dan's remarks years later bore out, the hurricane hit her unprepared, and she was helpless. Heavy seas and the hurricane-force winds threw *Glory* over more than 45 degrees, shifting the cargo. Dozens of grain sacks burst, choking the main pumps, and making it impossible to keep the water down in her bilges. In telling his version of the mishap, McLaughlin related how *Glory* was hove to on her beam ends for a full sixteen hours before the crew could fully trim the cargo.[16] She had indeed proved once again that she was a staunch ship to come through such a storm afloat, a further tribute to Donald McKay.

Twelve days later, on September 3, Captain Dan sailed his badly leaking ship into Valparaiso Harbor. In this South American port, normal port and repair costs were outrageous, and McLaughlin planned on attending only to the most necessary repairs. As soon as possible, he made arrangements to unload her cargo into lighters so that her hull could be repaired. During the month the crew, including Gribble, temporarily discharged 2,800 short tons of grain into the dozens of lighters that McLaughlin had hired, leaving the remainder in the lower hold, while the shipwrights worked on her. Once she was sufficiently unloaded, surveyors went below in the lower hold to figure out how to tighten her up enough to make her seaworthy. They estimated the damage at 6,000 dollars. The twisting of her hull had loosened many of her copper and iron fastenings, not only in the frame and knees, but also in the keel and keelsons, the backbone of the ship. Without permanent repairs, McLaughlin could not hope to keep her completely dry until he reached Le Havre. To restiffen her, the Valparaiso shipwrights added wood stanchions in her hold in hopes that these would offset the working of the strained hull, especially in the long, steep seas off Cape Horn.[17] Besides repairing her boat damage on deck, they also recaulked her main deck to stop the leaks topside. It wasn't until November that the crew could begin to reload her. Once the bills were in for the refit, the handling of the cargo, and general port expenses, the owners and the insurance companies had to pay out nearly 25,000 dollars *and* stand the loss of 5,000 sacks of water-damaged wheat from her 'tween decks which had been sold ashore.[18]

Glory sailed for Le Havre on December 2, this time rounding the Horn safely and finally reaching her destination February 17, 1882, seventy-seven days from Valparaiso. At the great French port, McLaughlin had further bad news for the owners and grain consignee. *Glory* had continued to leak badly the rest of her passage, and another 700 tons of cargo was damaged. It was auctioned off as animal feed at Le Havre. This swelled the cargo loss to 20,000 dollars, nearly 20 percent of the value of her cargo, and she had to undergo further repairs at Le Havre. From France, *Glory* sailed for New York via Brixham, England, where Captain Dan picked up 571 tons of coal for the ship. A month later, she arrived at New York and it appeared that the repairs at Valparaiso had stopped the leaks. Following her arrival in June, 1882, she was resurveyed and pronounced sound enough to warrant having her "A-1-in-Red" classification extended to the fifteen-year mark.

On July 2, 1882, *Glory of the Seas* sailed with general cargo for Williams Dimond and Company of San Francisco. On board was Daniel Carleton McLaughlin, the captain's twenty-one-year-old son. He was going out to California to settle at his father's and stepmother's home at Oleander. Young Dan had recently completed his education, and was leaving Malden, Massachusetts, where he had lived since the death of his mother when he was only six. At that time Captain Dan had felt that the lad needed the thorough shore education which he himself lacked. Although the captain had always written long and picturesque letters to Dan, he had only been ashore with him a few times during the ensuing fifteen years. The upcoming four-month passage to California would be the longest opportunity they had ever had to share a close relationship.

It was a voyage that Daniel Carleton never forgot, one that he mentioned with fondness and pride to his family in the years to come.[19]

On *Glory*'s arrival at San Francisco on November 7, 1882, 128 days out from New York, the Captain found that Sears Company had communicated with Josiah Knowles the wish to have a major refit aloft for *Glory*. As soon as her cargo was discharged, she was towed to a shipyard and stripped of her top-hamper. While other repairs were being carried out, sparmakers made up two lower masts for *Glory*, a fore and a main, out of massive, single Douglas firs which had been shipped from the Pacific Northwest.

By the end of December, *Glory of the Seas* was back in first-class condition again, ready to go around Cape Horn for many more voyages. In the eyes of insurance underwriters she was still a valuable piece of shipping property worth 60,000 dollars.[20] Considering that she was now more than thirteen years old and had originally cost her owners only 90,000 dollars, she had proved herself to be a sound investment. However, another problem now presented itself. Sears Company could no longer charter her for grain at a profitable rate. They were not alone. On December 30, 1882, forty-six square-rigged sailing ships were at San Francisco, most of them also finding it impossible to obtain a profit-making charter rate. Those of American registry particularly suffered, receiving less than 2 pounds per long ton. The outlook considerably darkened as new, economical English steel tonnage flowed into the trade and could be fairly content with low rates, mainly because they needed less money to keep in first-class condition. Even so, the foreign vessels received far better rates than the wood down-easters (on the average about 5 shillings [$1.22] more).[21] Slowly but surely, American ships were being forced out of the California grain trade. Even though *Glory* had just been thoroughly refitted, Josiah Knowles found it necessary to lay her up back of Goat Island.

During this interval, Daniel McLaughlin, his wife, and son were at Fresno doing more work on their vineyard and ranch. In February, 1883, Millie Chappell, the stewardess on *Glory*, joined them. She bought 10 acres of land from Captain McLaughlin, probably hoping that soon she could live ashore at Oleander while Frank went to sea.[22]

The afterguard still stayed by *Glory of the Seas*, thinking that she would be sailing for Europe before long. Among them was a new chief mate, Dick Martin, shipped since the return to the Golden Gate. Martin

was busy while his captain was tilling the land, and his activities were to
merit him a nickname which would stick — Slippery Dick. Basil Lubbock, an expressive maritime storyteller, told the tale in his book *The
Down Easters:*

> Martin was a first-class officer, a wonderful navigator and a linguist of
> some ability. He was also a swell dresser with all the outward appearance
> of a gentleman. But after he had sold a hawser, a new mainsail, and several
> coils of manila rope to a junkman at San Francisco, the "old man" of *Glory
> of the Seas* declared that though Martin was beyond reproach as an officer,
> he was a bit too "slippery" for him and he went on to remark that if he had
> not returned from his ranch when he did, he would have found that Martin
> had sold the "whole blooming ship."

By spring, 1883, the shipping situation on San Francisco Bay had only
worsened. A newspaper reporter had the following to say:

> The ships keep piling up in Mission Bay and there are now idle in that
> vicinity over twenty-five ships representing fully one million and a quarter
> dollars in value not earning a dollar and back of Goat Island there are six
> or eight first-class vessels in the same condition, which swells the amount
> tied up to fully one million and a half. Hard times is the word with them.[23]

Among the ships laid up were the cream of the American Cape Horn
fleet — the fast *Three Brothers;* both the sisters, *America* and *Triumphant;* the down-easter *Palestine;* and the *Glory of the Seas.*

Several months later, Daniel McLaughlin decided to end his seagoing
days and settle down at Oleander. He soon discharged the afterguard, and
Glory was left in the care of a watchman. The trade of sea legs for ranch-
er's boots was a difficult one for Captain Dan. He had a backlog of com-
missions earned as shipmaster, but the amount was eaten up in the early
years of establishing his vineyards. He was eventually forced to file a "declaration of homestead" and mortgage part of the property to Josiah
Knowles for 5,000 dollars. In time, though, the vines repaid him and he
became not only solvent, but a grapegrower with a solid reputation.[24]

In 1893, at the age of seventy, he decided to take Maggie to Grand
Manan Island, New Brunswick. They leased their ranch and vineyard
and shortly were on their way east. On arrival, they bought a house and
had three years of retirement together before Captain Dan died, sud-

denly, in January, 1896. Maggie died five years later at their Canadian home.[25]

Meanwhile, *Glory* had many long years ahead of her and many cargoes to carry. She was by no means nearing the retirement age, even though she had well over 350,000 sea miles in her thirteen-year-old hull.

CHAPTER X

The Last Cape Horn Voyage

I_N June, 1884, the shipping picture was generally bleak for everyone in the American merchant marine, but disastrously so for J. Henry Sears and Company. Two hundred and ten foreign ships left the Golden Gate laden with cereals for Europe, while only eighty-one American vessels chartered for grain during the season.[1] More than thirty first-class square-riggers continued to be laid up in San Francisco Bay, their average freight rate a mere 25 shillings 8 pence ($6.22) per long ton.[2] To make matters worse, the United States was in the middle of a major financial panic, many marine banks had failed, and the resulting shortage of money to finance deep-water voyages further destroyed the health of the nation's shipping.

At this time *Glory of the Seas,* the Sears bark *Ocean King,* and their ship *Titan* were laid up at San Francisco. In Cardiff, the two Sears ships that had managed grain charters for England, the *Imperial* and the *Grecian,* lay awaiting charters. All five of their vessels with a total gross tonnage of 9,000 tons not making a penny made bankruptcy a stark reality for J. Henry Sears and Andrew Nickerson. The crash came for them in the middle of the month. An agreement was quickly reached with their creditors to assign all company assets to a trustee, William P. Ellison, a junior partner in the Boston shipping firm of Howes and Crowell. On June 16, 1884, legal instruments were drawn up and recorded stating in part that J. Henry Sears and Company was "insolvent and unable to pay their debts

in full or at maturity."[3] All their shipping interests and real estate holdings were conveyed to Ellison as trustee.[4]

Despite low shipping rates, Ellison soon had the *Imperial* and *Grecian*
on voyages to China. For over thirty years his firm had owned or managed
dozens of successful clippers and down-easters ranging from the *Climax,*
the first ship built for them in 1853, and the *Comet* of 1869 to the ex-
steamer *Ericsson,* which they managed during the 1870's. But Howes and
Crowell themselves were doomed. Because of stiff steamer competition,
they would be selling all their shipping interests within a few years.[5] During the summer of 1884 the energetic company still had the capital to back
the three inactive Sears ships even though one of their own vessels, the
1,450-ton royal-yarder *Carrollton,* was also laid up at San Francisco.

In September, miraculously, Nickerson and Sears recouped their
losses and were allowed legally to retain their shipping and real estate interests.[6] In several months all their tonnage except *Ocean King* would
again be plowing through the seas of the world.

Before *Glory of the Seas* could become active again, she needed a captain who could maintain her reputation as the fastest ship in their fleet.
During the fall months important discussions on this matter were held
in the Sears offices on Commercial Street between J. Henry Sears, Andrew
Nickerson, and Captain Joshua Freeman. The three men were all originally from Brewster, Massachusetts, on Cape Cod and had known and respected each other for many years.

There were many solid reasons why Sears and Nickerson wanted
Joshua Freeman to command *Glory.* He was born at Brewster in 1835,
the seventh generation of Freemans living on Cape Cod. His ancestors,
of English Puritan stock, dated back to the 1600's in America and through
the years had intermarried with Searses, Crowells, and Knowleses, ex-
plaining some of the closeness of the families. When Joshua was only four
years old his father, who commanded square-riggers, died. His mother re-
married shortly thereafter, this time to one of the Dunbars, another seagoing family of the district. In the next few years Joshua received his
schooling at Brewster and on reaching the age of sixteen decided to follow
in his forebears' footsteps. He shipped out on vessels managed by the important East Dennis merchants Christopher Hall and Prince Crowell. In
a very short while he had made such a good impression on his employers
that he was quickly upgraded to a junior officer.

By the time Joshua Freeman was twenty-one he was already serving as first officer in square-riggers out of Boston. He was striking in manner and appearance. He stood 6 feet, was thin in build, and had a dark complexion, black eyes, black hair, and the beginnings of a full beard. Typical of his Puritan background, he was austere and commanded respect even at an early age. In July, 1856, he married a twenty-year-old Brewster woman, Lucy Anna Lincoln, who had been a childhood friend, and was, predictably, a member of a local shipping family. A warm-hearted, soft-spoken girl with dark brown hair, she was to be his complement for the next sixty years.[7]

In early 1857 Christopher Hall died. At the time a smart little medium clipper to be named in honor of the late merchant was being built by the Shivericks of East Dennis. She was a saucy three-masted square-rigger, 147 feet in length, spreading single tops'ls, a main skys'l, and flying a suit of stuns'ls. Prince Crowell, her managing owner, honored Freeman by giving him the new ship as his first command. In September and October, at the age of only twenty-two, the new captain proudly prepared his 649-ton ship for sea. In October Joshua and Lucy sailed for China in the *Christopher Hall,* returning to Boston the following fall. In 1858–1859 they made a second voyage in her, to San Francisco via Cape Horn. She completed her passage out from Boston in 127 days, arriving at the Golden Gate March 25, 1859.[8] Now twenty-four, Freeman was already gifted in making his ship a money-maker. Prince Crowell, once he trusted his captains, was noted for granting them free reign with their charters and expenses. Freeman fulfilled the trust, thriftily cutting expenditures whenever *Christopher Hall* was in port. In the next few years he called at many ports — Valparaiso, Melbourne, Calcutta, and Liverpool among them. In May of 1861, he was honored by being granted membership in the respected shipping fraternity, the Boston Marine Society. Four months later the Freeman's first child, Lucy Anna, was born at the home of Lucy's relatives at Boston. As the Civil War laid waste to the shipping industry, Joshua decided to relinquish command of the *Christopher Hall* and stay ashore for the duration. In May, 1865, a month after the war's end, Lucy gave birth to a baby boy in Boston, Joshua Eugene Freeman.[9] The following February Captain Freeman resumed command of merchant vessels, taking over the 181-foot *W. B. Dinsmore.* He made a fourteen-month voyage in the 1,041-ton wooden vessel and had left her shortly before she was completely destroyed by fire in 1867.[10]

That year Andrew Nickerson and J. Henry Sears persuaded their good

Captain Joshua Freeman with his wife Lucy and daughter Lucy Anna. Photo taken at Lima, Peru, in the late 1870's, when Freeman was master of the *Gold Hunter*. Courtesy Mrs. Barbara Bumpus.

friend to take command of a 180-foot down-easter that they were having
built in Waldoboro, Maine. Joshua and other Freemans from Brewster
all bought shares in the 1,258-ton ship, which was named *Gold Hunter*.
She was a trim, beautifully built vessel crossing nothing higher than royals and had built lower masts. By November, Freeman had her smartly
equipped and readied for sea. In the ensuing thirteen years, she proved to
be a relatively slow sailor in the Cape Horn trade. Joshua's fastest trip in
her from Boston to San Francisco was only 166 days in 1869; but he kept
her in top condition, a showpiece of the Sears fleet. In October, 1880,
she was in the China Sea bound for Hong Kong with a cargo of Cardiff
coal, when a strong gale sprung up, tossing her like a cork in an angry sea.
She piled up on a reef near shore and was completely in pieces in a matter
of hours. Fortunately, Joshua, his crew of nineteen, Mrs. Freeman, and
Lucy Anna, now a young lady of nineteen, made land safely in the boats,
where they were assisted by the islanders.[11] On returning to the wreck the
following day, Joshua was particularly chagrined to discover, among the
scattered wreckage on the beach, not a piece of brass or copper. The natives had looted it all, and every single personal possession which had
floated ashore. Before long, the captain, his family, and the crew were
making their way in the ship's boats to Manila in the Philippines. After
several weeks the Freemans sailed for Boston, arriving there in January,
1881.[12]

   On the voyage back to Boston, Joshua did a great deal of thinking
about the advisability of going back to sea. Once he and his family settled again at Boston, he decided to retire at the early age of forty-six. He
had invested wisely through the years in stocks, savings, and bonds, and
had made good profits in *Gold Hunter*. In addition he had bought interests in different square-rig vessels — all of which made his decision possible. Another landfall occurred in the months following his return. The
insurance company covering policies for the *Gold Hunter* paid him 7,500
dollars for his 3/16 interest in her.[13] But in three years the Marine bank
failures and the shipping crash that caused J. Henry Sears to become insolvent nearly wiped out Joshua Freeman, too. The mental pressures during the financial panic broke Freeman's health. During the summer, he
suffered a stroke that left his right leg paralyzed. During the following
months Lucy did all she could to help her husband, and by fall, 1884, he
could get around fairly well with a cane. His strong will served him mas-
terfully while he fought to recover from his crippling illness, and he refused to admit that his leg would never be the same.[14]

With the greater part of his savings and securities gone, Joshua found himself being forced to make the decision which other semiretired shipmasters had made recently, to return to sea. This was why his answer to J. Henry Sears and Andrew Nickerson was in the affirmative. He realized he was fortunate to be finding any first-rate ship command with the continuing decay of the American grain fleet, and he looked forward to boarding *Glory of the Seas* even though she was presently laid up on the West Coast as "unprofitable to operate."

Soon Captain Freeman, his wife, and daughter headed out to California, leaving nineteen-year-old J. Eugene behind to finish his schooling at M.I.T. On their arrival at the bay port, Josiah Knowles welcomed his old friends and escorted them out to *Glory of the Seas,* which still lay at anchor on the eastern side of Goat Island. As they came alongside the McKay medium clipper, it was obvious that inactivity had left its mark on her. A watchman had been the lone soul on board for nearly a year and only minimum upkeep had been done to her. *Glory* looked weatherworn, a sad state for a first-class Cape Horner. Once their possessions were safely aboard, Joshua began walking her decks to formulate what he would have to do aloft and to the hull to make his big command ready for sea. Meanwhile, as Lucy and Lucy Anna were busy back aft unpacking trunks, the little hot pot stove in the dining saloon warmed up the after cabin, taking out the chill and dampness in the air.

At the same time the *Titan* prepared for sea. She eventually sailed for Melbourne in November, leaving the big ships of the Sears fleet, *Glory* and *Ocean King,* in back of Goat Island; but soon, the only Sears vessel to be left in layup would be *Ocean King.*

The hum of activity sounded in the ship roadsteads at Sausalito, Mission Bay, and the eastern side of Yerba Buena. By the turn of the year the California grain crop was good and the freight rates were low but improved enough for many American square-riggers to afford to come out of layup and make the 14,000-mile voyage to Europe. As examples, the ship *Palestine* had lain in port the longest — for nearly twenty-eight months — but had recently been chartered for 38 shillings ($9.23) per long ton. The great 3,019-ton ex-steamer *Three Brothers,* which had been in port for over a year, finally received a charter. Joshua Freeman had high hopes *Glory of the Seas* would soon be joining these vessels at the grain wharves.

While awaiting word of a charter, Captain Freeman had wrought a transformation in his new command. He had wiped away the look of shab-

Broadway Wharf, San Francisco. Courtesy San Francisco Maritime Museum,
J. Porter Shaw Collection.

biness and had returned the aura of spit and polish from stem to stern. All her spars had been scraped clean and revarnished, including her lower masts, which now sported varnish even in the mizzenmast chappells. The white bulwarks, figurehead, and deck houses no longer showed their signs of rust stains and dirt. Her hull and rigging had been gone over as completely as possible. Workmen had even caulked her upper deck to offset any shrinkage in the seams caused by her long inactivity. Gilt shone brightly throughout, from the elaborate scroll work on the stem and the intricately carved after-cabin brackets to her beautiful McKay stern. As February, 1885, approached the last vestige of Daniel McLaughlin's command of *Glory of the Seas* disappeared from view — her new master covered up the 6-inch yellow band on her planksheer. Captain Freeman put the same degree of care in her that he had in the *Gold Hunter.*

During this interval the Freemans had some special visitors, Captain Josiah Knowles and his family. More than eight years had passed since Knowles's command of *Glory,* and changes had taken place in his family and financial standing. Captain Knowles was fifty-four years old, heavyset, completely gray-haired, but still sporting his full beard. Of his children, Mattie and Harry were sixteen; Mary, fourteen; the twins Alice and Thomas, eight years old; and Ruth, the youngest, was five. Many years later, Alice would relate how awestruck she had been when she went aboard the big square-rigger. She was overwhelmed by the windship with her lofty masts and lines crossing every unintelligible which way, and she was proud to say from then on that she had once been on board her father's ship. Of course, the person most interested in visiting *Glory of the Seas* was Josiah Knowles himself. She had been his favorite command and he was gratified to see that Freeman was already keeping her up very well. Indeed, Captain Freeman and Lucy were just as proud of their seagoing home as the Knowleses had been for the four and a half years they had lived on board *Glory* as a family.[15]

From William Dresbach, a San Francisco shipping merchant, J. Henry Sears and Company received a grain charter for *Glory* at 35 shillings ($8.51) per long ton the latter part of January. In a matter of weeks the freight rate for American sailing ships had dropped 3 shillings for wooden tonnage; and down to 37 shillings for iron and steel ships. Obviously, the grain trade was light-years removed from the days of 15 and 20 dollars per long ton.[16]

On February 11, 1885, as *Glory of the Seas* was being towed up to the

California Grange wharves on Carquinez Straits, bills of sale in favor of
Captain Freeman were being recorded at the Boston Customhouse. Once
a cargo had been assured, he had communicated with Sears and Company
his wish to purchase a 1/8 interest (approximately $6,250) in *Glory,* and
they had acted as his agents in buying the shares from the Whiton brothers
estate in Boston.[17] As of February 2, nearly everything Joshua and Lucy
Freeman had left from the shipping crash was invested in her. They had
firm hopes that she wouldn't let them down.

After being berthed at the grain wharves that were near Crockett,
large stevedore crews began loading 3,000 long tons of wheat in her 'tween
decks and lower hold. A contemporary newspaper article described the
steady action at Port Costa: "Wheat is being poured out of cars, warehouses, and barges for nine hours a day, six days a week."[18] *Glory* was not
the only ship thus being loaded. The British iron ship *River Nith* was
farther up Carquinez Straits receiving in excess of 1,600 tons of grain.
Because of the fairly fast loading methods, *Glory* had a full cargo on
board in four days.

As the first rays of sunlight shone hazily through the dense fog on San
Francisco Bay on February 22, there was an eerie silence over the water,
disturbed intermittently by the deep blare of foghorns. In those early
morning hours a renewal of activity took place on *Glory of the Seas.* Sails
that had lain unused in the sail locker were now bent expectantly waiting to be filled with a fresh ocean breeze. Captain Joshua stood solemnly
on the after cabin top making sure that everything was in order as *Glory*
prepared to get under way. Her tug now came alongside and took her
under tow. Then, as the great ship began to rock gracefully in its wake,
she came fully alive again after her long hibernation. Once sufficiently
outside the Gate, she cast off the towboat hawser, freeing her at last from
land for the first time in two years. *Glory* was now ready to obey every
wish of her new master. Four months later, she came to anchor at Liverpool on June 19, 119 days out from San Francisco. Freeman had made a
fine passage, beating a number of English and American grain ships to
England, some by a week, others by a month. In comparison, the big
Sutherlandshire, a smart 1,549-ton, iron lime-juicer, arrived three days
before her, but made her passage in 124 days. She was a longer ship than
Glory by 18 feet, more heavily rigged, and only three and one-half years
old. The 1,785-ton *Brodick Castle,* which Daniel McLaughlin had beaten
to England in 1876–1877, bettered the McKay clipper by two days this

year. She sailed from San Francisco four days after *Glory* and arrived at Liverpool two days after her. Though Freeman had broken no records, he had made a fine run in the old ship.

The United States Government at this time was becoming concerned with the continued downgrading of her wooden sailing ships in the grain trade. Earlier in the year, the Assistant Secretary of State in Washington, D.C., sent communiqués instructing the American consul at Liverpool to compile detailed lists of all grain vessels entering the River Mersey from the Pacific coast of the United States. The Government, after many years of complacency, was vainly trying to fight the discrimination shown against down-easters in cargo insurance and freight rates. At the close of 1885, the American consul sent a letter and chart to Washington in which he wrote in part: "that the information will be sufficient to assist the Honorable Secretary of the Treasury in determining whether or not grain can be carried in wooden vessels in the trade between the Pacific coast and Europe as safely, speedily, and economically as in vessels built of iron."[19] In his letter he wrote that the condition on arrival of the cargo on *Glory of the Seas* was "excellent" and that "about 15 tons" had been "slightly sea-damaged." Of the three other American wooden ships arriving within weeks of her, the two-year-old *William H. Smith* had "about 60 tons, slightly sea-damaged"; the 1881-built down-easter *Charmer* had "about 60 tons" damaged; and the eleven-year-old *C. F. Sargent* had only "about ten tons." In comparing the condition of *Glory of the Seas* with these down-easters and with the other American ships calling at Liverpool in 1885, Joshua Freeman could easily prove that after fourteen years of hard driving, *Glory* still remained a sound cargo carrier.[20]

However, *Glory* no longer had her special A-1-in-Red insurance classification. It had expired in October, 1884, at the fifteen-year mark, but she could still carry grain for several years to come because of proper maintenance over the years and the sound construction Donald McKay had given her back in 1869. British Lloyds had never officially recognized her as a specially classified ship for any of this fifteen-year period,[21] so her age made little difference to them, as long as cargo damage remained low. To make sure that she continued in fine shape, Freeman had her docked in July, 1885, in one of the graving docks at Liverpool. There she was stripped of all sheathing, thoroughly recaulked, and then resheathed with yellow metal. She sailed from Liverpool on August 2, bound for San Pedro, California, with a cargo of Lancashire coal for the Southern Pa-

cific Railroad. She made a fair passage of 129 days, coming to anchor in
the outer harbor of this growing port on December 8, 1885. During the
following weeks, the crew and shore personnel busily discharged the coal.
At this time the inner harbor of Los Angeles was too shallow (a 15-foot
depth at high water) to permit entrance of heavily laden sailing ships, so
all deep-water cargoes had to be discharged into lighters. To eliminate
this, the United States Army Corps of Engineers had been constructing
and enlarging two jetties since 1871 in order to scour out the Los Angeles River channel as far as the towns of San Pedro and Wilmington,
then the principal ports of Los Angeles County. Vast improvements were
needed before this area could ever grow commercially and in popula-
tion.[22]

While *Glory of the Seas* lay out in San Pedro Bay at anchor, Joshua
Freeman wrote to Josiah Knowles, Andrew Nickerson, and J. Henry Sears
regarding the future of his command. More and more, American ships
entered the grain trade only if a shortage of tonnage existed and if halfway
favorable rates could be secured. Large three- and four-masted foreign
vessels constructed of iron and steel now carried the greatest percentage
of the grain from California and the Northwest Territories. As a general
rule, a wooden ship was unfit for the perishable cargo trade by the time
she reached eighteen to twenty years, though there had been exceptions
to this rule, the *Young America* being a notable one. American down-
easters only eight years old now had difficulty securing cargoes.[23] Many
shippers did not care to take the chance of cargo damage with wooden
ships and refused to pay as high a freight rate as they would with a similar
iron or steel ship; consequently, a large percentage of American shipowners continued turning to the Pacific coast coal and lumber trade for temporary employment between grain charters. Joshua Freeman seriously
contemplated taking *Glory* permanently out of the Cape Horn trade even
though she was still sound. Facing the cold facts on paper, he saw that a
grain charter would henceforth gross only about 20,000 dollars for a wood
ship the size of *Glory of the Seas* — less than half that of ten years before.
The average freight rate of 28 shillings ($6.80) was not enough to meet
the expenses of an older wooden ship for insurance on ship and cargo,
port expenses, crew, and general upkeep, especially when she could carry
grain only once a year.[24] The Pacific coast coal trade, however, presented a more lucrative future. Commerce from Puget Sound and British
Columbia was increasing at a fast pace and freight rates were excellent

for a short-term voyage, averaging $3.50 to $4.00 per long ton.[25] Freeman figured that *Glory* could easily make at least five voyages a year, almost doubling the money she could make in the grain trade during the same period. All these factors were thoroughly discussed by Sears, Nickerson, Knowles, and Freeman and the resulting decision left the captain sad but resigned: *Glory of the Seas* would be withdrawn from the grain trade. In later years Freeman told his family how he had hated doing this, but that no alternative was open to him if he wanted her to make reasonable profits. It was a big step down for him to have his command turn into a regular coastal coal drougher.[26]

In early January, 1886, Josiah Knowles chartered *Glory* to Robert Dunsmuir and Sons of British Columbia to carry a load of coal to San Francisco. On the twenty-third with a crew of twenty-nine on board, *Glory of the Seas* weighed anchor and stood out from San Pedro Bay bound for Departure Bay, British Columbia.

Glory had ended a career that spanned sixteen years; her prime was past, but she still had more tnan two-thirds of her life yet to live.

CHAPTER XI

Beginning in the British Columbia Coal Trade

Dᴜʀɪɴɢ the middle of February, 1886, *Glory of the Seas* neared, for the first time, one of the most dangerous places along the Pacific Ocean coastline — Cape Flattery, at the extreme northwesterly point of Washington Territory. Joshua Freeman, having fought rainy, blustery weather for more than two weeks all the way up the coast, now stood prudently well off the cape, waiting for the tides and winds to allow him to enter the Straits of Juan de Fuca, the 13-mile-wide channel leading to Puget Sound and the Straits of Georgia. He had much respect for these treacherous waters, knowing well that the coastline lay strewn with the wreckage of numberless ships, which had either piled up on a lee shore during a dense fog, or floundered with all hands during one of the frequent heavy gales. When the weather and tides were right, the Captain carefully piloted her into Juan de Fuca Straits, coming to anchor at Royal Roads, the ship roadstead at Victoria, British Columbia. He was eighteen days out from San Pedro.

Five days later, during the early morning hours of February 19, the Dunsmuir Company tug that would be towing *Glory* to Nanaimo came alongside and passed her hawser. It was the sleek, 170-foot, 192-ton side-wheeler *Alexander,* the biggest vessel of its kind on Puget Sound. Once she made her line fast on *Glory,* the towboat's 160-horsepower walking beam engine began chugging away. Simultaneously, her paddle wheels,

20 feet in diameter, churned the water of Royal Roads as her stately charge slowly got under way. So began the nearly 90-mile tow to Departure Bay. After passing to the south of Victoria, the *Alexander* headed north up Haro Strait. Knowing about the tricky currents and unpredictable winds of the winter months, Joshua Freeman had been well-advised not to attempt to sail *Glory* to Nanaimo his first passage. Behind the tug's hawser, she set a few steadying sails to allow her to make fair headway up the narrow strait. Late that afternoon, as the *Alexander* and *Glory of the Seas* entered the Straits of Georgia, about 2 miles east of Saturna Island, the two crews saw a heart-rending sight: the big, three-skys'l-yarder *John Rosenfeld* hung up on a reef less than a mile away with her tug, *Tacoma*, standing by. It was indeed pitiful to see this beautiful vessel helplessly heeling over to starboard as her crew desperately tried to lighten her of her 3,905-ton cargo before she sank. The *Tacoma* had been towing the heavily laden ship from Nanaimo to the open sea and had senselessly tried to take a short cut at high tide, running the *Rosenfeld* on a chartered underwater reef at 6 knots. The big down-easter's bow was stove in and she was taking water, but the captain, James G. Baker, was still hoping to save her. The master of the *Tacoma* signaled the *Alexander* for help, but the latter refused, fully aware of the seriousness of *Tacoma*'s blunder, but not wanting to leave *Glory of the Seas* unattended in the treacherous tidal waters. The two-year-old *John Rosenfeld* was left to her fate. The next low tide sealed her doom, hanging her up on the reef again and breaking her back amidships.[1]

On entering Departure Bay late that evening, *Glory* dropped anchor on a signal from the *Alexander*'s captain. As soon as possible, they made known the plight of the *John Rosenfeld,* but it was already too late to avert the tragic ending for the nearly new ship. Early the next morning, Captain Freeman had his crew busy discharging ballast over the side before loading the bulk coal. Although for thirty years the deep and spacious bay had been receiving thousands of tons of ballast, there was no danger of its filling up. Surrounded by vast forests and occasional commercial vicinities down to the water's edge, the beach ran out to a point and then abruptly dropped off to a considerable depth.

On the north side of the bay just west of the Brandon Islands stood the Dunsmuir coal wharves, a series of three narrow piers, two of which were T-shaped, so that coal droughers could come alongside to load. The narrow-gauge coal trains came down from the shaft sites located near the

The paddlewheel tug *Alexander,* which often in the late 1880's towed *Glory* to or from Departure Bay. Courtesy Provincial Archives, Victoria, British Columbia.

The down-easter *John Rosenfeld* aground on a reef. Courtesy Provincial
Archives, Victoria, British Columbia.

community of Wellington, about 2½ miles away. Nearing the loading site at Departure Bay, a railroad engineer ran his train on a switchback, and then backed the coal cars onto the wharves where their contents were dumped into the holds of ships by Chinese laborers. There were two other coal facilities nearby. One was at the southwestern part of Departure Bay, and the Vancouver Coal Company wharf was several miles south, adjacent to the city of Nanaimo. The production of the three mining companies owning the loading docks was rising at a fast rate: in 1885, 365,000 tons of bituminous coal were mined, 238,000 tons of which were shipped to California, Portland, Alaska, and Hawaii. Although the Washington Territory mines produced more coal as a whole, British Columbia was fast catching up.[2]

Since *Glory of the Seas* would be in port for a month, there was not enough activity to warrant keeping to the regular watch system used at sea of "four on, four off." Instead, Freeman had his whole crew busy discharging ballast from dawn to dark. Occasionally, in the evening when shipboard duties were completed, some members of the crew launched the ship's boats and rowed to a small finger pier on the west side of the bay. Just off the beach was a place to "wet their palates," the Bay Saloon. This was a typical old-time tavern with a long, high bar where drinks were served to *Glory*'s crew. A decrepit but ornate piano plunked out rip-roaring tunes for their background music. The visit of Captain Freeman and his crew to Departure Bay was the first of many that, in the years to come, would greatly endear *Glory of the Seas* to the saloon owner and vice versa.[3]

While the ship loaded cargo, the Freeman family was invited to James Dunsmuir's thirteen-room mansion overlooking Departure Bay. There they met some of the supervisory staff of the Wellington Colliery, among them Dunsmuir's right-hand man Frank "Dib" Little, who managed all machine operations of the colliery.[4] Lucy, the captain's daughter, was formally introduced to the quiet Scotsman and made an immediate impression. Frank Little decided this would not be the last time he would see Lucy.[5]

By the third week of March, *Glory of the Seas* had her full cargo of 3,300 long tons of coal on board and lay prepared to sail for San Francisco. Once a tug arrived to tow her out to Cape Flattery, Freeman weighed anchor and she silently left Departure Bay. Nearing the entrance of Boundary Pass, off Saturna Island, the crew once again saw in the distance the remains of the *John Rosenfeld*. Barges were lying alongside to load coal from the wreck, now stripped of all salvable gear. The *Rosenfeld* was pathetic, completely broken in two just abaft the mainmast. As Freeman, his wife, and daughter viewed the disaster, it brought them sorrowful memories of the wreck of the *Gold Hunter*. They could well appreciate the heartache of Captain Baker when he had seen that saving her was hopeless. Once *Glory* was let go off Cape Flattery, she made a fine passage down to San Francisco, arriving there March 26, six days from Departure Bay. So ended her first voyage in the Pacific coast coal trade.

Following their arrival, Joshua Freeman was informed that the *Ocean King* was soon to be reactivated after three long years at San Francisco. Josiah Knowles now held an interest in her and had recently chartered her for the British Columbia coal trade, relegating two Sears ships to the coal drougher ranks. However, *Ocean King* was to have a sadly brief career. In just thirteen months she would spring a bad leak off the coast and flounder in heavy weather.[6]

The Southern Pacific Railroad now chartered *Glory* to load coal at Tacoma, Washington Territory. She arrived there in ballast on May 9, and came to anchor in Commencement Bay, next to "Old" Tacoma. This large natural harbor in the southern part of Puget Sound afforded excellent anchorage for deep-sea sailing ships and like Departure Bay had more than sufficient depth to hold ballast dumped over the side.[7] Tacoma had the distinction of being the leading lumber manufacturing city on the Pacific coast at that time, and saw innumerable sailing ships come and go; moreover, the Carbon Hill (Carbonado) coal miles, owned by the Pacific Improvement Company (a subsidiary of the Southern Pacific Railroad), had extensive mining operations 30 miles from Tacoma. These were connected by train to ample loading wharves, located just below Stadium High School. *Glory* and the bark *Aureola,* which had arrived at Tacoma the day after her, both loaded Carbonado coal for San Francisco. More than a dozen additional ships, barks, barkentines, and schooners lay in this busy port, several of which were loading at the Tacoma Mill Company wharf. Among them were the bark *Canada* and the stately old clipper ship *Dashing Wave*. There was bound to be sailing rivalry between Captain Conner of the 181-foot *Dashing Wave* and Joshua Freeman. The main skys'l yarder had the reputation of being the fastest ship on the coast. Although she was half the tonnage of *Glory of the Seas* and thirty-three years old, few ships with the exception of the clipper *War*

Above. Wharves of the Carbon Hill Coal Company, Tacoma, in the 1880's. Courtesy Fort Nisqually. Below. Tall ships berthed at Tacoma in the 1880's. *Dashing Wave,* nearest the camera, was by reputation the fastest square-rigger on the Pacific coast. Courtesy Fort Nisqually.

Hawk, which had been destroyed by fire three years before at Discovery Bay, Washington Territory, gave her any competition up and down the coast. The *Wave*, as she was nicknamed, had been bought shortly after she had made her last Cape Horn passage in 1869–1870 by the Hanson-Ackerson Company of San Francisco, owners of the Tacoma Mill. This brought to a close seventeen strenuous years filled with many mishaps in the East India and Cape Horn trades. Her new owners converted her into a lumber drougher at San Francisco, partially resparring her, and cutting two large lumber ports in her transom, so that she could henceforth load massive sticks out of the forests of Puget Sound. From that time onward, she generally carried 650,000 to 750,000 board feet of lumber per voyage from Tacoma, and made seven to eleven voyages a year, which meant that she had paid for herself ten times over.[8]

Two and a half weeks after her arrival on the sound, *Glory* lay out in the stream laden with 4,000 long tons of coal, drawing more than 28 feet. Proudly the *Tacoma Ledger* wrote, "This is the largest cargo of coal that ever left any port on Puget Sound on a sailing vessel."[9] For a ship her age she was overloaded; however, for a week's hopefully fair-weather run down the coast, Freeman thought he would see how she handled. The more coal she carried, naturally, the greater profits she would make. At 6:30 P.M. on May 26, the screw steam tug *Tyee* took *Glory* in tow and the following afternoon let her go at Cape Flattery. The *Dashing Wave*, heavily laden herself, with an 8-foot deck load, was towed out to sea May 27. *Glory of the Seas* arrived at San Francisco June 3, seven days from Tacoma, beating the *Dashing Wave*, which arrived at the bay port late in the evening of June 4, eight days from Puget Sound. Although her overloaded condition had caused *Glory* to work and leak much more than usual, her beating the *Wave*, even under unfavorable circumstances, started a competition which would span fifteen years.

On her third voyage in the coal trade, Robert Dunsmuir and Sons again chartered *Glory*. She made a round voyage from San Francisco of forty-six days. Three and a half weeks were spent lying at Departure Bay, so Lucy Anna Freeman and "Dib" Little had a further chance to acquaint themselves. It was evident from their encouragement of and friendliness to Little that Joshua and his wife approved of him, even though he was quite a bit older than Lucy. Frank was short in stature, dignified but quiet, and had a handle-bar moustache. Lucy, who had been partly educated in England, was a stately and reserved young woman, a proper

Dunsmuir wharves at Departure Bay, British Columbia, in the 1880's. Courtesy Provincial Archives, Victoria, British Columbia.

Nanaimo and its harbor, ca. 1890. Courtesy Provincial Archives, Victoria, British Columbia.

upper-crust New Englander. She was slightly taller than Frank, slim like her father, and noticeably attractive. While *Glory* lay in port, "Dib" came to court Miss Lucy, riding an old mule, his mode of transportation. Long walks were a hardship for him because of an injury suffered in a mine explosion at Wellington. During the three-and-a-half-week interval, the couple had several occasions to build a romance from their chance acquaintance.[10]

Glory made one more complete voyage to Departure Bay for Dunsmuir in October and November, bringing to a close her first four voyages as a coal drougher. She had carried 14,300 tons of coal to San Francisco and made a gross profit of nearly 50,000 dollars, vindicating Freeman's decision to withdraw *Glory* from the grain trade. She was far more successful financially than she ever could have been during the same interval in the Cape Horn trade.

At the beginning of the new year, 1887, she lay in Nanaimo harbor awaiting her turn to load at the Vancouver Coal Company wharf. John Rosenfeld, one of the most colorful shipping men on the Pacific Coast, had persuaded Joshua Freeman to carry coal for him this voyage. Rosenfeld, besides using the many square-rigged ships in his fleet, both Cape Horners and coasters, very often chartered outside tonnage to fill the growing needs of the Vancouver Coal Company, an English concern home-based in London. Their small facilities at Nanaimo could hardly compare with those at Cardiff, Liverpool, or Newcastle, Australia; their production was snail-paced, a mere 400 tons per day. Only 120,000 tons were being shipped out annually from the Vancouver Coal Company mines, but at least a large percentage of this was being carried in American square-riggers.[11] In January three ships lay out in Nanaimo harbor waiting to load — *Glory* and the down-easters *Richard P. Buck* and *Iroquois*. The 1,491-ton *Richard P. Buck* being used as a coal drougher was another example of the few grain charters and poor rates offered American tonnage. Though not even five years old and well kept up, she could not make a profit-making voyage to Europe, and her owners had recently placed her in the coast coal trade, a source of revenue that she would not be leaving for a two full years.[12] First, *Glory of the Seas* was berthed next to the long Vancouver Coal Company wharf. Then, a few days later, the *Richard P. Buck* also came alongside. Enough coal had been stockpiled from the nearby mines so that both ships could be loaded fairly rapidly. The *Buck* finished her cargo first and sailed for San Pedro the latter part of January, laden with 2,340 tons. *Glory,* larger and able to carry more cargo, remained on the berth until she loaded 3,387 tons, and then sailed for San Francisco.

On February 8, *Glory* doggedly bucked headwinds one day out from San Francisco, while the ships *America, Kennebec,* and the *Richard P. Buck* lay out in San Pedro Bay discharging their cargoes into lighters. During the night a terrific southwester struck the southern California coast, seriously damaging the three anchored ships. The three skys'l yarder *America* ran ashore and was pounded on the San Pedro inner bar. Severely strained, she was subsequently towed to San Francisco and sold for 10,400 dollars at public auction, because her managing owners, Thayer and Lincoln of Boston, considered her unrepairable.[13] Her buyer was Charles Goodall, president of the Pacific Steam Whaling Company, who with others including Josiah Knowles planned to refit her for use in the Pacific Coast coal trade. Soon after they completed the transaction, Knowles had the 2,054-ton *America* in a Bay shipyard under repair. Pacific Steam Whaling could well afford to spend money on her, having bought her for such a paltry sum. Besides having her hull extensively tightened, Knowles had *America* rigged down to royals to cut down the number of crew needed to handle her at sea. At the same time the riggers replaced her "built" fore and mizzen lower masts with solid sticks from the Pacific northwest. Within months, the *America* would join *Glory of the Seas* in the British Columbia coal trade, giving Joshua Freeman some additional keen sailing competition.

On June 4, *Glory* arrived at Victoria. Soon after, the *Alexander* towed her up to Departure Bay where she was to load Wellington coal. Not only Joshua, his wife, and daughter were on board this voyage, but also J. Eugene Freeman. A forthcoming family event had prompted J. Eugene to take time off from his job as a draftsman with a prominent San Francisco building architect. Lucy, within days, was going to become Mrs. Frank Little. On Tuesday, June 15, the Freemans and all the other invited guests assembled in the spacious parlor of James Dunsmuir's home to witness the union of Frank and Lucy Anna. After the ceremony was over, the couple went on a brief honeymoon, and on their return would make their home at the mining community of Wellington.[14]

Glory of the Seas lay at Departure Bay discharging ballast and lying under the coal chutes off and on for thirty days this voyage, which meant that the crew made more than one visit to the Bay Saloon. In fact, the fo'c's'le crowd, even though they were, for the most part, different men each passage, became such regular customers that the tavern owner now had a painting of *Glory* up on the saloon wall. During the month of June, other square-rigger crews made up the noisy sailors' crowd evenings at the Bay Saloon. The down-easters *Sintram* and the two-year-old *St. Charles* likewise lay in the bay. Neither ship had picked up a grain cargo, so their owners had chartered them to Dunsmuir to make some money at least until they could afford to enter the Cape Horn trade again.

On July 1, the news spread aboard the coal ships at Nanaimo that the proud ex-Cape Horner *America* was being towed up from Royal Roads. Josiah Knowles had placed one of his best square-rig masters in command, Captain James S. Gibson. Thirty-one years old, Gibson had been a master mariner for less than four years, but Knowles felt he was a good choice to command this ship. Even though Gibson had lost the ancient square-rigger *Belvidere* just nine months before by striking a reef during a dense fog on the Vancouver Island coastline, Knowles knew him to be industrious, quick to learn, and with his commands always looking exceptionally smart.[15] As *America* came to anchor in Departure Bay, the crews on *Glory*, *St. Charles*, and *Sintram* had to admit that with her graceful lines, round stern, and white figurehead, few vessels could compare with her in beauty. Everything about her was well painted and trim in appearance. In fact, before *America* left port coal-laden three weeks later, Gibson had fo'c's'le hands hanging over her side in boatswain chairs painting her black hull fore and aft.[16] Because she had finer lines than *Glory*, she would be averaging about 400 tons less coal per passage in the years to come, but even at that, 3,000 to 3,100 long tons of coal were a big cargo for a sailing ship that had practically been resurrected from the dead. The success with *Glory* as a coal drougher, besides the recent loss of the *Ocean King*, had helped Josiah Knowles's decision to place *America* regularly in the British Columbia coal trade. *Glory* grossed close to 12,000 dollars per passage.[17] Her regular complement, besides captain, was two mates, a carpenter, steward, cook, and nineteen A.B.'s. Although she and the *America*, which carried a crew of about twenty-two, were now considered tramp ships in the maritime social ladder, they still paid their way.

Gibson and Freeman were fast friends, but this did not mean that they ever missed an opportunity to race down the coast together. Many years later, Gibson commented on *Glory* in the Seattle shipping weekly *Marine Digest:*

> We often went down the coast under full sail, with timbers, spars, and rigging creaking and groaning. The *Glory* under full sail was a sight to warm the heart. The *America* could beat her in moderate weather, but the old *Glory* was the more weatherly and the faster when winds and seas were roaring high. The *Glory* could carry sail till the whole world was blue.[18]

They also never missed an opportunity to race up the coast, when both vessels were in ballast. Freeman was never content to let a square-rigger pass him, and he rarely admitted that *Glory of the Seas* could be beaten. He would keep sail on her as long as possible, especially if it could mean he would beat another square-rigger.[19]

As the months slowly passed, both Dunsmuir and John Rosenfeld kept *Glory* busy. First, one chartered her for a voyage and then, after a few trips, the other followed suit. On May 15, 1888, she lay at Departure Bay when the Freemans' first grandchild was born at Wellington. Lucy Anna Little bore a baby girl, who was named Marguerite. With J. Eugene living in San Francisco and Lucy Anna in British Columbia, Joshua and Lucy Freeman had no incentive to take *Glory* into offshore trades. Although the Freemans could have headed deep sea, they now just did not care to do so. Both Freemans were well known and liked in the Nanaimo area and *Glory* was a common fixture, either lying in Departure Bay or near the Vancouver Coal Company wharves. Frank and Lucy Little always made the Captain and his wife feel most welcome and encouraged them to stay ashore at their home in Wellington when in port.[20]

Although a different fo'c's'le crowd was shipped every voyage, they all learned quickly to share an epithet for Joshua Freeman. Safely behind his back, he was known up and down the Pacific Coast as the Prophet Elijah. His stern bearing, explosive temper, piercing look, and long white beard had earned him the title and also made its secrecy imperative. Mrs. Freeman also had a nickname — Tooty — but it was used only by close relatives in the Freeman clan and was a term of endearment. She accepted it with good grace.[21]

The winter storms along the Pacific coast in 1888 were more than up to expectations. As a reporter wrote in the *San Francisco Bulletin,* "Unusually bad weather has prevailed on the coast for the past month. Old sailors say that there had not been such weather for years."[22] Decades later Captain Gibson of the *America* told a graphic tale in the *Marine Digest* about these stormy months:

> There were 24 or 25 sailing vessels in the coal fleet. In November or December, 1888, we left Nanaimo one after the other. Weeks began passing and none of us had reached San Francisco. Revenue cutters were sent out to relieve us, as it was known that our food supplies must be running short. The delay was due to storms and headwinds. Then the whole overdue fleet arrived in San Francisco on the same day. Some of the ships were 38 days from Nanaimo. My *America* was 25 days out. As we entered the Golden Gate, the *Glory of the Seas* was with us. She had started weeks behind us and made the run in six days, escaping the adverse weather. Most of the fleet was badly battered. Two had their rudder heads twisted off. They were steering with jury rudders. Others had sails gone or spars missing, but the *Glory* came into port spick and span as ever.[23]

Not only coal ships had been in that fleet. The lumber-laden *Dashing Wave* was also battered by the heavy weather. Following her arrival on December 24, the same day as *Glory* but twenty-one days out from Tacoma, tugs berthed the old clipper at Folsom Street Wharf in a badly leaking condition. Her crew had pumps going steadily and she had a heavy list to starboard.[24] Even the regular Cape Horner *Joseph S. Spinney* had to put into San Francisco for repairs before she could resume her passage to Queenstown, Ireland.

After three successful years as a coal drougher, the good ship *Glory of the Seas* had further proved that she was not the white elephant some shipping firms had called her back in 1870, shortly after Donald McKay had put her up for sale to the highest bidder. Though she now neared the twenty-year mark, she looked exceptionally trim, even while unloading her grimy cargo at San Francisco. Changes in economics had made no changes in Joshua Freeman's ideas of how a smart ship should be kept up. At dockside, although her lower yards were cockbilled for unloading bulk coal into portable hoppers on the adjacent wharf, he had her upper yards squared to a T. All her sails were snugged up in a neat harbor furl. Even the giltwork on her cutwater and stern shone brightly, living up to the name that her builder had given her nineteen years before.

Deck view of *Glory* facing aft, ca. 1898. She was then lying at Howard Street coal wharves, San Francisco. Captain Freeman stands atop the deck house, and Goat Island is visible over the stern. Courtesy Robert A. Weinstein.

CHAPTER XII

Life Aboard a Coaster

As spring of 1889 wore on, coal shipping rates on the coast dropped nearly 50 percent, and Freeman laid *Glory* up for three months until the market would necessitate a raise in rates again. During this interval the captain spent some time in the fast-moving city of Seattle on Puget Sound. On April 3, while he was still down sound, three Nanaimo "mossbacks" (elder citizens with antiquated ideas) were persuaded by Captain Hughes of the 150-ton steamer *Ferndale* to take a jaunt to Puget Sound. Leaving Nanaimo at 1:30 that Wednesday afternoon, the travelers found the voyage to Seattle quite uneventful until that evening when they sat down to a friendly game of poker. Much later, all three had extremely long and sad faces when they left the gaming tables practically cleaned out. At ten o'clock the next morning, the little screw steamer swung into Elliot Bay and discharged its passengers at downtown Seattle. Soon after landing, the three old gentlemen saw Captain Freeman and attached themselves, almost childishly, to him as he walked along the waterfront looking dapper in a finely cut suit, a hat, and his ever-present cane. He showed great kindness to the old mossbacks, spending much time with them, putting his local knowledge of Seattle at their disposal. They had chosen a fortunate time for their tour, because in just two months, much of the downtown business section they were enjoying would be wiped out by fire. This city of 28,000 people boasted a cable car, the first north of San Francisco, and it was to this line on Yesler Way that Joshua Freeman took the trio. The captain was greatly amused as he viewed them gleefully

145

Deck view of Glory facing forward, ca. 1898. The youth on the deck house is
unidentified. Courtesy Robert A. Weinstein.

riding the newfangled contraption from downtown Seattle to Lake Washington and back. Indeed, time had little dulled their capacity for enjoyment. There was plenty of spice left. Captain Freeman heard one of them remark, as he looked earnestly at a specimen of the fair young ladies of Seattle, "Lots of 'bustle' in this town. Hee! Hee! Hee! After leaving Joshua, the mossbacks embarked on visits to other towns on Puget Sound and finally returned the following Monday to Nanaimo on the *Ferndale,* well satisfied with their escapade.[1]

Glory made her next voyage for Dunsmuir between the months of May and August. Rates had gone up to $2.50 per long ton, which would be the average coal shipping rate for 1889–1890.[2] About the middle of May, Joshua and Lucy had gone south on a Dunsmuir steamer to activate *Glory of the Seas* at San Francisco, and they sailed on May 25 from the bay port bound for Departure Bay.

On her arrival, while Captain Freeman and Tooty visited the Little family, the chief mate oversaw the discharge of about 500 tons of rock and sand ballast *Glory* had loaded for the run north. First the carpenter, who also doubled as donkey man, opened the after end of the donkey room so that special block and tackle, which had been rigged from her cockbilled mainyard, could be made fast on the cargo winch just aft of the donkey boiler. Then the donkey engine was stoked. Once "Chips" had a head of steam up, the mates kept most of the crew busy 23-odd feet below in the lower hold loading rock and sand into massive wooden tubs. Using large scoop shovels, they bent their aching backs through the day, filling each tub with well over a half ton of ballast. Once the crew had filled a tub, the carpenter was ordered to haul away. He then put the cargo winch in gear and up swung the ballast tub through the hatchway and out over the water, where it was upended and its contents fell with a great splash into Departure Bay. This same monotonous and backbreaking operation continued for three or four days until *Glory* lay ready to receive her coal stiffening.

On June 26, she was lying under the coal chutes when an ungainly tramp steamer chugged into the bay. It was the collier *Wellington,* a Dunsmuir-owned self-trimmer. With machinery spaces situated well aft and her pilothouse set forward, the 239-foot vessel in ballast looked much like a miniature tanker of the twentieth century. She regularly made more than one run per month from British Columbia to San Francisco and was a steady money-maker.[3] Since according to charters, a sailing ship's time was not generally so valuable as a steamer's, the *Wellington* hauled *Glory* off the T-wharf to an anchorage out in the bay, and then completed her own cargo first. Three days later, she sailed for San Francisco laden with 2,500 tons.

Although the sails on *Glory* remained bent, she did not sail back to the wharf. Instead, the crew loaded a kedge anchor in one of her 26-foot longboats, attached a 3-inch manila line from the ship to the mud hook, and ran the line out full length by rowing in the direction of the wharf. Then the anchor was dropped into the bay, and they heaved the ship up to it with the donkey boiler cargo winch. It was a slow method to warp *Glory* in, but it was the only sure way they could move her in a calm without a tug. Less than two weeks later, the Chinese laborers had her fully loaded and she was on her way to San Francisco.

After discharging cargo at the Howard Street coal wharves, Freeman had *Glory* docked for an insurance survey. The inspector opened her up and found her surprisingly sound. A young naval architect happened to see her in dock and humorously called her "a wall-sided old pot."[4] If Joshua Freeman had heard this, he would have "called down fire from heaven." Though he knew she had her imperfections, he wanted no one to tell him so.

In October, as *Glory* came to anchor at Departure Bay, the 278-foot steamer, *Costa Rica (Bristol)*, running mate of the *Wellington,* lay berthed under the Dunsmuir coal chutes finishing up a 2,500-ton cargo. She was also a tramp collier and together with the *Wellington* carried nearly a third of the Dunsmuir coal exported to California.[5] The 1,983-gross-ton, iron-hulled screw steamer had been built in 1875, at Stockton, California. Originally bark-rigged, she was now fully steam-powered and normally made average runs of eighty-five to one hundred hours up and down the coast laden with "black diamonds." The cheaply run tramp steamers were slowly but surely forcing sailing ships out of the coastal coal trade, even at this early date. Steamers normally needed no tugs, provided a much easier living for their crews, and could afford to pay better wages. It was sad to admit but wooden full-riggers were fighting a futile battle for survival, and had but few money-making years left.

In the 1920's, the *Boston Herald* printed a humorous reminiscence of a voyage an old shellback made up the coast in *Glory:*

> In a letter to the [New York] *Times* an old sailor now in Jersey City recalls a trip he made aboard the *Glory of the Seas* in 1889. Captain Freeman

"from down Brewster way" was the master, well on in years, tall and thin. The writer relates how one night in a heavy squall, the captain came on deck in a hurry to see how the second mate was handling the ship, which was in ballast and high out of the water. When the *Glory* took a sudden roll to starboard "the skipper only saved himself by clutching the mizzen royal backstay" and the inadequacy of his attire was amusingly revealed.[6]

Joshua customarily wore a long nightshirt, and one can picture how the driving rain and wind drenched him to the skin and billowed his flannel nightshirt high into the air. Knowing the captain's personality, once he was back safely on the deck the air must have vibrated in the immediate vicinity as he blustered and fumed over being soaked and nearly pitched to a watery grave.[7]

During the height of the bad weather season in 1889–1890, Freeman's name was added to the list of famous shipmasters who established records in their finest commands. On December 16 at San Francisco *Glory* began her voyage north by putting well out to sea so that she would have no fear of being blown ashore by heavy southeasters. *America* sailed from San Diego the day after her, but this was one passage during which Captain Gibson's ship stood no chance of catching up with *Glory of the Seas*. On nearing the rugged Washington coastline, the sound of "watch-oh-watch" rang out as Joshua's crew heaved the head lead to take bottom samples to determine how close *Glory* was to land. Freeman then took the first opportunity to clear Cape Flattery and get inside. The winter winds were with him all the way as his weather-worthy ship came to anchor at Royal Roads. Conscious of the good time he had made to date, the captain grew impatient waiting for a tug and decided to sail *Glory of the Seas* up to Nanaimo through the treacherous inside passage. Few sailing shipmasters would have attempted this even during the fine weather months, but Freeman had accomplished it before, and would do it again several times.[8] His youngest granddaughter, Lucy, was told of just such an occasion: "It was a gala day when the *Glory* arrived there. Grandfather insisted on sailing her right into the wharf and the harbor was quite 'blue' with his vocabulary to the crew until this was accomplished."[9] Three weeks after sailing from San Francisco, a tug towed her out to Cape Flattery and let her go. Freeman then stood well out to sea and raced down the Pacific Coast about 100 miles off land. Seven days later, on January 15, 1890, she came to anchor in San Pedro Bay, 600 miles southeasterly of San Francisco. The round voyage was thirty days, a superb passage and another record for *Glory of the Seas* to add to the New York-to-San Francisco and San Francisco-to-Sydney record passages.

On January 23 while Freeman busily superintended his crew discharging coal at San Pedro, many of his shipping friends met at Lick House, the plush San Francisco hotel, to hold a meeting of the Pacific Coast Shipowners, Stevedores, and Shipmasters Trust. Commodore Theodore H. Allen, San Francisco stevedore magnate, shipowner, and one of the famous forty-niners of gold rush days, brought up the subject of Freeman's record passage in *Glory of the Seas* and suggested that all forty men present sign a special commemoration scroll in honor of his feat. The signatures of many prominent men appear on the 18-inch by 30-inch piece of drafting linen: John, Henry, and Louis Rosenfeld of Rosenfeld and Sons; Millen Griffith, tugboat owner and a big shareholder in Pacific Steam Whaling; J. Eugene Freeman, twenty-four-year-old son of the captain and already a promising architect; Josiah Knowles and his now twenty-one-year-old son Henry. Josiah in signing his name called attention to his two records in *Glory of the Seas,* reminding his fellow trust members that she was no ordinary ship.

Fourteen other shipmasters also added their names to the scroll: Captain Jordon of the Dunsmuir collier *Wellington;* Captain Porter, master of the Pacific Steam Whaling Company tender *Jeanie;* Captain Bob Merriman of the 2,390-ton Cape Horner and "bloodboat" *Commodore T. H. Allen;* Jim "Shotgun" Murphy, the fiery, Irish master of the smart three skys'l yarder *W. F. Babcock,* who would shortly be taking the big, 300-foot four-poster *Shenandoah* off the stocks; Captain James G. Baker, remembered for having lost the *John Rosenfeld* in British Columbia waters, added his name to the list. His beautiful command, the English-built, four-masted bark *Kenilworth,* was being refitted as an American vessel after being burnt out at Port Costa. Also on the list were Rowland Clapp, skipper of the Rosenfeld-owned *India:* the masters of the *Elizabeth, Jabez Howes,* the British ship *New York,* the down-easters *George Stetson* (Ebed Murphy in command), *Kennebec,* and *Carrollton;* and George Goodwin of the ship *Sterling.* Of course, James Gibson of the *America* was there to honor his good friend. Although keen rivalry was an aspect of their relationship to one another, nonetheless they were quick to praise when praise was due. The extravagant words to which they signed their names read as follows:

TESTIMONIAL

TO

Captain Joshua Freeman
of the Am. Ship
GLORY OF THE SEAS

At a meeting of the Pacific Coast Shipowners, Stevedores and Shipmasters Trust — held at the Lick House, San Francisco, Cal. the 23rd day of January, A.D. 1890, Commodore T. H. Allen presiding, to take action on the unprecedented quick voyage of the good ship *Glory of the Seas* from San Francisco to Nanaimo and thence to San Pedro, and to present a suitable testimonial to Captain Joshua Freeman.

Resolved: that we tender to our friend and fellow member, Captain Joshua Freeman, our congratulations upon the very successful voyage he has just completed and we are pleased hereby to bear testimony to his skill, seamanship, and untiring energy shown by him during the many years he has been amongst us, and in particular on this voyage wherein he has broken the record in making the voyage from San Francisco, Cal. to Nanaimo, B.C. and San Pedro, Cal. in thirty days. That we drink to his health and success this night in the good punches prepared at the Lick House Bar. That upon the Captain's return to this port we present him with a suitable testimonial, for which his old friend, Commodore T. H. Allen, is appointed a committee of one on selection and purchase.

That we cause these resolutions to be handsomely engrossed (in duplicate) one copy of which shall be hung in a conspicuous place in the Lick House Wine Rooms, the other to be forwarded, postage paid, to our honored friend the subject of these resolutions.[10]

This record passage was the first of eleven voyages to San Pedro which *Glory of the Seas* made for Rosenfeld and Sons from 1890 to the early part of 1892. During that period Freeman averaged five voyages a year. The New Vancouver Coal Company at Nanaimo, of which John Rosenfeld was a large shareholder, had taken over the wharves, offices, and mining facilities of Vancouver Coal Company, and was then rapidly increasing their mine output and the amount of coal shipped out of British Columbia. *Glory* averaged nineteen days in port counting time discharging ballast and under the coal chutes — a far cry from thirty years before at Nanaimo, when sailing ships had been loaded out in the stream from coal baskets brought on board from Indian canoes. Now a special loading platform, designed for rapid dispatch, was being constructed; eventually it would compare with the monster loading platforms at Cardiff and Liverpool.[11] Shortly following the change in management, nearly a dozen Rosenfeld-owned sailing ships as well as *Glory* and a half-dozen chartered steamers were needed off and on to fill the demand for New Vancouver coal in California, the Hawaiian Islands, and Alaska. Freight rates stayed at about $2.50 to $3.00 per long ton up until the spring of 1892, meaning that vessels like *Glory of the Seas* had no worry about steady employment.

On one of her voyages during this time, *Glory* was sailing into San Pedro Bay laden with coal when one of the worst storms ever known in that region hit. The great rock breakwater which now protects the bay had not yet been built and there was no shelter from the force of the terrific southeaster nor a way for *Glory* to get far out to sea. Just such southerly winter winds had caused the stranding of the *America*, the *Richard P. Buck,* and the *Kennebec* in 1887. Now it was *Glory of the Seas'* turn. The tremendous force of the wind and the waves roaring high lifted her completely clear of the small rock jetty connecting Deadman and Terminal (Rattlesnake) Island. Miraculously, she landed inside the shallow harbor channel and came to a sluggish stop undamaged. Once the storm had abated, Freeman discharged her coal cargo into lighters, but she remained stuck in the mud. The channel in that particular area was too shallow for her even when completely empty of cargo. After several days, the tide rose high enough for tugs to haul her off into deep water, little the worse for her close call.[12]

Another incident occurred at Nanaimo while she lay at anchor out in the stream waiting her turn to go under the New Vancouver coal chutes. Though the Pacific Coast Seamen's Union had been organized back in 1885, many sailing ship captains in the '90's still refused to subscribe to their terms and Joshua Freeman was one of this number. Because *Glory* was a regular coaster, union organizers in British Columbia decided to make an example of the captain, even though the ship "had a good name among sailors who served in her" and her master paid fair wages to his foremost hands, an average of 25 to 30 dollars per month.[13] The late Ralph "Doc" Cropley wrote in the *New York Sun* what happened when a young Mickey Rooney of a sailor came on board.

> Union organizers wanted to get the crew off her, tie her up, and bring "old Freeman" to terms, but no one could get aboard to talk to the crew; for Freeman had one helluva temper, and kept an arsenal handy of

"pirates." And it was a case of not only getting aboard the *Glory* but to "deodorize" Freeman's guns.

It was known that Freeman badly needed a cabin boy. Tho' an able seaman, Buckley was small enough and young enough to pass as a "cabin tiger." Seeking the job, Buckley was allowed aboard on *Glory,* got it and speedily set to work, as galley dishes hadn't been washed for days.

While making up the cabin bunks, Buckley found the arsenal stacked on the wall of the chief mate's cabin. It didn't take him long to ram corks down the barrels and get on with his work as if nothing had happened.

After evening chow, Buckley was permitted to go ashore for his gear. That's where Captain Freeman made his mistake. For once ashore, and telling what he'd done, union organizers started for the *Glory.* On their approach Freeman and his mate, both heavily armed, warned them off. As they still came on, the first mate fired first. Both barrels of his shotgun exploded. Captain Freeman fired. Same thing happened, only he wasn't hurt as bad as his mate.

Well, the union leaders not only got the crew off the *Glory,* got them not only to Nanaimo, but during the nite, over across to Vancouver across the Straits, a job Buckley also had to do with a small sloop, before the night was over....[14]

To top off the story, in about 1910, Joshua Freeman and his good friend Captain W. F. Buckley, a well-liked and respected Puget Sound pilot, were having dinner together in the posh Rose Room of the then swank Butler Hotel, just a block north of the Smith Tower in downtown Seattle. Buckley had lately decided that he could no longer withhold his identity as the man who, twenty years before, had spiked the arsenal on *Glory of the Seas.* Before he blurted out the truth, he realized he would have to be wary. Even though Joshua was past seventy-five, his temper had not cooled with the years. Buckley nervously kept his eye on the heavy water bottle on the dinner table. Just as the past was laid bare, the captain made a grab for the bottle and would have brained his companion, but the humor of the situation squelched his wrath. The old man sat back and laughed his head off to think that a man he'd been longing to kill for that gun affair had been one of his best friends for years.[15]

During the summer of 1890, Joshua and Lucy Freeman spent much of their free time at Cumberland, British Columbia, about 60 miles northwest of Nanaimo. Near the little village of Cumberland, "Dib" Little worked as a general superintendent of the Union Colliery, a new Dunsmuir mine that had been opened in 1888. Since the start of operations, the town of Cumberland had grown with the increased importance of the mining activities. The first buildings in the region were a boarding house for the miners, and a two-story office, the upper part being reserved for "Dib" and his family. They lived there for 18 months until the home that he and his family would eventually call the Red House was built.[16]

In 1890, Marguerite Little was two years old and greatly attached to her grandmother. Tooty persuaded Lucy, her daughter, to let Maggie go on a voyage on *Glory of the Seas* that summer. In fact, Marguerite spent much of the next five years on board *Glory* between the spring and fall equinoxes, except while the ship was in port. Joshua Freeman no longer wanted his wife to make the somewhat dangerous and uncomfortable passages up and down the coast during the bad weather months from November to March; so she and her granddaughter stayed at Cumberland during that part of the year.[17]

Life aboard a coaster was a glittering adventure to the little girl. Her very first experience was during the summer of 1890 when she learned the grim importance superstition plays on board ship. She vividly recalled, "I couldn't play on deck except in harbor, as the first time grandfather took me out, my hat blew off and that would have been the worst of bad luck if it had gone overboard. It was a willow straw hat with buttercups with some elastic under the chin."[18] Nonetheless, she managed her glimpses of deck life. One day she and her grandmother were in the after cabin when one of the forward doors had been inadvertently left open. The child was transfixed by the sight and sounds of a half dozen fo'c's'le hands going around the capstan just forward of the mizzen hatch. Led by the song of the chanty man, they pushed in rhythm on the capstan bars and lustily sang along.

She was also confined to quarters when *Glory* unloaded at San Pedro. Marguerite, who later became Mrs. Hespard Twigg, wrote, "She was always clean between trips. Remember, she was loading coal, so she may have been dirty while loading or unloading. Grandmother and I were never allowed on deck while the stevedores were working."[19]

Marguerite found other captivating aspects to her new life. Donald McKay's swinging oil lamp which never upset no matter how the ship bucked or rolled was a marvel to her. For bedtime she had the same special little trundle bed that Josiah Knowles had built in his cabin eighteen years before. Her grandmother thoroughly enjoyed pulling out the drawerlike bed, arranging the covers, and tucking her in every evening.

One of Marguerite's unpleasant memories was of the night she nearly set the ship on fire. She woke up and was walking sleepily with a candle that somehow found its way to some tapestry on a cabin door. It flared up, but adults came to the rescue in time and nothing worse than a scorch resulted.

The weather, Marguerite Little recalled, was not always peaceful during the spring and summer months. On one voyage, *Glory of the Seas* was caught in a very bad storm. The captain normally carried a few chickens on board to provide fresh eggs for their breakfasts, and on this particular passage, all were washed overboard by unusually heavy seas engulfing her decks. Her grandmother told her at the time that *Glory* was not equipped as *Gold Hunter* had been for her long voyages in the China trade. Then, besides chickens, Joshua and Lucy had carried a milking cow and a goat. In addition to the usual fresh eggs, Marguerite remembered that all the food was excellent, and that the setting for meals was extraordinary. A massive, 3-foot-in-diameter mast stuck right through the center of the dinner table.

She had just two friends on board, but they were especially kind to her. She wrote, "The only people I was allowed to play with or talk to were the Negro steward and the Swedish carpenter."[20] The jovial, middle-aged steward, Edmund Dixon, was a favorite of the Freemans' and of Maggie's. He had been part of the regular afterguard on *Glory* since 1887, and was highly respected; his pay scale was the same as the first mate's — 55 dollars a month. Dixon had been born in Mississippi in slavery twenty years before the Civil War and after the emancipation had shipped to sea as a steward. The carpenter, Ole Olson, a 200-pound Swede from San Pedro, likewise had a little admirer in Marguerite. He showed great kindness to her on many occasions by giving her souvenir gold coins he had gathered from all over the world.

Tooty kept her little granddaughter busy with many enjoyable time fillers. Much of the day they knitted and sewed as their seagoing home droughed up and down the coast. Lessons were a part of the easy regime, and the little girl was taught her ABC's at an early age, although her hard-of-hearing grandmother was never entirely successful in detecting whether or not Maggie was correct in her use of "e."

Maggie's memories of her grandmother give a good picture of the domestic side of life aboard a square-rigger. The warmhearted, bespectacled old lady, devoted to her husband and contented with her life, made sure that the after cabin was neat as a pin despite the rheumatism which

Above. Lucy Freeman Little (hand on hat), Marguerite Little (beside her), and Frank "Dib" Little (next to Marguerite) viewing Union Bay from a Dunsmuir wharf, ca. 1900. Courtesy Mrs. Barbara Bumpus. Below. Coal Wharves at Ladysmith in the early 1900's. Courtesy Raymond J. Knight.

troubled her in later years. She was meticulous when it came to planning meals, and adequate stores of delicious food were always on board. In her early days of housekeeping on *Glory* she had removed the mattress from the bed in the middle stateroom on the port side, and now regularly carried a variety of preserves inside the frame.

Maggie recalled one meal that was a testimony both to her grandmother's skill at planning a menu and her resourcefulness under trying conditions.

> I remember sailing from San Francisco one Thanksgiving Day with the whole crew drunk, even the steward. Grandmother cooked the dinner with a two-burner oil stove and a tin oven in the bathroom as Grandfather would not allow us to go to the galley. Oysters, soup, chicken pie, turkey, vegetables, pumpkin pie, fruit, and nuts. She was nearly the age I am today and I don't know how she did it.[21]

With Joshua's help Lucy had placed a long plank on the ship's bathtub and had set the oil stove and the tin oven on top of it. Both of them were disgusted at old Dixon for being drunk, but, of course, after a few days at sea, he was back in their graces.

Mrs. Freeman was also a creative lady with a talent for making the best of her time and the materials which were handy. Using the multitudinous varieties of seaweed found along the Pacific coastline, she made exquisite pictures on pieces of 5- by 5-inch white cardboard. In the long days and evenings at sea and at port Tooty carefully clipped and pasted the dried seaweed to mount many designs ranging from various spreading tree shapes to the circle wreath common during the Christmas holidays, in the muted marine colors of maroon, green, black, and yellow.

The captain's wife was as susceptible to superstition as any mariner. She had been told in her youth that sharks never attacked black people, so she always carried a pair of long black stockings to wear in case *Glory* should ever go down at sea.

Marguerite Little also had great love and respect for her grandfather. She attested to his usual somber, quiet, Puritannical mien and the violent exceptions to that nature. However, her younger sister Lucy said, "The children never paid the slightest attention to my grandfather's blustering. He was sort of the Pied Piper for free."[22] Marguerite could picture him sitting solemnly at the high table in the after cabin, writing out data in his sea logs. After his stroke and his return to sea, he necessarily had to take good care of himself and after getting up in the morning and making sure everything was shipshape on board, he would usually take a short nap in the daybreak cabin, just forward of the bathroom. To break the monotony of the same old trip, he would often take an old friend or his son Gene along for company, putting the guest up in one of the spare staterooms off the dining saloon.

Glory of the Seas arrived at Nanaimo in September, 1891, and from there, the Freemans and Maggie took a steamer up to Union Bay, the loading port for the Union Colliery. Several weeks later, the captain sailed for San Pedro without his wife and granddaughter on board. The bad weather was due in force before long, but an even more important reason kept Lucy ashore: on October 23, her daughter gave birth to another girl, who was named Helen. Once she grew out of the diaper stage, she, too, would join her sister on board *Glory*.

Quite often advertisements like the following appeared in the Nanaimo *Free Press* while *Glory* was in port, and with good reason:

> SHIP Glory of the Seas
> Neither the owners nor the undersigned will
> be responsible for any debts contracted by
> the crew of the above named vessel.
> J. FREEMAN, Master[23]

Shortly after midnight on Sunday morning, May 8, 1892, fo'c's'le hands from *Glory of the Seas* banged heavily on the door of a building just outside the main business area of Nanaimo. Freeman had arrived at Nanaimo on May 5 and from that day until Saturday evening had kept the crew busy discharging ballast. At that point, the captain gave nine seamen shore leave, but by the time they got to town, they found all the saloons closed. Finally, seeing a light in a nearby window, they decided to ask directions on how to get back to the waterfront. A man answered the door, took one look at the group of rough and ready sailors, and quickly turned round and ran inside to hide, leaving the door wide open. The sight *Glory*'s crew beheld was a paradise to them. The building was a brewery. Bottles and kegs of beer beckoned the thirsty group, and the hapless brewer, in hiding, had to watch in pained silence while the sailors from *Glory* drank at least five dozen bottles of beer and started in on several kegs.

At 1:00 A.M. the proprietor of the Empire brewery, Mr. Peter Weigle, arrived at the scene, found the front door agape, empty beer bottles strewn all over the floor, and the crew from *Glory* staggering off with a keg of beer, which they hadn't yet fully consumed. The men naturally ignored his command to stop, so Weigle stomped in, unearthed his brewer, and sent him flying off to get the police.

The crew from *Glory* was finally located parading (staggering rather than marching) down Commercial Street, the main business street in Nanaimo. They were too drunk to resist the constables, were collared and escorted to the Bastion, an old Hudson Bay fort that served as the town jail, and were locked up until Monday morning.

On Sunday morning, Joshua Freeman was informed that he had best appear in police court Monday, along with the brewer, the two arresting officers, Mr. Weigle, and, of course, his now sobered crew.

On Monday morning, they all gave their stories and excuses in court. The magistrate deliberated all the facts in the case and then decreed that each sailor be fined $5.25 for being drunk in public; the brewer be fined $20.00 and $5.00 costs for selling beer during unlawful hours (he had sneaked out of hiding long enough to accept $1.80 from the sailors), and Captain Freeman ended up paying for all of the damage, though he informed the court that his crew would be docked in wages until he was paid back in full. Small wonder the incident ended with the above advertisement in the *Free Press*.[24]

From February through May, 1892, Joshua made a final round voyage to San Pedro. *Glory* arrived at the Southern California port eighteen days from Nanaimo on March 15, the last time for the next fifteen years that she would be entering San Pedro Bay. The financial condition of the nation was poor and was injuring the coal trade. Freight rates between British Columbia and San Francisco were down to an all-time low of $1.25 to $1.50 per long ton.[25] However, this did not mean that the economic situation had defeated Joshua Freeman a second time. He sorely needed a break from the monotonous run, and he looked forward to a change that would net fair profits for *Glory*.

CHAPTER XIII

The Mellowing Years

THE month of July, 1892, found *Glory of the Seas* bound north to Alaska in a new facet of the coal trade. Her destination was Dutch Harbor, Unalaska, in the Aleutian Island chain. Twenty-two days up, she majestically came to anchor in the deep bay near the headquarters of the Alaska Commercial Company where she was to unload a cargo of New Vancouver coal for the Pacific Steam Whaling fleet. After lying in the northern port for several months, Freeman weighed anchor and sailed for Cape Flattery. Arriving September 17, at Port Angeles, then a small village on the Washington side of the Straits of Juan de Fuca, the captain anchored *Glory* for several days while he made arrangements at the customhouse for her to continue her voyage under a charter to Dunsmuir. Four days later, she sailed into Departure Bay after a two-year absence. On the coast the coal market had changed for the better and freight rates were soon to begin climbing to the 3- and 4-dollar mark once again. *Glory* would continue to load for Dunsmuir for the next twelve years.

During her stay at Departure Bay, Lucy Freeman brought Marguerite down from Cumberland to make a voyage in *Glory* before the winter storms began. The little girl, now four, had missed the three-and-a-half-month trip to Alaska and looked forward to spending the next thirty days with Tooty. Shortly after she came on board, she noticed Grandmother going up on deck with a large furry bundle in her arms. Lucy had discovered that her expensive wardrobe of beautiful furs had been devastated by moths on the voyage north. Salvage was hopeless and they were destined for burial at sea. Just in time Maggie's eye caught a glimpse of pretty white fox; she pleaded plaintively and her grandmother gave in, but the rest ended up in Departure Bay.[1]

In September, the old extreme clipper *Ericsson* lay next to the New Vancouver coal wharf at Nanaimo. Although her forty-year-old hull was still in fair shape, her days as a lowly coal drougher were numbered. She had been in the coal and lumber trade for over six years now, running between British Columbia or Puget Sound and California with an occasional voyage to Australia. Earlier in 1892, Captain George Plummer, her owner and master, had sold *Ericsson* to Boole and Company of San Francisco. Her new owners were now trying to get a few more years out of her, and, being ruled by profit, were overloading her by 200 to 300 tons by Plummer's standards.[2] As could be expected in a ship her age, the main skys'l had been sent down and her single tops'ls had long ago been replaced by upper and lower tops'ls, but her fine clipper lines still gave an idea of the beauty she had once been. On October 6, she sailed for San Francisco deeply laden with a cargo of 2,372 tons of coal on board. Five days later, *Glory of the Seas* followed her. *Ericsson* made her run down the coast in eleven days while *Glory* had a better elapsed time of nine days from Departure Bay. In November both Freeman and Captain Bennett of the *Ericsson* sailed for Nanaimo once more, but the venerable ex-caloric steamer was never to arrive. The *Victoria Colonist* of Monday, November 21, 1892, told why:

> By the time the *Colonist* reaches its readers this morning, the shattered timbers of the old ship *Ericsson* will in all probability be strewn along the shores of Barclay Sound or tossed far out on the wide Pacific, for when the familiar old vessel was last seen at noon on Sunday, she was in such a position that her immediate destruction seemed inevitable. She had been caught in Friday night's gale while bound from San Francisco to Nanaimo for a coal cargo, driven into Barclay Sound, and pinned between the rocky shore of Entrance Island and a narrow ledge skirting it. . . . from the position of the ship, it was evident that she must soon go to pieces. Her bow rested clear out of the water on a gigantic boulder, while her stern was awash, the ship being exposed to all the prevailing winds of the Pacific.

Glory of the Seas, now in her twenty-third year, had outlived another game competitor.

In April, 1893, *Glory* made a passage to the Golden Gate with two
small visitors on board, Marguerite and Helen, now one and a half years
old. Having both girls on board added spice to life on the old ship. Years
later Marguerite recalled that "Grandfather used to rage at my sister and
I, and then say, 'what to do you want?' and give us twice as much as what
it was."[3] With the mischief the two youngsters stirred up in the course of
a day, Joshua Freeman had good reason to seek peace and quiet during
the morning hours in his daybreak cabin; meanwhile, *Glory* beat down
the coast and eventually came to anchor off Oakland, nine days from her
coal port.

On May 1, *Glory* would mark an achievement of the United States
Army Engineers. She would be the first large vessel to enter the newly
dredged channel separating Alameda and Oakland, called Oakland
Creek or Estuary by mariners. Prior to this, deep-water ships always had
to lighter their cargoes into the wharves fronting the estuary. In 1874 the
Army Engineers had started building two training walls 900 feet long and
had dredged a channel 200 feet wide and 10 feet deep, which could ac-
commodate shallow-draft bay craft; but with the growing importance of
Oakland, the United States government saw the need of deepening the
channel to admit ocean-going vessels. By May 1, 1893, the estuary was increased in size to a width of 300 feet and a depth of 20 feet at low tide, and
Glory of the Seas prepared to enter Oakland Creek under tow. For several
days previously, stevedores had lightered out part of her cargo to bring
her down to the 19-foot draft mark. Now, on May 4, she entered the estuary and was warped to the city dock. Here she discharged the remainder
of her cargo for the Oregon Improvement Company.[4]

The following month found her sailing past Nanaimo, and entering
Baynes Sound between Vancouver and Denman Islands, where she came
to anchor in adjacent Union Bay, the loading port for the Union Colliery. As in Nanaimo, Joshua Freeman did things his own way no matter
what others might think. His granddaughter wrote, "One thing I do remember. Grandfather would always go up to the wharf with no tug to
help him, much to the dismay of the harbormaster."[5]

The "city" of Union Bay was pretty much a one-horse town, consisting
of one hotel, one school, one post office, one policeman, and one small
jail. The largest structure in the region was the 700-foot-long coal
wharf, which jutted out into the bay. Dunsmuir had designed it so that
ships could come alongside to load directly from coal trains that had been

backed out on the wharf; to the northeast was a low-lying dock specifically constructed for loading and discharging passengers and freight from small steamers.

Joshua, Lucy, and their two grandchildren soon went ashore at Union Bay and waited for a coal train to take them 14 miles to Cumberland. On their arrival at Frank Little's Red House, Lucy Anna was extremely happy to see her little girls, but her display of enthusiasm was checked by her New England self-restraint. Her formality was a fond family joke. Although her daughters often heard their mother call their father "Mr. Little," he in turn, nearly always called her "Madam," a habit which continued until the day he died.[6]

On October 26, 1894, *Glory* sailed into Departure Bay ten days up from San Francisco. Shortly thereafter Joshua planned to continue up to Union Bay, but meanwhile, his big wind ship lay at anchor with the crew, the Freemans, and their two grandchildren on board. Without warning three-year-old Helen took deathly sick, suffering excruciating pain throughout her small body. Joshua and Lucy Freeman were helpless to assist her, and quickly conveyed word to the Littles' family doctor at Cumberland. He came down the coast 60 miles by Indian canoe, boarded *Glory of the Seas,* and prepared to take Helen ashore. His diagnosis was the dreaded spinal meningitis. In time the little girl seemed to have recovered, but then fell prey to pneumonia, and died on Saturday, November 10. In sorrow the family gathered together, and quietly buried her in the family plot at Cumberland.

Marguerite made three voyages with her grandparents during the spring and summer months of 1895, but the time had come for her to begin her formal schooling. A final voyage that summer brought to a close five wonderful years with the Freemans on *Glory of the Seas.* The first week in September, *Glory* arrived in British Columbia waters to load Dunsmuir coal at Union Bay. Captain Freeman, his wife, and their now seven-year-old granddaughter made the familiar trip to Cumberland. Two weeks later, on September 21, Lucy Little gave birth to another baby girl. They named her Lucy Anna, the third-generation Lucy Anna in the Freeman line. Although she was never to go to sea with her grandparents, she was to have many chances to be with them during her childhood while *Glory* lay in British Columbia waters. Several years ago, Lucy Anna Little Sutherland added her reminiscences about Joshua and Lucy Freeman:

They lived with my parents always when on shore. I never remember life without them. They were the most lovable people imaginable. Grandfather was a great blusterer and grandmother such a gentle soul, but full of character too. They used to keep me entranced with their tales of the sea. One particular story used to fascinate me. Grandfather used to say, "Did you know? Your grandmother was the belle of Bar Harbour? She was the only girl in port when Admiral Dewey and the American Navy were also in port," and then go off in gales of laughter.

Neither of them used to like people who talked about their aches and pains. Grandmother would quietly say, "We were in Valparaiso [in the *Gold Hunter*] once and I was really sick. They took out my gall bladder and we sailed on time."

Every time they came back from a trip Grandfather immediately got interested in horses and they were always the bad ones that we had to look after. His favorite book was *David Harum* by Edward Noyes Westcott [a novel about a man who had bad luck with horses] and when reading it he would laugh for hours. They both loved to play poker and my mother was horrified that they taught me to play when I was only seven. From them both I learned my love of horses and to hold my own in the game of poker. I might add that my grandmother was the better player.[7]

In March, 1896, Captain Josiah Knowles wrote the following communiqué to the Arctic Oil Works in the Protero district of San Francisco.[8] It mirrors the care given to ships under his management:

San Francisco
March 16, 1896

J. N. KNOWLES
Shipping & Commission Merchant
No. 30 California St.

In reply to your favor of the Arctic Oil Works.
Protero, City
Dear Sirs:

Please deliver to ship "America" on Tuesday morning, at Arctic Oil Works wharf the following goods.

                    100 lb. White lead
                     50 "   Zinc White
                    100 "   Black paint
                     15 gals. Raw linseed oil
                     15 "   Boiled linseed oil
                     20 "   Stockholm tar
                     15 "   Coal tar
                      5 "   Turpentine

10 "   Fish oil
25 lb. Red oxide (in oil)
4 cases Headlight oil

Please mark ship's name on goods.

Yours very truly,
[signed]   J. N. KNOWLES

Besides the regular Pacific Steam Whaling steamers, Knowles continued to manage the shore affairs of *Glory*, still a valuable piece of shipping property at 24,000 dollars; the 1,031-ton down-easter bark *J. D.
Peters*, of which he owned a 17/64 interest (4,250 dollars);[9] and the *America*, in which his wife held a third of the shares. Apropos of the *America*,
Noah Harding was now her master, having moved up to command when
James Gibson left her in 1891 to go East to take another vessel. Knowles
had been using her through the years as he had *Glory of the Seas*. Up until 1892, she was continuously chartered for the British Columbia–California coal trade and made four or five voyages annually. Because of the
shipping slump that year, Knowles had sent *America* as well as *Glory*
north to Alaska with coal. Since then, *America* had been used as a cannery tender in Bristol Bay during the summer months and in the coast
coal trade the remainder of the year.[10] Both she and *Glory*, even though
they were in the mellowing years of their sea lives, were neither semiretired nor neglected. Josiah Knowles saw to that.

Joshua Freeman and Knowles were still the best of friends. Whenever
Glory lay at San Francisco, the now elderly gentlemen nearly always
spent some time together but their meetings were numbered. *Glory* and
Freeman both were about to assume roles in the closing days of their confederate's life.

On Saturday, June 6, 1896, Josiah Knowles and his eighteen-year-old
son Tom sailed from the bay aboard the Pacific Steam Whaling tender
Jeanie. Their destination was the Bering Sea, where Josiah planned to
inspect the salmon canning operations of the company in the Bristol Bay
region. Since they would be gone for a few months, the captain had hired
a private tutor for Tom to enable him to continue his schooling. When
the *Jeanie* left, the elder Knowles had a slight cold that was more of a
nuisance than anything else, but by Sunday he could tell it had developed
into pneumonia. Deciding the best place for him was home near a doctor, he told the master of the *Jeanie* to turn back. The steamer arrived off

San Francisco Heads Monday evening, and was met by the pilot boat. As Knowles made ready to board the pilot boat, he told Tom to stay on the tender since he "really wasn't very sick." Soon, the whaling tender's running lights receded in the distance as the pilot schooner sailed through the Golden Gate. A few hours later, they entered Oakland Creek, a convenient place to disembark for the Knowleses' home, but the tide was low and defeated their purpose. In the near distance at the foot of Franklin Street lay *Glory of the Seas,* tied up next to the Dunsmuir coal wharf. The pilot boat headed for her, lay alongside the great windship, and hailed the watch to drop a Jacob's ladder over the side for Captain Knowles. He was helped aboard, crossed her 40-foot deck, and made his way down her port gangway, his last walk on the decks of *Glory of the Seas.*[11] When he arrived home, he went directly to bed. The following morning he seemed much improved, or so his wife and daughter Alice (Tom's twin sister) thought. Later that morning he got up and had a pleasant talk with Alice during which he told her that in a few days he would take her and "Momma" on a trip down the coast. She left the room happily thinking that he was recovering rapidly, but one hour later an apoplectic stroke struck her father down. A doctor was called but nothing could be done. The great Captain Josiah Nickerson Knowles, clipper shipmaster extraordinary, record breaker in *Glory of the Seas,* and outstanding shipping merchant, was dead at the age of sixty-six years.[12]

On Saturday, June 10, his funeral was held at the family home on Jackson Street; a simple service where the minister gave a short sermon. No great flower wreaths were displayed — just a small bouquet of sweet peas fastened with a lavender ribbon called attention to the sorrowful event. Since it was a private funeral, only the closest friends and business associates attended. Among the eight grieving pallbearers was Joshua Freeman, who had held up sailing *Glory* so he could pay his last respects to Josiah Knowles. The links with the past were slowly being broken for *Glory of the Seas* as she lived beyond the lifetimes of the men who had made her famous.[13]

On the arrival of *Glory* at Departure Bay in June, 1896, Joshua and Lucy Freeman once again traveled up to Cumberland. The sound of hammers and sawing greeted them as they approached the new three-story home that Frank Little was having built to house his family and his in-laws. It was an immense Victorian structure, designed by the Freemans' son J. Eugene. Set against tall evergreen trees, the "weathered-shingle," rustic look of the structure mirrored the original ideas that had already made Gene Freeman a sought-after architect in San Francisco. Marguerite Little was especially proud of her new home because it had running water and indoor toilets instead of the usual privy that served most houses in the region. On the second story were the shore quarters of Joshua and Lucy. Although the Littles considered them a close part of the family, the Freemans lived with the Littles by choice, not by necessity, and paid Frank Little 300 dollars per month to help with the expenses. Since *Glory* was regularly employed by Dunsmuir, Captain Joshua no longer had to concern himself overly about finances. Ten successful years in the coal trade had more than recouped his losses from the panic in 1884. Now with advancing age and its resulting infirmities he and Tooty were content to spend all the hours away from *Glory* with their family on Vancouver Island. These were happy, mellowing years for them.

But *Glory,* too, was feeling her age. As she headed up the coast in ballast in May, 1897, she began leaking forward so severely that the crew had to stay at her pumps without letup all the way to Victoria. On May 22, she anchored in Esquimalt Harbor after fifteen harsh, headwind-bucking days up from San Francisco. On seeing her out in the stream, even a landlubber could tell she needed repairs. She lay well down by the head, thrown off even keel by the amount of water in her hold. A steady clank, clank, clank rang out as Freeman kept the main pumps going by a rope messenger connecting the donkey boiler and the pump wheels. The only way to stem the leak was to put her in drydock, but the captain had another problem. Bullen Limited [ship repair] were using their marine railway to tear apart a steamer and there were several more weeks of work yet to go. Both Freeman and Bullen recognized the difficulty of keeping *Glory* afloat, so Bullen arranged to rent the public graving dock at Esquimalt, just west of Victoria proper. On May 31, *Glory* was hauled into position so the dock could be pumped dry. The donkey boiler was still going periodically as the leaking ship slowly came to rest on bilge and keel blocks. At the same time, workmen shored her up with regularly spaced timbers from the ship's side to the tiered walls of the stone dock.[14]

The repairs to the old ship were to be thorough. Besides having the leak stopped, Freeman arranged to have her recaulked and resheathed with yellow metal, since her old suit had been on her for nearly twelve years. Once they stripped the metal off, it was easy to see why *Glory* had leaked and worked more and more each voyage as the years passed. Most of the rotten and smelly oakum in her seams was long past the point of keeping her dry. The various maritime tradesmen — shipwrights, caulkers, and laborers — busied themselves for a full week on her hull, carefully inspecting the maze of seams and butts for dry rot and damage from toredo, the voracious marine boring worms, inside and out, caulking her underwater body completely, and repairing the leak. Then she was sheathed up to the 17-foot draft mark. Since she and the *America* spent so little time fully loaded, Joshua Freeman and Harry Knowles (who now managed the shore affairs of both vessels at San Francisco) had felt there was no need to expend money to sheath her up to the 22-foot mark. On June 7, a much dryer and freshly painted *Glory* was hauled out of the Esquimalt dock and towed toward Union Bay to load coal and coke.

After making a complete voyage following her bottom work, the month of August found her again out in Union Bay. Meanwhile, down on the Seattle waterfront, a decrepit wooden sidewheeler, the *Eliza Anderson*, prepared to head north. The Alaska gold rush was on. Hundreds of rapacious fortune hunters were willing to go north on almost anything that floated. Just a few months earlier, this thirty-nine-year-old, 249-ton vessel had been resurrected from a ship graveyard on Puget Sound, docked, given a generous coat of white paint to help cover the nearly rotten state of her tired hull, and overhauled down below where her antiquated boiler and walking beam engine rested. The *Eliza Anderson* sailed from Seattle late in the afternoon, August 10, overflowing with passengers bound for the gold fields. At Port Townsend she made a brief stop where the fo'c's'le crowd smuggled enough liquor on board to ease the rigors of the trip ahead. The next day, the little 140-foot sidewheeler with its 60 horsepower steam engine chugged and wheezed into Union Bay to coal. With the crew steeped in alcohol, the master was forced to use his steward department to load the ship's coal bunkers. As could be expected, they stowed her fuel incorrectly, and she cast off from the wharf with a heavy list to starboard. Her port paddle wheel was nearly out of the water, the pilot could not head the rudder properly, and the venerable old scow helplessly drifted out into the bay with the current. In short order she was careening dangerously close to *Glory of the Seas*, laying peacefully at anchor. Joshua Freeman yelled over the water, "Where the hell are you a-heading with that damn tub?" Absolutely out of control, the old steamer relentlessly kept coming. Then a loud crunch ac-

companied with the sound of splintering wood resounded over the water.
As the *Eliza Anderson* crashed against the side of *Glory*, a large section of
the starboard paddlebox broke up. In her own time her remains drifted
clear, but all through the ordeal, the steamer crew had to endure a
continuous flow of adjectives from Joshua Freeman as he cursed at the
top of his voice the incompetence of the "steam kettle" and its drunken
crew. No damage resulted to *Glory*, again proving she had been built to
take punishment. The *Eliza Anderson*, after temporary repairs and a
correction of her list, headed out of the bay bound for Alaska. No one
on *Glory* regretted her departure.[15]

During the years 1898 and 1899 *Glory of the Seas* sailed both to Departure Bay and Union Bay. She loaded coal at the latter port where ovens
capable of producing 100 tons of coke per day were now in full operation under the supervision of Frank Little. *Glory* made six voyages annually in which she loaded a yearly average of 20,000 tons of cargo. She was
not slowing up even as she neared the thirty-year mark.

By 1898, she was the only merchant ship built by Donald McKay still
sailing. *Sovereign of the Seas* had just recently been cut down to a towing
barge and would have to suffer the degradation of being a coal scow on
the East Coast until February 19, 1903 when she would founder off the
coast of New Jersey.[16]

On November 30, 1899, *Glory* had her final meeting with a McKay-
built ship, the steam-powered U.S.S. *Adams*, off Cape Mendocino, about
220 miles northwesterly of San Francisco. *Glory* was 28 days out from
Union Bay and short of provisions. The *Adams*' official log tersely reported:

> At 9:30 [A.M.] sailing ship on port beam made international signal
> D.P.G.M. "Can you spare provisions." Left course and headed for her. . . .
> On coming near ship stopped engines, lowered whale oat and sent her 300
> lb. flour ($4.50) and 16 gal. of beans ($3.00), these being the provisions
> asked for. They were paid for in cash ($7.50). The ship was the *Glory of the
> Seas*, Joshua Freeman, master and H. K. Knowles, San Francisco, agent. At
> 10:40 hoisted whale boat . . . and went ahead full speed on course.[17]

The two vessels then parted company, never to be seen together again.
Glory of the Seas finally arrived at San Francisco four days later, 32 days
from Union Bay, which was the longest voyages she would ever make
between the two ports

On Sunday, July 22, 1900, an enterprising maritime photographer

Glory's bow and figurehead, photographed in 1900 at Howard Street wharves, San Francisco. Courtesy Robert A. Weinstein.

went down on the San Francisco embarcadero (East Street) to take pictures of the various sailing ships in port. Just south of the Ferry Building lay *Glory of the Seas* at one of the Howard Street coal wharves discharging cargo. The photographer went out on the dock, set up a tripod, carefully aimed his camera lens to take in the bow of *Glory,* and then flipped the shutter. His finished product told a great deal about the old ship, now past thirty. Her days of "spit and polish" were over. The constant use as a coal drougher and the increased maintenance expenses meant she was no longer valuable enough to be kept in first-class condition. All evidence of gilt on her cutwater scrollwork, trailboards, and nameboards had been covered up by black paint years before. The Greek goddess, although still strikingly white with gilded arm bands and necklace, was minus her outstretched right arm. A collision had broken off the arm and had damaged the ship's stem and elaborate scrollwork. Now, two 8-foot-long steel rods spiked in a makeshift manner from her fo'c's'le head buffalo rail to the heavy cutwater assembly marred the fading beauty of *Glory of the Seas*.[18] Aloft, the bright, rich color of natural wood coated with varnish no longer caught the eye. All her spars had been painted the common mast or tan color, a shade generally used on steamers and older square-riggers such as *Glory* in the closing years of full-rigged sail under the Stars and Stripes. Both she and her master had just a few years left.

CHAPTER XIV

The End of an Era

I N June, 1901, while *Glory of the Seas* discharged coke at the great Selby lead smelter on Carquinez Straits, a fifteen-year-old boy in San Francisco made a decision to go to sea on a sailing ship. Young Walter Ehrhorn had stowed away on an American troop transport bound for the Philippines two years before, and now he longed to learn what life on a square-rigger would be like. The following story written by Ehrhorn many years later shows how he found out that the life of a hard-case, rough-and-ready, deep-water sailor wasn't for him:

I thought that taking a trip on a sailing ship would be adventuresome and exciting. Many was the time I would go down to the waterfront and size up the ships tied up at the different wharves. After seeing all these, some beautiful and clean, and some really dirty ships, I said, "I'm going to get a job as a deck boy and take another trip somewhere." But everytime I would ask someone in authority on a ship for a job, the answer was, "You're too young." This never discouraged me in the least. At last I was directed up the sailor's home at First and Harrison Street. This home was located on a large knoll. There I was told to get permission in writing from my mother which I did. Then I was told to stay at the home overnight. This was done to test my grit and see if I'd get homesick. So, the next morning, two men, I remember, decided on what kind of a ship I should be put on — a British ship taking eight months to go around Cape Horn or a sailing vessel flying the American flag. It was decided to ship me on the one flying "Old Glory" and, by the way, the ship turned out to be the *Glory of the*

Seas, an old windjammer even in those days and this was in the year 1901. The morning I left home (June 29), I went aboard a Red Stack towboat called the *Sea King* and headed for Port Costa where I went on board the ship and was introduced to the quarters I was to occupy. Then, the first job to do was to coil up all the ropes lying about the deck. I was given my first lesson on coiling ropes by the first mate, Wallace, and naturally, I coiled them from right to left and soon learned to coil them properly from left to right. I never saw so many ropes in all my life. When this job was done, I got to washing paint on the officers' cabin. I thought that this was fun as I was now one of the crew and on a sailing ship. It didn't take long to find out what a mistake I made and many times considered myself lucky that I didn't get shipped on an English ship.

The tugboat finally towed the *Glory of the Seas* to a pier in San Francisco and then it laid tied up for about one week when a crew was taken aboard. What a rough neck crew it was from the very first day (July 5). The crew were nearly all drunk and fights were continuous. I was about to beat it off the ship but was afraid to desert as another kid came aboard and said that when deserters were caught, they're put in the brig, shot, or dumped overboard. This frightened me, so I decided to stick it out for one trip.

At last, we finally sailed being towed out through the Golden Gate one afternoon. When well outside the Heads, sail was set and the ship was on its own. I was ordered to stand watch the first four hours the same as an able-bodied seaman. With night coming on and darkness having set, I was ordered to help a sailor lash down the anchor on the forward deck over the fo'c's'le [head]. We were heading north in a choppy sea with all sails set and seemed to be making good headway, when on looking ahead through the darkness, I suddenly noticed a light that seemed to be coming straight for the ship. I called the seaman's attention to this and he immediately ordered me to notify the Captain who was in his quarters aft. Captain Freeman was his name, an elderly man, white-haired, with a white beard, who came out of his berth in pajamas. I told him a light was seen by me that was coming directly toward our ship. When upon seeing it, he started swearing like a trooper. He gave all hands on deck orders to go below as he thought we were going to have a collision. Sure enough, the mast of the sailing boat hit us. (It turned out to be a pilot boat as found out later when we returned to San Francisco.) Well, the mast just struck the lower yard of the mainmast and Freeman thought it would break off, so he started to yell at the crew of this sailing boat and his words, I'll never forget, were, "Hey! There on board sailor! What the hell's the matter with you down there?" (This deck was much lower than ours.) "Can't you see where you're going, you blankety-blank G——D—— fools?" But no response and the captain said to me, "They must be all below deck drunk."

That sure was exciting for the first night out. He told me then to "keep a sharp weather eye open as we may run into some more damn fools," so forward I went to resume my duties with the sailor.

When it came time after four hours on watch to turn in, I had to toll the bell and then waken the other sleeping members of the crew one by one. With only an oil lamp to see by, I had to climb over all kinds of sailor's baggage, grips, bags, boxes, and all kinds of junk. Then I turned in. What a night to try to sleep. We had four hours on and four hours off, two shifts of crews. Well, I no sooner turned in, and mind you, I never knew I had to furnish my bedding. I thought it strange that the sailors had all come on board carrying their own mattresses and blankets, but I was not informed that I should furnish my own. It wasn't long before I found out to my sorrow why they outfitted themselves with this equipment. I was no sooner asleep than something started to annoy and bite me. To my amazement I discovered that the mattress I was sleeping on was infested with bedbugs. It was alive with them and to sleep was out of the question. The next shift that I was to turn in, I decided to sleep on top of the sailor's quarters out in the open with a piece of canvas for a covering. The second night out found me sleeping or trying to sleep with the rain coming down in buckets full, I getting soaked to the skin. The only thing I could do was to go back in the fo'c's'le and try to sleep on one of the benches used by the crews to sit on, but with the smell of the oil lamp and the musty smell of the interior of the cabin, this brought on sea sickness, and I was sick! As sick as I was, I had to go on deck and work just the same. The crew saw to that. But I finally found a better place to sleep and that was on top of the galley alongside of the stack that came up through the cabin top. It was warm. When a squall came up suddenly, especially when we were off the Columbia River, a large, mountainous wave engulfed the whole ship and washed her clean from one end to the other. This happened at about three A.M. I was fast asleep when this wave struck broadside. The ship must have got in the trough of the sea because the wave came right over the place where I was. Before I knew it, I was washed off onto the deck 8 feet below right up against the railing on the starboard side. Why I wasn't carried right over the rail into the ocean, only God knows, but I think it was because the ship righted herself just before I landed on deck. I was pretty well bruised but thankful that I was still alive and safe on board. I was given first aid by the cook (Edmund Dixon), who was called out of bed to attend to me, and whose life I afterwards saved. But that is another story.

It was my job to serve the food to the crew in the fo'c's'le at meal times. I would go to the galley and bring the food, if one could call it such, and place it on the deck of the fo'c's'le where the men sitting around on the benches would help themselves — mush every morning with brown sugar, no milk or cream, in large pans. I recall one instance when I brought in a pan of mush all cooked up fit for a poultice. As the men dug into the gruel, a couple of cockroaches were headed downward in the mush with their bottoms up. When the men saw this, that was the start of a fight I've long remembered. First, they sent me back with the pans of mush to tell the cook to eat it himself and to bring some clean mush. The cook took the cockroaches out but sent the mush back. As a kid would, I told the men what he had done. That started the fight. The cook afterward started carrying about six or eight large knives with him so the crew wouldn't get their hands on them. They thought that he was arming the officers who came on deck to see what the trouble was. As they gathered around the cook, one of the officers reached out to release the cook of the knives. The crew took this as a clue that a free-for-all fight was imminent. The men of the crew ran in all directions and began to pull belaying pins out of the rail to arm themselves. In the meantime the cook took off to the galley to hide out of sight, but a couple of men spotted him and after him they went. If it hadn't been for me, a kid jumping in between the men and the cook, he would have been murdered right there and then. I put my foot out to protect the cook, standing in front of him. One man made a swing with a pin in his hand. I stuck out my foot and tripped him, causing him to fall to the deck. By this time some of the officers came to the cook's rescue. The first mate, Wallace, with a pistol in his hand, said, "The first man to touch the cook will be shot!" He grabbed me by the collar and flung me to one side telling me to "get the hell out of the way." Things started to quiet down a little by this time. The captain read the riot act to the men and ordered them to return to their quarters. They finally did but they sure had it in for the cook.

On the way up the Straits of Georgia to Union Bay, the ship was taken in tow by a tug. During this time, the crew including me, had to go below in the hold and empty ballast of earth and rock. This was put into large buckets by hand, hoisted up and dumped overboard. By the time we arrived at Comox (Union Bay), B.C., our destination, the ship was empty and ready to load coal and coke. The ship was soon tied up at the wharf. When we arrived, the captain made a big mistake. He was approached by some of the crew who wanted some spending money from their pay. This he readily consented to, so the crew took off. No stores of any kind were at the coaling place where some Chinese lived. The crew bought whiskey and whatever liquor they could get and returned to the ship drunk. Some acted like crazy men. What they didn't consume off ship they finished on board with about twenty men all drunk and fighting mad. Some drew their knives from their sheathes and started to swing them in every direction. One man in particular, I recall, placed his left hand against the bulkhead of the forward cabin and with fingers spread apart plunged the knife into the spaces between them. One time he missed and the knife went in his finger. The blood flowed profusely but this didn't stop him. He kept it up for some time. Then, he threw his knife up in the air and a few times was all

that was required for him to stop this. The knife came down point first
and landed on his head. This knocked him out stretching him out on the
deck. There he lay 'till others of the crew who were not too drunk managed
to drag him into the fo'c's'le where they threw him into a lower bunk.
What happened to him after that I don't know. I took this all in while hiding out on top of the cabin where I made my headquarters, too scared to
go on deck.

The coal [1,500 tons] went below and the coke [1,068 tons], being light-
weight, went in the 'tween decks. We were tied up for about two weeks at
the bunker. During this time the first mate, Wallace, being quite a fisherman and trolling his hobby, had me busy. He was a heavy-set man weighing about 200 pounds. Every day when work was done he'd get me to tow
a large round bottom lifeboat that belonged to the ship with him laying
back in the stern smoking his pipe and a troll line with about twenty
hooks on trailing in behind. I would row him down Union Bay (Baynes
Sound) for about 5 miles and back again, no matter how tired my arms
would get. I'd tell him so, but it made no difference. When he was ready to
go fishing, I had to be "Johnny on the spot." This kept up day after day so
long as the ship was at the dock. Once, when a coal steamer tied up on the
other side of the pier I tried to get a job, earn for no pay, to help the cook
for return passage. When the cook heard I was signed up on the *Glory of
the Seas* he said, "Nothing doing." So I had to stay with the ship 'till it returned to San Francisco.

The return trip [twelve days] was uneventual [sic] except when entering the Golden Gate under sail as darkness was coming on. We were cours-
ing head on for Alcatraz Island, when about to drop anchor the anchor
chain fouled. Great excitement took place on board as we were getting
closer and closer to the island. Suddenly, the chain cleared itself and down
went the anchor into the water. The ship began to drag the anchor for
quite a distance before it grabbed onto the bottom of the bay. In the morning at daylight [August 28] the ship was scarcely 300 feet from going ashore
on this island in the middle of the bay.

It didn't take me long to get ashore. I immediately went to the office of
the owners of the ship [Pacific Steam Whaling offices at 30 California
Street], got my wages for about two months (20 dollars), and set out for
"home, sweet home" again, none the worse for my experience but much
wiser. This to date has fulfilled my desires to sail before the mast. Never
would I want to do it over again; yet I wouldn't take a thousand dollars in
exchange for the experience and knowledge that I gained.[1]

In October, 1901, Joshua Freeman signed on another chief mate,
George Ekrem, a deep-water veteran for most of his forty-one years. He
had been born at sea on his father's Norwegian square-rigger, just before

the Civil War. Shortly after completing his education, he came to the
United States and joined the U.S. Navy. Following his four-year hitch in
the late 1870's, he received his master's ticket in the American merchant
marine and subsequently took command of the coasting schooner *American Girl* in 1882.[2] During the ensuing nineteen years he had become a
competent shipmaster and impressed Joshua Freeman as a man he could
trust with his old ship. Of medium build and height, Ekrem was debon-
air, neat and well-dressed. He did everything in an easygoing manner
whether it was walking, talking, or working. He was not a tough-shelled
"bucko" who ordered men up the ratlines at the point of a pistol, but he
made sure the crew carried out their duties properly. Freeman soon found
that Ekrem liked to joke in his gruff, typical mate's manner. He also discovered, once *Glory* was at sea heading up the Pacific Coast, that his
mate always kept one accessory with him no matter whether he was wear-
ing oilskins during a heavy blow or attending to shipboard duties during
fine weather — his pipe. Ekrem was an enjoyable human being and a first-
rate officer, and once *Glory* arrived in British Columbian waters, he was
left in command as the old captain went ashore to stay with Lucy and the
Littles until the spring equinox of 1902.[3]

During this period in the British Columbia coal trade, very few
square-rig sailing ships called at Nanaimo, Comox, or Ladysmith, the
new Dunsmuir loading port that had replaced Departure Bay. Almost
all exports by the New Vancouver Coal Company were carried on tramp
steamers; only an occasional full-rigged sailing ship or bark picked up a
Dunsmuir charter. The most regularly employed coal droughers for
Robert Dunsmuir and Sons in the year 1901 were the steamers *Wellington* and the *Costa Rica* (renamed *Bristol*). Both vessels often made two
voyages to California a month. *Glory* continued on her long-term charter
to load for San Francisco, while the dashing 1,496-ton iron bark *Antiope,*
also on charter, regularly carried coal to the Hawaiian Islands.

The glorious days of Yankee square-rigged sail were continuing to
fade as fore-and-afters and steamers eclipsed the American square-rig
fleet. More and more of the older full-riggers were even being forced out
of low revenue bulk trade except for those few shipowners and captains
who had an in with the proper people. Joshua Freeman was indeed fortunate to have Frank Little, the new superintendent of all Dunsmuir mining operations, for a son-in-law.

The Dunsmuir coal fleet was reduced to three in January, 1902. The

Captain George Ekrem, 1903. Courtesy Mr. and Mrs. Carl Woodward.

collier *Bristol* was steaming at 11 knots on the night of January 2 in Chatham Sound, Alaska Territory, when the storm-tossed vessel piled up on a reef with a full cargo of coal and a crew of twenty-seven souls on board. Wedged in between a rock ledge, she seemed to be afloat, but her bottom was ripped out. Once the fierce storm rocked the *Bristol* loose from her perch, she sank like a stone, taking the captain and six others down to a watery grave.[4]

During the first week in January, *Glory of the Seas* headed up the coast with newlyweds on board oblivious to the storm up north. Several days previously, while stevedores had been unloading the ship at San Francisco, Captain Ekrem had welcomed aboard a special visitor from Olympia, Washington — his fiance, Miss Ada Woodard, daughter of a pioneer dentist. She had come down the coast to make the coming voyage as Ekrem's wife, and *Glory of the Seas* became a honeymoon ship for the first time in her thirty-one-year career. Though Mrs. Ekrem suffered seasickness on the trip up the coast, the weather remained quite mild; on the return passage, however, *Glory* almost joined the *Bristol* in a watery grave.[5]

On January 30, 1902, the coal-laden *Glory* was towed out to Cape Flattery. Immediately, the tough, old square-rigger began plowing through storm-whipped graybeards as she fought her way well off the coastline. Several days out, she ran into bad weather and labored heavily as mountainous waves many times rendered her helpless in making headway. Caught in the teeth of a winter gale, she lay off Cape Blanco on the Oregon coast for fully seventeen days. Besides causing general seasickness on board, especially to the bride of Captain Ekrem, the stormy weather nearly reduced *Glory* to a derelict. Part of her bulwarks were smashed. A large wooden water cask next to the forward house went adrift and pounded her main deck pitilessly before going overboard; gigantic waves washed her decks; and the creaking and groaning ship opened up in her seams and began to leak a great deal. Even so, her troubles had just begun as the crew fought to keep her afloat. At latitude 42°26′ north, longitude 127°18′ west, the gale winds further took their toll on the old square-rigger. Her mainmast broke in the hounds, 50 feet above the main deck. Unless it could be secured, *Glory* stood a good chance of losing everything above her lower masts. While part of the crew kept at her pumps, Ekrem directed other men in laying spars next to the broken mast and amply lashing them with dozens of feet of chain wrapped around and

around it. Next, the rudder head sprung, putting her further at the mercy
of the gale. Once that was jury-rigged, the preventer tiller went adrift
also, reducing her to the same helpless condition. Then, miraculously,
the weather moderated. The crew secured the mast, although they had to
rig her down partially, and the rudder was jury-rigged for the third time.
Finally Ekrem could slowly nurse his storm-battered ship down the coast
to San Francisco. Thirty days after she left Union Bay, *Glory of the Seas*
passed through the Golden Gate, completing what was by far the most
damaging passage she would ever make between British Columbia and
California.[6]

Joshua Freeman had anxiously awaited news of *Glory* at Victoria fear-
ing the worst since it had been generally acknowledged that the winter
storms off the North Pacific coast had been extremely bad this year. He
received word of her safe arrival with vast relief. Meanwhile, Ekrem directed her refit in a bay shipyard. Her broken mainmast had to be replaced and was pulled with shear legs. On its removal the customary 20-
dollar gold piece, which had been placed beneath it following her refit in
1882, was revealed and pocketed, but later on, when they stepped the
new mast, Ekrem short-changed the old clipper by placing a mere new
four-bit piece under it. Many years later, when George Ekrem was asked
why he hadn't returned the 20-dollar gold piece to its proper spot, he
explained that "hard times" didn't justify spending "big" money on an
old ship.[7] Once she was fully rigged again, she had a new appearance, yet
a further sign of advanced age. Her main skys'l yard and mast had been
sent down, reducing her height from keel to truck by 14 feet. The repairs
had taken nearly a month. Upon their completion Ekrem sailed for
Comox, arriving there on April 17, nine days from San Francisco. There
he quit *Glory* to take command of a lumber schooner, a rig that he was
to sail exclusively for the next thirteen years until his retirement from
the sea. Although he had almost lost his life on her and despite the four-
bit piece, Captain Ekrem in later years called *Glory of the Seas* the finest
vessel he had ever commanded.[8] Upon his retirement to Olympia, Washington, he made a superb detailed painting of her in oils — a shipmaster's opinion of how well the old ship looked under sail.

While *Glory* was under repair, another of her old competitors neared
retirement. On many occasions during his years on the coast, Joshua
Freeman had raced with the lumber drougher *Dashing Wave*. *Glory of
the Seas* had won on some voyages; at other times, the gold rush clipper

had proved the winner. On March 15, 1902, this relic of the clipper era
sailed from San Francisco in ballast under command of Captain Richard
Lancaster, who had earlier been mate of the *Ericsson*. Like both Knowles
and Freeman, Lancaster carried his family with him although the *Wave*'s
after cabin was 5 feet shorter fore and aft and 6 feet narrower than *Glory*'s.
For a vessel nearly fifty years old, the main skys'l yarder still looked fairly
well kept up and painted, but now had a noticeable hog in her keel. More
than 200 voyages in the Pacific coast lumber trade had taken a gradual
toll on her tough old hull. *Dashing Wave* was well worn and could not
compete in upkeep with the cheaply maintained coastal lumber schooners. Following her arrival on Puget Sound on April 2, 1902, she was
turned over to new owners for conversion to a utility barge, having
brought only 6,000 dollars in the transaction.[9] The old vessel was rigged
down to lower masts and her oaken keel was eventually hogged until she
had no sheer left, a disheartening end for a ship that had been as dashing
as her name.

In October, Joshua Freeman made a passage that closed an era in his
life, his final voyage as captain of *Glory of the Seas*. Sailing from San Francisco on October 5, he beat up the coast, fighting storms and fogs all the
way and finally came to anchor at Union Bay fifteen days later. On November 1, forty-five years after having taken command of the medium
clipper *Christopher Hall*, Freeman prepared to leave *Glory*. This year he
would not return to her in the spring. As the sixty-seven-year-old captain
and his mate, John Pinding, a naturalized American originally from Fin-
land, made out papers at the customhouse at Cumberland that transferred command to Pinding, Joshua had understandably mixed feelings.
Glory had been the outstanding ship in his career. He knew that he would
miss her in his life — her creaks and groans, her leaks, and her sailing pe-
culiarities both good and bad; but advanced age was catching up with
him. His walking cane was more in evidence as he used it to support his
right leg and his slightly stooped frame; his eyes, although still bright
and piercing, had the look of hard years in them. It was best now that he
enjoy the leisure of life ashore with his family. He could say with pride
that he had added further polish to the shining reputation of *Glory of the
Seas*. In eighteen years he had made eighty-one voyages in her with re-
markedly few mishaps. Now she had to sail without him.

After turning over the command to Pinding, the captain took the
Esquimalt and Nanaimo Railroad train to Victoria where his wife waited

Dashing Wave, reduced to a hulk, under tow in Seattle harbor, ca. 1910.
Courtesy Joe D. Williamson.

for him. In this picturesque city the elderly couple were to spend much
of the remainder of their years. Since 1901 when Lucy had stopped going
to sea, their home had been the beautiful three-story mansion on fash-
ionable Rockland Avenue overlooking the straits lying east of Victoria.
Both now looked forward to happy times with their granddaughters —
and little Lucy's lessons in poker were about to begin. By no means,
though, had the Freemans seen the last of their beloved *Glory*. With their
superb view of the straits and the sound from various vantage points in
Victoria, they could look forward to seeing *Glory of the Seas* every time
she came to anchor at Royal Roads before loading coal at Comox or
Ladysmith. It can be safely assumed they took advantage of the oppor-
tunities.

CHAPTER XV

Deep-Sea Sailors

WITH Joshua Freeman no longer a part of *Glory of the Seas*, she began deteriorating at an accelerated rate. The coal trade from British Columbia and Puget Sound to California continued to become increasingly unprofitable for old full-riggers. It was hard to believe that not even two years before a dozen sailing ships had hauled coal on a regular basis from the four major "black diamond" ports of Seattle, Tacoma, Ladysmith, and Union Bay. Now many of these same vessels were either broken up, in the offshore trades, being used as Alaska cannery tenders, or were degraded towing barges. Had it not been for Freeman's and Knowles's close friendship with the Dunsmuirs, *Glory* herself would probably not have been sailing. Because of the low net profits for the old ship, Captain Pinding and Harry Knowles cut costs wherever possible.[1] With little upkeep and money put into her, *Glory* had no choice but to go slowly to pieces.

In March, 1903, after completing three passages under Pinding's command, she lay alongside the Howard Street coal wharves at San Francisco ready to ship a new crew to take her to British Columbia. One young able seaman who signed on this trip was George Webb, a tough and cocky 6-foot Englishman. Several years ago, the author interviewed this old shellback at his beautiful estate just outside of Sonoma, California. His recollections were descriptive of the decay in the American square-rig fleet at the turn of the century.

George Webb and his pal of several years, Gus Swenson, were looking for a way north one day in March, 1903, after having had their fling on the Barbary Coast. Both were larger than the average man of their generation, and gave the impression of being well able to take care of themselves either at sea or on shore. Webb called Swenson "the Swede" and stated that "nobody could describe that one. Big Gus stood about 6 feet tall and was about two axe handles across the shoulders. We had a lot of fun together." Swenson had once been an officer in the Swedish Navy, but had gotten into some woman trouble that had meant the end of his commission. Webb was the first to come out to the Pacific Coast, sailing on the crack lime-juicer *General Roberts* in 1897. Both men were seagoing, devil-may-care deep-water sailors, and since teaming up, had shipped together many times on the regular coasters.

Nearing the vicinty of the coal wharves at San Francisco, the two shell-backs caught sight of *Glory*. Webb said, "She was laying there on the Embarcadero with her bowsprit sticking over the roadway." His first impression of the old clipper was, "She's an old bucket, I hope that we get there with it. But she was a matter of transportation to me. I wasn't so sure that I'd picked a good one." Going on board, they found that because of poor shipping conditions in British Columbia she was making a one-way run, and Pinding was signing on a crew of runners. Webb said, "I think the deal we made was fifteen dollars for the trip up, a dollar a day."

Asking Webb about John Pinding, the author was surprised to learn that the old sailor had thought for all these years Pinding was the chief mate. The captain sailed shorthanded for the run up to B.C., with just a mate, Edmund Dixon, and twelve ship runners, and had stood the port watch in place of a first mate. Webb said regarding Pinding:

I don't remember him very well. We didn't see him about three or four days out going up the coast. I suppose he was drunk. Maybe he was sick, but we didn't see him at all. We called him "the Finn." He looked square and broad. He'd be tough like most. He didn't know how to be hard-case, not on the coast. The second mate, Peck, mentioned being in a couple of crack ships I had known when I was in the Cape Horn trade.

There were really never any watches. It took twelve men anytime to do anything. I think I was in the starboard watch [Peck's], when they picked us outside the gate. It must have been just before sunset, because I remember we got out of the Golden Gate and the Red Stack tug dropped us a couple miles offshore. It was still light when we got the kites on her. She was very badly run down. I don't know whether they had any insurance on her. In fact, we didn't have any ourselves. The hull was in good shape. The old saying is, "while she creaks, she holds." It's when they don't creak, you look out. They get so rotten you don't hear them and they come apart on you. I say, she creaked. The first time I was laying in my bunk in the fo'c's'le, she was creaking away with a heavy sou'easter behind. I said, "Well, fellows, I think we picked a good one. She creaks." The fo'c's'le wasn't clean, plenty of bedbugs, so I never unpacked my grip 'cause I didn't want the bedbugs to get into it. She was dirty, nothing like the old Cape Horners, which I was raised in, that were perfectly good ships, perfectly run, perfectly officered. It was a shock to me, but I was just going places and I didn't gave a damn!

Glory found herself in typical winter weather outside the gate, Webb said:

We packed it to Cape Flattery. Blew a couple of kites away that were ready to go anyway. Rotten sails in bad shape and rigging in bad shape. We had plenty of splicing because the rigging was pretty rotten. You had to serve a rope splice or you'd cut your finger on it some day. We had a pleasant trip, like I say. We had everything we needed. It wasn't a Cape Horn trip. We weren't on sea rations. We had left San Francisco with plenty of potatoes and fresh beef. We were a peaceable gang, well fed, but you never run a ship in your life with something not wrong with it according to the fo'c's'le. Everybody beefed about everything. They used to say, "the more you beef, the harder you work."

Giving a little background on the fo'c's'le crowd, Webb said:

This bunch we had were all mostly Scandinavians who worked the coastal schooners. They went south every winter to dodge the bad weather at the logging camps. They were mostly fishermen who would go up north to Nome or Bristol Bay in the summer and make hundreds of dollars and then come down in the fall, catch a ship to San Pedro or the cities like San Francisco, and spend the winters in luxury; then catch a boat back to Bristol Bay and catch more fish. We weren't together long enough to know each other and the only one I knew was the terrible Swede I shipped with. We didn't have a carpenter and sailmaker. We were just twelve runners taking her up the coast. There was a good cook but greasy. He gave us a good breakfast every morning.

We used to sing the chanty on the old Cape Horners. You have to sing a chanty to get everybody to pulling at the same time. The best tops'l halyard chanty was "Blow the Man Down." That was always the tops'l chanty.

Webb now sang in a rich bass voice:

> When I was a-walking down Paradise Street
> To my way, haye, blow the man down

That's the way we did it with a string of men on one rope, all pulling at the same time. The chanty man would sing another verse. Two were fine.

> Give it some time boys. We'll blow the man down.

You couldn't hoist a heavy sail with a small crew unless you had a chanty. You have to have a chanty man. The other way — one, two, three, one, two, three — wouldn't work.

Giving an idea of how much *Glory* leaked and how she handled at the ripe old age of thirty-four, Webb said,

> We pumped okay. All the time. We had the pump running a lot, but she wasn't leaking too badly. Well, believe me, I think we made a pretty good passage. Weren't over twelve days. Passed a couple steamers coming south and passed a bald-headed schooner, as I remember. The rocks [ballast] stayed where they belonged. She was lying very high and dry, and very cranky, because she had very little ballast. We never got the upper t'gallants'ls all the way up. We took all the men in the fo'c's'le to put a mains'l on her; all there was, including the mate and second mate. We didn't blow her out, thank God, but we had to haul up the mains'l a couple of times, but never reefed her up. We had four stays'ls, a main fores'l, four tops'ls and once in a while, the main'l. Generally we were hauling that up. The mate was very careful with [the sails]. He pulled them up before danger arose, because he was afraid of them. The mate tried to get the t'gallants on her but she was so light that we never made it.

As *Glory* neared Cape Flattery, Pinding told the lookout to watch for a tug. Webb said, "The only place we wore ship was off Cape Flattery. Cape Beale's near there [across the straits]. It's all up and down cliffs, you know. That's where a lot of ships have piled up." A tug was soon sighted and before long had *Glory* in tow. On the arrival of the old medium clipper at Union Bay, Webb explained, "We just made a harbor stow, not a very good one, and that was good-by. We just left the mates and the cook aboard. I never knew what happened to *Glory* after that, don't know whether she got a cargo of coal or what. It was unfortunate, but it was just a matter of transportation to me."[2]

Following her arrival, *Glory* was laid up for four months in British Columbia waters, not only because of a mine strike, which lasted for two months; but also because of a general decline in coal shipping during

Above. Coal sacked for shipment on the Ladysmith waterfront. Courtesy Provincial Archives, Victoria, British Columbia. Below. *Glory* about 1908: the only known photograph of her under sail. The original was owned by Captain Freeman. Note her "patched and patched and patched" canvas. Courtesy Mrs. Barbara Bumpus.

that summer. On Puget Sound at the same time lay eight California Shipping Company down-easters disengaged: the ships *Henry Failing, Reuce, William H. Smith, St. David, S. D. Carleton,* and the barks *Carrollton, Sea King* (both ex-ships), and the *St. James.* These charterless vessels made up nearly a third of the great San Francisco-based merchant fleet. Once the temporary slump ended, not one of them would carry coal. All were eventually to sail offshore with lumber.

The coal exporting trade for square-rigged sailing ships continued to fade even more. A peak in exportation had been reached at the turn of the century, but by 1903, because of the steadily increasing use of oil as a fuel for factory and home, the few tramp steamers in B.C. coal trade had pushed out most of the square-riggers with the exception of *Glory* and the *Antiope,* which regularly ran to the Hawaiian Islands. In May, the coal situation even forced Dunsmuir to lay up the collier *Wellington* for a while.

In the middle of July, Harry Knowles chartered *Glory* to load coal for Alaska. She was towed to Ladysmith Harbor, 60 miles north of Victoria, to take on cargo there for the first time. The 4-mile-long harbor afforded an interesting sight for Pinding and the rest of the afterguard that had stayed by *Glory* during her long layup. The town of Ladysmith, carefully laid out on a steep, once densely wooded slope to the west, had just began to bustle. It had been built at the turn of the century specifically to house the families of miners who worked by the hundreds in the great Extension Mine about 10 miles north. A massive coal wharf almost 800 feet long jutted out from the land in a southeasterly direction, and ships of practically any size and draft could come alongside to load. Immense copper-sheathed pilings, 100 or more feet long, supported the great structure. Another coal-loading platform jutting out to the east added to the fast-loading facilities, and five average-size sailing ships or steamers could load at the same time as the need arose. Off and on during the last two weeks of July, *Glory* took on cargo at the efficient facilities.

On August 11, after Pinding had shipped a crew, she headed north, bound for Dutch Harbor. Communications in Alaskan waters were so limited and slow at this time that outgoing and incoming ships were the major source of news. One steamer, sailing from Dutch Harbor in the middle of September, arrived down the coast and gave Knowles the first clue that nothing had been heard from *Glory of the Seas* for over a month. Her manager feared the worst and was just about to post her overdue and reinsure her at 5 percent when word was received that the old ship had finally dropped anchor at Dutch Harbor on September 16, after thirty-six long days up from Ladysmith. About two months later, after discharging his cargo, Pinding sailed for Puget Sound, making a fine passage of eleven days to Cape Flattery.[3]

On March 8, 1904, *Glory* completed the final leg of another voyage from Ladysmith by sailing through the majestic Golden Gate. Late that evening, Pinding anchored her just off Black Point, about a quarter mile north of the present-day San Francisco Maritime Museum. This proved to be a grave mistake. With the coming of dawn and low tide, the heavily laden craft lay hung up on the beach, much to the embarrassment of Pinding and his crew. She heeled over a ways, but fortunately stood no danger of sinking or breaking up. Pinding sent distress signals aloft at dawn and before long, two Red Stack tugs, the *Sea Queen* and *Sea Rover*, came to her assistance in the early morning hours; meanwhile, it became the talk of the waterfront that the old *Glory*, one of the best known and respected square-riggers on the coast, was hard aground. Late in the afternoon when the tide had sufficiently risen, the two tugs succeeded in pulling her loose and then towed her to the Howard Street wharves for unloading. *Glory of the Seas* had once more seemed indestructible.[4]

As the second week in April approached, Captain Pinding prepared for another voyage. Among his able-bodied seamen was a stalwart big Swede, Fingal Larson. Although only twenty-two, Larson already had nine years at sea behind him. By October, 1958, when the author interviewed him, he had spent fifty-three years as a seaman, sailmaker, and boatswain on dozens of ships ranging from the barkentine *Irmgard* and the bark *St. James* to the Matson luxury liner *Lurline*. The interview took place on the decks of the colorful full-rigger *Balclutha*, now owned and restored to her former Cape Horn glory by the San Francisco Maritime Museum Association which keeps her berthed near Fisherman's Wharf. This was a fitting place indeed to talk about the past. Arrangements were made to meet Larson on a Saturday afternoon. As the author stepped down from the starboard gangway onto the weathered main deck of the 256-foot *Balclutha,* he saw an elderly man still straight and tall standing near the foremast bitts. Though now emaciated by asthma, Larson looked nowhere near his eighty years. He once explained his rugged constitution to Karl Kortum, director of the Maritime Museum — "We lived tough, but we didn't get no ulcers!"[5]

Once we settled in the ex-donkey-boiler room of the *Balclutha,* now a
shipboard office, Larson held the author in complete fascination as he
spoke in a heavy Swedish-American accent of his days on *Glory* and other
vessels, years before. To begin with, he told of being tatooed from
"head to toes." He said about a tatoo on his chest, "I got dis one standing
up against a bar in London. Spent all my life at sea. The last time I
shipped out in 1948 on the *Lurline.* Now I do not'ing." Despite the difficulties of his asthmatic condition, Larson displayed admirable patience
in telling his experiences on the *Glory of the Seas:*

> *Glory* was my first American ship. Well, ya see, there was a strike going
> on in the spring of 1902, and we shipped on her, but then the strike took
> us off. It lasted ninety days. We had to get off, sailors, teamsters, and steve-
> dores, so I didn't go out in her. I went around Cape Horn in a lime-juice
> ship, and came back here in 1904. Then, I shipped in the *Glory of the Seas*
> again the second time, and we went to British Columbia to load coal for
> San Francisco. She was getting old so they couldn't send her around Cape
> Horn any more. That's the way she was running.
>
> She was gettin' pretty old and shaky, the rigging and all. The hull was
> pretty good, but the rigging was going. She had wire standing rigging and
> hemp running rigging. [There was] always something chaffing and going
> in the rigging, 'course, if the ship is getting old, they let the rest of it go. A
> sail blow away — ya have to go up and renew the sail. Always something
> going, always something parting — patched and patched and patched. You
> have to go up and put a patch on the sail, ya know, wouldn't renew any-
> ting, ya know. She was getting old and what good in spending money on an
> old ship. The deck was clean, but no "holing stone" work was done. She
> was past dem days. Still she was a smart ship. Ya know, she was leaking in
> her later years, leaking quite a bit. [Major repairs] didn't pay. Caulk her
> and recaulk her, that didn't pay. We sound her so many inches and we had
> to pump her out. Of course we sounded morning and night and every
> watch.
>
> I was with Captain Pinding, John Pinding. I think he was a Russian
> Finn. He couldn't speak very good English, the son of a gun, but by God,
> he could write good English. Well, he was all right in a way, ya know,
> 'course, he was not one of dose hard ones. You couldn't be that way on the
> coast. Dem days were gone on the coast. 'Course, deep water was different.
> On the coast they had to behave themselves, both the mates and skippers.
> Up and down the coast they had to lay low. They couldn't pull all that
> stuff they did on Cape Horn. [There was a] first and second mate, a donkey
> man to run the donkey engine, cook and a cabin boy, and sixteen men be-
> fore the mast [five ordinary seamen and eleven able-bodied seamen]. Char-
> lie Svankey's the only man I can remember was with me on the *Glory of*

the Seas. He was an A.B. same as me. He stuck around here the rest of his life. I used to go with him times after that in steam schooners and one thing another like that. He died last year [1957]. 'Course, you had to be tough, that's all there was to it.

Speaking of fights, he said, "You might fall off in a gin-mill. We had no trouble with the first and second mates."

He was proud of the old square-rigger days of "four on, four off," a rough watch around the clock compared to that on American deep-water ships today. Now sailors work eight hours an entire day with a four on, eight off shift. Less than fifty years ago, deep-water sailors worked twelve and more hours out of the twenty-four.

> We got towed out to about the Farallones, and up the coast we sailed in five days. She was a smart ship. Dem were good old days. We went off shore a long way off. In a windjammer you're afraid of land. Never hove to. We shortened down to lower tops'ls, goosewinged them in heavy weather. A Puget Sound tug, a steam tug, took us in. It was laying out there. Lighthouse report you, *Glory of the Seas,* at both Ladysmith and Comox. At both ports, we layed beside a dock. Nanaimo too was a big port. Well, I tell ya, the Alaska packers used to come in there. Three other ships were there in May [1904]. I think I have a discharge for that month.

On the main deck of the *Balclutha,* he described in detail how a half-century before, sailors had discharged ballast from ships like *Glory:*

> We had what we called ballast tubs. Also, we had the yardarm cockbilled as a boom. For unloading we had a span between the main and fore, see, and a block in the middle of the hatch. Then, we had the donkey boiler [fired up], and took up so far as it would go. Then, you slack it out on the burton out on the yardarm, and over the side the ballast went.
>
> At Ladysmith and Comox we were loaded with a little over 3,000 tons. Didn't take no time at all. Three days she was loaded. Shoot it down, ya see — comes down through the chutes. Different kinds of coal, I t'ink. They loaded the hold until she was filled to the Plimsoll mark. They could load dem just so far. That's the law.[6] Taking up the tops'l yard, we used to sing a chanty, "Away, my boys and we're homeward bound." Sixteen men to get her up. For the setting of the mains'l we'd sing, "Whiskey for me, Johnny," all hands on the main yard strung along. That's a big piece of canvas.

About the steering gear, Larson said:

She was old-fashioned with rope gear and blocks. She didn't have steering gear with the screw, ya know. You had to [periodically] renew the ropes and the drums. Dat's the way they steered dem days. We had what we called "peggy," to keep her clean. We divy up the rooms and quarters. Sometimes my week I done it, the next week you did it.

The author asked him about Edmund Dixon. Fingal said:

He was a good guy. He fed well, fresh bread every day. American ships were always good for eats; they had to on the coast. Those lime-juicers were the worst goddamn [tubs] afloat, hungrier than hell. On the coast food was very good. On a long trip it's lousy.

The author asked him whether sailors on coasting craft made sailing ship models in their off hours. He replied:

No, not on the coast. That was deep water, when you're coming around the Horn four or five months, 120 to 250 days. Oh, God, you ain't got no time to pass, not on the coast. You're at it all the time on the coast.

That was a British tug that towed us out to Flattery. The run down the coast, coal-laden, was a little longer 'cause we happened to get down in the sou'easters. I don't know how many days it was, but it was at least nine days, before we got back to 'Frisco, headwinds, ya see.

On the arrival of *Glory*, Captain Pinding discharged the foremast hands. Larson said, "If ya wanted to stay for another trip, all right, but as a rule we all got off. Well, ya know, burned up. We'll take another one, a schooner or something else, or we'd want to go to Australia or Africa, the hell with this!"[7] *Glory* on the decline was a one-voyage vessel to her crew. The days of pride were over.

There was bad news for John Pinding and *Glory* as the old ship lay at the foot of Howard Street. The coal bunkers at San Francisco were overstocked, which meant that Dunsmuir would be laying her up again. Joshua Freeman, the new marine superintendent for Dunsmuir Collieries and naturally an old and close friend of *Glory*'s, hated to do it but it was either her or the *Wellington*.[8] And, of course, the *Wellington* herself would be temporarily laid up for six weeks in July and August because of little demand for coal. But for *Glory*, the coal trade, as regular employment, was as good as dead. Her so-called temporary withdrawal from the coast coal trade would be permanent. She was no longer useful.

Her fate at this point had become the same as her American wooden sisters'. Not a wooden full-rigger had been built in the United States since 1892. Furthermore, as the statement of a statistician in the 1904 *Hearings before the Merchant Marine Commission* revealed: "As for sailing vessels, the loss is appalling. On January 1, 1870, we had 2,295 square-rigged vessels, and by the records of the Bureau of Navigation we had, on June 30, 1903, 350, and most of them that were not wrecked were uninsurable."[9] Of the above number only *Glory* and about seventy-two other vessels still retained their classification as wooden full-rigged ships. The only thing that she and her remaining sisters could look forward to was a lingering death. They were a dying species that in a few years would be completely extinct, dinosaurs of the sea.

CHAPTER XVI

Reprieve

THE summer of 1904 found *Glory of the Seas* in a ship graveyard, Oakland Creek, the estuary separating the bay cities of Oakland and Alameda. In these murky, sewage-filled waters, many a sailing ship had reached a last harbor. After her cargo was discharged, *Glory* had been towed deep into the estuary to the vicinity of Government Island where she was run up on the mud at high water. A line secured ashore to couple her with her intended beaching was the most convenient way of making sure she would not drift off. The summer months passed slowly as Captain Pinding patiently waited for word of a coast coal charter that was not to come. Nor was a voyage to Alaska in the offing this year. Less than a half dozen square-riggers and fore-and-afters were to sail with coal from Puget Sound for Alaska before fall set in. Other prospects were dim for *Glory*. She could not head offshore because she was in generally poor condition aloft, and although her hull was still sound, Harry Knowles did not feel any large amount of money should be spent on her because of the stiff competition between the few remaining low-revenue bulk trades open to full-riggers. The Russo-Japanese War, then in all its fury, had created a need for tonnage to ship war supplies, but American vessels in better repair than *Glory* had nudged her out. Steamers, both iron and wood, continued to make heavy inroads on the Pacific Coast bulk trades. Schooners, barkentines, and lime-juicers had the edge on *Glory* and her aged sisters because of lower operating costs. Even the subsidized French square-rig "bounty" fleet could afford to make voyages financially foolish for a ship of her type. The American wooden square-rigger was obsolete.

As winter of 1904 approached, *Glory* was joined by dozens of other tired and shaky sailing vessels, seasonal cannery tenders flesh from the Bristol Bay region, and a few remnants of the past great New England whaling fleet, which now sported the port of San Francisco on their ancient transoms. Once the tenders and whalers left Oakland Creek during the spring of 1905, a few ships remained, among them *Glory of the Seas* and the thirty-seven-year-old down-easter *Two Brothers,* a nearly worn-out ex coastal coal drougher. Her last activity had been a 1903 voyage between San Francisco and Astoria, Oregon. Since that time, the 1,203-ton vessel had been slowly rotting away as she lazily swung at anchor in the ship graveyard. By the end of 1905, it became an established fact among coast shipping people that the general use of square-riggers in the coastal coal trade was finished. This gave further reason to conclude that both *Glory* and *Two Brothers* would end up as towing barges in the not too distant future.

In the early part of March, 1906, Captain John Barneson, then one of San Francisco's prominent shipping men, voiced his interest in buying *Glory* to Harry Knowles. Barneson had seen her laying up on the mud in Oakland Creek and thought that she would make a sound towing barge for his growing fleet, which operated under the corporate name Barneson-Hibbard Company. John Barneson was no stranger to the decks of a square-rigger. After spending much of his childhood on his father's lime-juicer, he himself reached command of the full-rigged ship *George Thompson* in 1885 at the age of twenty-three. He came ashore in the 1890's, first making his headquarters as a shipping merchant and owner at Port Townsend and then later transferring his operations to San Francisco.[1] During the Alaska gold rush he successfully managed the old down-easters *Seminole* and *Prussia* in their last days. At the turn of the century he owned three British-built four-posters, the near sisters *Drummuir; Drumburton,* lost in 1904; and *Drumcraig,* posted missing in April, 1906. Early in 1906, Barneson had felt that he needed additional tonnage for his fleet, which, as of March, consisted of the old down-east bark *Sea King,* acquired in 1904; the *Two Brothers,* which he purchased in February, 1906; and the *Drummuir.*

Old faces were soon to fade from the life of *Glory of the Seas,* and new ones to appear once all her owners decided to sell their interests. She

Glory as painted by W. A. Coulter, 1906; the Barneson-Hibbard house flag is prominent at her masthead. Courtesy Washington State Historical Society, Curtis Collection.

must have meant something to Harry Knowles, for she had been almost a part of his family for nearly thirty-six years, but he had to view the situation realistically and admit that she was just a delapidated old "pot," still worth a few dollars, 8,550 dollars to be exact,[2] that could be traded and retraded like an old horse long past her prime. During March and April, Knowles gathered bills of sale from her various owners conveying their interests to him. Of those shareholders who had bought into her in her days of glory, only J. Henry Sears and Joshua Freeman remained. All other shares were in the hands of descendants,[3] which included the interest Harry Knowles had been conveyed from his mother at her death in 1903.[4] *Glory* had certainly outlived most of the people who had been closest to her, but her days as a sailing ship now seemed literally numbered.

At 5:16 A.M., on April 18, 1906, a terrifying catastrophe struck San Francisco and won a reprieve for *Glory of the Seas*. During that precise minute, the first shock of an earth-shattering quake rolled and buckled its way throughout much of the city. Electric lines snapped; trollies and cable cars were derailed; gas lines broke; large buildings, including the stately City Hall, collapsed; but the worst was not over. Tremendous fires broke out and raged for three days, leaving in their wake hundreds dead and the greater part of the business section a smoking ruin, including the offices of Harry Knowles at 30 California Street.[5] The damage was estimated at half a billion dollars, as insurance claim adjusters gloomily surveyed the vast piles of ashes and rubble. Though most of the magnificent buildings of old San Francisco were completely demolished, the hardy spirit of her survivors certainly was not. Rebuilding on a large scale began immediately.

Millions of board feet of lumber were needed to reconstruct many of the nearly 30,000 buildings destroyed by the fire and earthquake; but not enough tonnage was available on the coast to fill the demand. Coast seamen were in the middle of a serious labor strike, which obviously meant that many available vessels could not be sufficiently manned. So great was the need for lumber following the fire that in a matter of months the freight rates jumped from $4.50 to $6.00 per thousand and were expected to go higher. This is what gave *Glory* her chance. The purported profits were high enough to meet voyage expenses for a wooden square-rigger.[6]

As the weeks after the great conflagration passed, John Barneson decided that he could afford to repair *Glory* so that she could make a few voyages under sail. The decision to use her meant that the *Two Brothers,* evidently in worse shape aloft than *Glory,* was to be barged before the year was over. As to cargo capacity, no comparison could be made between the two vessels. *Glory* could handle well over a half million more board feet of lumber than the smaller vessel. In August *Two Brothers* would be chartered and begin a new existence as a towing barge.

About the middle of May, Barneson transferred Henry Gillespie, master of the *Two Brothers,* over to *Glory of the Seas.* This middle-aged man, who hailed from Portland, Maine, had followed the sea much of his life. Since the days of the California gold rush, his family had produced shipmasters, though not of the caliber of the Knowleses or Freemans, nonetheless of respectable reputation. Gillespie had a wife and two young boys who were eventually to sail with him on a voyage. In May and June, Captain Gillespie occasionally brought his sons on board *Glory* as she underwent her refit.[7] Despite her poor state of repair, the Gillespie boys were soon to be able to say with pride that their father was master of a clean and taut ship in the midst of a decayed wooden square-rig fleet.

Much had to be accomplished in a minimum of time to prepare her for sea. Along with general rigging overhaul, the chain halyard ties in her upper tops'l yards were necessarily replaced with wire rope, which, though not as permanent as chain, did the job satisfactorily. The main deck needed recaulking because the hot sun had melted the pitch in her seams; two years of accumulated rust, bubbled and flaked paint, and filth had to vanish before Gillespie would deign to set sail on her, so an ample coat of flat white paint on her houses, bulwarks, and rails was applied to cover up a multitude of sins on deck. Her spars were freshly painted mast color and her sides sported a new coat of black paint from the waterline up. The old ex-Cape Horner was transformed; her deeply carved marks of age were well concealed. To prepare *Glory* for her new role as a lumber drougher, Gillespie had shipwrights cut two large stern ports with hatches 5 feet by 7 feet under her counter so that she could load 100-foot timbers in her 'tween decks. By July, *Glory of the Seas* looked trim for a wooden vessel thirty-six years old, smartly fitted out for the voyages lying before her. That month, Barneson chartered her to the E. K. Wood Company to load lumber for San Francisco at their Bellingham, Washington, mill. The charter price was nearly 6 dollars per thousand, vindicating the money Captain Barneson had put into her.[8] During the last few days prior to his sailing date, Captain Gillespie tried to dredge up a crew to take the old ship up the coast. With the strike still going strong, he had quite a problem recruiting experienced hands, but by July 20, her day of departure, a conglomeration of drunken semisailors, landlubbers, skid-row wharf rats and the like, totaling fourteen hands before the mast, were on board attempting to put sail on her under the prodding of the mates.[9] This day was a triumph for *Glory* as she began her run up the coast. As time at sea passed, Gillespie naturally experienced troubles, not only because of strong headwinds, but also because of the many green hands which he and the mates had to train after a fashion in a few days. Two weeks later, after doggedly battling the elements on board and off, *Glory* lay in a pea-soup fog off Cape Flattery, a natural occurrence in that general region during the summer months. It was not until she was fully seventeen days out from the Golden Gate that she took a slant into the Straits, passed Tatoosh Island, and picked up a tug.

In mid-August, Puget Sound was an extremely busy place. Twelve ships alone were loading timber cargoes for San Francisco. At the Bellingham E. K. Wood wharves lay *Glory,* three schooners, three barkentines, and the ex-ore barge *Chinook,* which had recently been converted to haul lumber. No one could have missed this ugly duckling, because her name stood out in box-car letters along her bow. An old friendly competitor of *Glory*'s, the full-rigger *America,* was also berthed at Bellingham taking on lumber. She had recently completed a seven-month voyage to Callao, Peru, with lumber from Puget Sound under command of Captain Hagen F. Astrup. This once-proud Cape Horner, now under charter to the Bellingham Bay Lumber Company for the lump sum of $8,437.50 was, like *Glory,* to be used for a few voyages during the coast lumber boom.[10] From 1902, when Pacific Steam Whaling sold their tender fleet and Alaska canneries, her owners had been the Pacific Packing and Navigation Company of Seattle, which had exclusively sent her north to Nushagak, Bristol Bay, through the 1905 fishing season. When that firm went bankrupt, their fleet was taken over by the Northwestern Steamship Company, which formed a subsidiary, the Northwestern Fisheries, to supervise operations. Under their ownership she made her deep-water voyage to South America, sailing from Everett in December, 1905. Now she was under general management of James Griffiths, a pioneer Puget Sound shipping magnate.[11] Both *Glory* and *America* loaded cargoes of a million and a half board feet of lumber and sailed for San Francisco during the first few weeks in September, 1906. The primary reason they did not sail earlier was that neither Captain Astrup nor Gillespie could corral enough hands to take their lumber-laden ships to sea, the labor shortage on the coast still being critical.[12]

In October, John Barneson received a second charter for *Glory* from the E. K. Wood Company, at $7.50 per thousand.[13] Arriving November 7, off Tatoosh, she was again towed to Bellingham to load. In mid-November extreme Chinook winds blasted upper Puget Sound, accompanied by a deluge of rains. Bridges washed out. Trains were delayed, and of course, *Glory,* along with other vessels in port, was caught right in the middle of the storm as they rode at anchor or took on cargo at the docks. The force of the wind and seas caught *Glory,* which lay berthed stern first at the mill wharf, and caused her great bulk to snap her forward moorings. She swung helplessly against the mill wharf and pilings, damaging them enough to create cargo-handling problems during the following week. No damage resulted to the venerable ship, but her loading had to be delayed for repairs to the wharf.[14]

During the first week in December, the British steamer *Virginia,* the 1,857-ton British ship *Fairport,* and *Glory* were all loading at the mill wharf. Seeing the two windjammers berthed next to each other gave a fair idea of the difference twenty-five years had wrought in sailing ship construction. The stumpy-masted, steel-hulled *Fairport* spread nothing higher than double t'gallants, and with less canvas and newer, up-to-date equipment on board was an easier and not so costly ship to handle at sea. The typical, mock gunport-painted full-rigger was loading for Callao, and on the coming voyage would be sailing with only about sixteen hands all told. Though *Fairport* was certainly no clipper in comparison to *Glory* in her heyday under Josiah Knowles, she stood a far better chance of getting cargoes than ships with wooden bottoms.

By the end of the mill working day on December 6, 1906, *Glory of the Seas* had loaded 1,500 tons of lumber over her normal 500 to 550 tons of ballast. She was within days of taking on deck cargo and sailing for San Francisco when a furious sou'easter hit upper Puget Sound during the dark early morning hours of December 7. With gale force winds tempestuously blowing and a heavy sea rolling into Bellingham Bay, the tall ships began struggling at their moorage bonds. At about 4:00 A.M. the *Fairport,* berthed between *Glory* and the *Virginia,* broke loose and loudly smacked her stern into the latter vessel, breaking a hull plate and bending a frame on the steamer. On swinging back, she struck *Glory* on the starboard bow, wreaking havoc in her head rigging and hull planking, and crumpling her own taffrail. She was speedily resecured before she could destructively swing her stern again. The following day, the damage to *Glory* was estimated at 3,000 dollars, a considerable amount for a vessel valued at only 22,000 dollars and insured for 5,000 dollars.[15] In a few days, shipwrights and riggers were busily at work on her while she lay at the mill wharf. Two weeks later, she had her 8-odd-foot main deck cargo securely lashed down and sailed bound for the Golden Gate, where she arrived safely on January 1, 1907.

The discharging of her lumber at San Francisco took five weeks. The city was rapidly taking on a new face from the fire-blackened, gutted appearance of eight months before. Much of the building rubble (going to sea as ship ballast) had already been cleared for dozens of blocks, so that the bleak city streets stood out oddly, emptily waiting for the many new buildings under construction to be finished. In February Captain Barneson chartered *Glory* to the Southern Pacific Railroad for $9.25 per thousand.[16] She loaded 1,400,000 board feet of cedar railroad ties at the Puget Mill Company wharf at Bellingham.[17] Her discharging port was San Pedro, which had continued to grow in shipping importance on the Pacific Coast, especially because of the extensive railroad work being carried out in lower California and Arizona. The arrival of *Glory of the Seas* off San Pedro on April third marked the first time she had visited these waters in fifteen years. Many changes had taken place. There was now a safe harbor in all weather because a huge rock breakwater nearly 2 miles long encompassed most of the bay. A tug soon towed *Glory* to the Southern Pacific Railroad wharf on the west side of the inner habor where she lay being discharged until the latter part of April.

By spring of 1907 the Pacific Coast lumber boom had moderated to the point where too many ships vied for the available charters, and the rates had dropped. This prompted Barneson to charter *Glory* to John J. Sesnon and Company of Seattle to load coal for the contingent of U.S. Army troops stationed at Nome, Alaska.[18] *Glory* was not the only square-rigger heading north to Nome. James Griffiths had likewise chartered the *America* for coal.[19] Both vessels were to be towed to Alaska, because of bad ice conditions in the Bering Sea. Not reinforced like an icebreaker, a typical square-rigger on her own hook stood a good chance of being stove in by heavy pack ice. This would be the last voyage the old *America*

Above. Mission Street wharves, San Francisco, ca. 1910. Courtesy San Francisco Maritime Museum. Below. E. K. Wood Company's mill and wharves, Bellingham, Washington, 1906. Courtesy Puget Sound Maritime Historical Society.

would make classed as a full-rigged ship; in just a few months, Griffiths planned on cutting her down to a schooner barge for his new firm Coastwise Steamship and Barge Company. *Glory* was to lose another friend to the hulk ranks. *America* would soon look very much like a certain old leaky barge that kept afloat at sea or in port by a prominently displayed windmill pump. Filthy and rust-stained, she had sailed behind a tug from Tacoma on May 29, 1907, also bound for Nome. The vessel looked in mourning, her houses, boats, and deck gear painted a dull black. The only remainders of her beautiful past were faded white letters on her transom and quarters wistfully admitting the name *Dashing Wave*.

Before *Glory* headed north in the middle of June, Gillespie had her docked and painted at Esquimalt by Bullen Limited.[20] At the same time the captain purchased a faster action eccentric pump which could throw a large amount of water from her leaky bilges on the coming voyage. Since she would have a skeleton crew, using a "whirly-bird" (windmill pump) was the cheapest way to keep her creaking and groaning hull fairly dry out in the North Pacific. Bullen's workmen permanently dismantled her flying gangway aft so that the windmill pump could be easily installed near the break of the poop after she was clear of land. Most square-rig masters were hesitant about exhibiting this obvious evidence of infirmity while in port or near shore and Henry Gillespie was no exception to the rule.

Once *Glory* had loaded 3,000 tons of sacked coal at Ladysmith, the combination passenger-freighter *S.S. Ohio* took her in tow.[21] Both vessels arrived at Nome in June, and anchored about 2 miles offshore, according to common practice, so that should a storm arise they would have a good chance of standing safely out to sea. After discharging passengers and freight, the *Ohio* weighed anchor and sailed for St. Michael, her next port of call, leaving *Glory* at anchor. Soon, word went out along the streets of Nome — "The *Glory of the Seas* is here with coal for the fort. They're going to need men to unload her." One of the recruited laborers was William Beeman, a young adventurer seeking his fortune in this gold dust town. Many years later, he told the author about the method used to discharge cargo from *Glory*.[22] Since she lay so far out, small, blunt-nosed barges, each about 75 feet long with 50 tons displacement, were used to lighter her black diamonds ashore. After a barge was loaded with hundreds of sacks, a small tug pushed it ashore, leaving in its place an empty lighter. According to Beeman, the biggest part of the job was not the direct unloading of the ship, but discharging the lighters once they bumped ashore near the fort. A long, narrow plank was laid between the barge gunwale and the beach so that Beeman and the other men could each shoulder a 100-pound coal sack ashore. Occasionally, Beeman recollected, they had more than sufficient reason loudly to curse the coal company at Ladysmith. Besides using the normal 100-pound sack, they had also filled 200-pound coffee sacks with coal. In trying to tote the big sacks ashore via the most unsteady plank, several men fell into the frigid Arctic waters, along with their 200-pound burden. On being hauled out, they were drenched to the skin, shaking like a leaf, turning the air blue with profanity, and were beet red from the freezing cold. At that time of the year, daylight lasts almost twenty-four hours, so Beeman and the other laborers worked nearly around the clock for close to a week, until all of the 60,000-odd sacks of coal were ashore.[23]

In mid-September, *Glory* arrived back on the sound to await word of another charter. Toward the end of the month, Captain Gillespie received orders from Barneson's Puget Sound agent that *Glory of the Seas* would soon join the *Sea King* and *Drummuir* in the offshore lumber trade. Barneson-Hibbard had chartered her to the Puget Mill Company at $12.50 per thousand for a voyage to Antofogasta, Chile, for orders.[24] At about the same time, the *Sea King* was chartered to load lumber for Valparaiso, Chile. Captain Barneson planned to use both *Sea King* and *Glory* on triangle voyages: from Puget Sound to South America; thence to Newcastle, Australia, to load coal; and then return to Puget Sound for their final port of discharge. After lying at Port Townsend for two weeks, a tug towed *Glory* to the large lumber mill at Port Gamble, where she loaded a million and a half board feet of lumber. Barneson had been fortunate with the timber charters for his ships. In October, the shipping industry became involved again in a nationwide financial panic, which was eventually to deal the death blow to many of the American square-riggers still actively trading.

During the final weeks of November, *Glory* lay at anchor at Port Townsend being readied for her first deep-sea venture in over twenty years. Heading deep-water put her in a different shipping classification from being a coaster. Now Gillespie had to pay a high premium to a boardinghouse master for each of his seamen. It was against the U.S. Navigation Laws either to levy this shipping fee against a vessel or to permit shanghaiing, but the laws were impossible to enforce. Port Townsend may have been but a miniature of the infamous Barbary Coast, but the same kind of shanghai artists that plied their trade on the San Francisco waterfront worked just as efficiently on Puget Sound. Townsend's equally infamous Water Street sported all the comforts that Jack Tar wanted in port — bawdy saloons with their watered-down liquor, half-worn-out prostitutes sashaying up to any sailor to sell their wares; and crimps who shanghaied any man, sailor or landlubber, foolish enough to get within their clutches. Water Street was a typical sailor's town.

Glory had been towed up from Port Gamble on November 21 to ship a crew. Gillespie had made arrangements with the New Sailor's Boarding House to supply fourteen hands at 40 dollars a head, in addition to the general "dead horse," which in Port Townsend consisted of a straight $16.67 per A.B.[25] That evening, the boardinghouse master and his crimps carefully liquored up eight men — all he could round up — put them under lock and key for the night with sufficient rot-gut whiskey to dull their senses, told them they were going to sea on the *Glory of the Seas*, an old-time clipper ship, and rowed them out o her the next morning. On tying up to her port quarter gangway, they were kicked enough to arouse them to the importance of getting out of the boat. Then, as they stumbled and lurched up the gangway, all the time cursing the ship, the master, the rotten whiskey, and mostly the boardinghouse master for shipping them on an old "bucket," they went on board *Glory* and dumped their meager gear, which was primarily a "donkey's breakfast" (a straw-filled mattress and a plug of tobacco), into the bug-infested fo'c's'le. With bloodshot eyes, aching heads, and mouths that felt as if turpentine had been poured in them, they were then signed on. Four days later, on November 26, the rest of her foremast crowd were shipped by the same method. Fourteen hands in addition to her six afterguard were pitifully few men to take a full-rigger the size of *Glory* deep-water; that was less than half the number she had on her first Cape Horn passage, but she was not alone in her predicament. With few exceptions, American full-riggers always voyaged undermanned in the closing days of sail. It was understandable that men seldom willingly joined a full-rigger heading offshore, because they knew they would be worked to death on them.

Slop chest stores were quickly depleted from the ship as the sailors purchased gear and supplies at greatly inflated prices from Gillespie. In a matter of days they had bought fourteen sets of oilskins from him. Evidently, the carpenter had volunteered his services for this voyage under duress, because "Chips" even had to buy a set of tools, naturally deducted from his future wages, from the captain. Tobacco sold for 75 cents per pound, an outrageous price, but with the "use now, pay later" method of buying things, the ignorant sailor felt no pain. An A.B. received 25 dollars per month, but normally by the time he was paid off, his gross wages had dropped at least to a third because of slop chest debits.[26] But no matter what he received, in a week or so on the beach a sailor had usually blown everything he had earned by living high. Henry Gillespie obviously lost no money with his floating general store. His monthly wages were not the best, 125 dollars at the most, but with slop chest profits and a small percentage of the cargo profit, he made a good income.

Late Saturday evening on November 30, a tug took *Glory of the Seas* under tow at Port Townsend and then headed toward Cape Flattery. They passed Tatoosh Island at noon the following day and on getting far enough out to sea, *Glory* was let go on her own hook. Such bad weather prevailed off the Washington Coast during that Sunday that incoming ships lay well off until the storm had moderated. With her big, clumsy deckload, it was no easy task to work the old vessel's sails, especially with so few hands. Time and again heavy seas swept her from stem to stern, as she buried her bow and pitched and rolled wildly. Though it was not so cold on Cape Flattery as on Cape Horn, the two regions had much in common. The pounding seas, fogs, and storms of both places had claimed their share of broken ships and lost men. Waves are long and steep at the Horn; while at Cape Flattery they are short and steep, producing a "bucking bronco" effect on wooden windjammers. As *Glory* slowly made her way far out to sea, she did her share of creaking, groaning, and leaking, just as she would on Cape Horn.

During the "death watch" from midnight, Monday, December 2, the second mate's watch of seven men were on deck attending to the ship. At about 1:00 A.M., Townsend, the second mate, and two hands went precariously forward over her deck cargo as the ship pitched wildly and labored heavily. Townsend was about to go out on the jibboom when all at once the ship buried her bow in the frothy green water and he disappeared (according to the two men who were supposedly farther aft). Townsend had fallen overboard without a breath of a chance for survival because the ship was almost 90 miles from land. In a bad storm, a big sailer like *Glory* had no way to brake like a car in such an emergency. A man falling over the side in such weather rarely survived for any length of time, and the second mate was no exception. It was commonplace for sailors still drunk or sobering up from their last night ashore to be killed shortly after a ship sailed; it was also not uncommon for a man to be disliked enough by members of the crew to be silently shoved over the side when the opportunity arose. Who would have told or admitted what actually happened in the disappearance of Townsend? The corpus delicti was not around to testify in his own behalf. After the loss of the second mate was reported to him, Gillespie made no effort to search for him. A man's life just did not mean much on some ships. Next morning, as per custom, Gillespie auctioned off Townsend's meager possessions and promoted a foremast hand to second mate. Ironically, he was one of the two men who had reported Townsend missing from the fo'c's'le head the night before.[27]

Henry Gillespie had taken his family on this passage and made sure his two sons did not idle away their time. Both he and his wife placed a high value on education, and she daily taught the boys their three "R's." Seven-year-old Harold Gillespie was so deeply impressed by his father's old square-rigger that she became one of the factors helping him make up his mind to follow in his forbears' footsteps. He eventually reached command of the Matson Line luxury liners *Lurline* and *Mariposa*.[28]

Evidently, the ship's food did not appeal to all the crew. Gillespie reported on January 1, 1908, in his official log, a little altercation between the cook — no longer Dixon, who had retired in 1904 and was completely blind by 1906 — and a young foremast hand. He wrote that the seaman "on this day made murderous threats in the presence of C. Kuse, mate, and Fagan, second mate, that he would chop the Japanese cook's head off and on this I find it necessary to see that the cook is protected."[29] One wonders not only how Gillespie "protected" the cook, but also how bad the food must obviously have been to have caused the outburst.

Glory of the Seas arrived at Antofogasta on February 22, eighty-four days from Puget Sound — a slow voyage in which she had averaged about 80 miles per day and had put in a long stretch in the Pacific doldrums. After receiving orders from the Puget Mill agent there, Gillespie sailed for her port of discharge at Callao, where she arrived March 8, and found no future destination in the offing. The panic back in the States had finally caused worldwide repercussions. Once Captain Gillespie got a clear picture of the shipping market, he decided that there was no reason to keep a crew on board, so after debiting their slop chest accounts, he discharged all hands including the officers by "mutual consent" four days after their arrival.[30] This meant an outlay of nearly a thousand dollars for wages. Meanwhile, *Glory* was unloaded and towed to an anchorage in the open roadstead of Callao harbor, there to wait with other laid-up full-riggers for better times. Because charters had become few and far between, the prospects for either *Glory* or *Sea King* to haul Newcastle coal back to the United States were slim. The captain of *Sea King* subsequently chartered his vessel to a Valparaiso firm to load a cargo of coal from Australia for them, but with the expenses of such a long voyage ahead of her, there was not much chance that she could make a profit, and this ultimately proved to be the case. Henry Gillespie weighed the prospects of a coal charter to a South American port but decided against it. After laying her up for over two months, he received instructions from Captain Barneson to sail back in ballast to Puget Sound for further orders.

During the final week of May, Gillespie arranged with a Callao boardinghouse master to get him a crew of runners for the return voyage. Only eleven A.B.'s were eventually shipped at the low rate of 15 dollars per month. The first mate, who was also recruited by the same boardinghouse master rated only 50 dollars per month. With eleven seamen, a carpenter (donkeyman), two mates, a cook, a cabin boy, and Gillespie, seventeen all told, the passage was bound to be strenuous.[31] *Glory* weighed anchor and stood out for sea on June 1. From the first day the crew had difficulty setting or keeping any sail on her. If a sudden blow hit, they simply could not clew the sails up fast enough, and the only alternative was to keep her under shortened sail all the way to Puget Sound, more than two months away. On this voyage no melodic sea chanties were sung by her crew to lighten the heavy work aloft. There was just plain cursing and grumbling over the drunken day they had signed on her. On August 9, she arrived off Cape Flattery where an amateur photographer on a tug took a candid photo of her while she sailed on her starboard tack. His picture told a great deal about the general condition of the old ship. High in the water because of little ballast on board, *Glory* ran under shortened sail with her coal-stained upper and lower tops'ls, inner and outer jibs, and the main stays'l set well. The "patched and patched" main stays'l pulled very hard as she steadily ploughed through the choppy seas on her in-shore tack. She was close-hauled; that is, lying as close to the wind as she could and still keep her sails full. A square-rigged ship that is too close drifts sideways like a crab. She was sailing at about six and one-half points of the wind, which is good for a full-rigger. With a fresh storm blowing from the south, *Glory of the Seas* was a majestic sight running at about 8 knots, looking fairly clean and well kept for an old ship. Surprisingly, she finished this passage in seventy days. But, in comparison, Captain Astrup of the *America* in 1906 sailed from Callao in ballast with a crew of twenty-two men at about the same time of the year and arrived off Tatoosh Island in only fifty-nine days. Being undermanned made a big difference in the efficient sailing of a full-rigger.

In two years of continual operation, Captain John Barneson's initial investment in *Glory* had proven worth every penny, despite the shipping slump. The gross profits had been ample for all four charters, her last one from the Puget Mill being over 19,000 dollars. *Glory of the Seas* was still hanging on far beyond the time of the average American full-rigger. Though most maritime men looked upon her as an old leaky "bucket," they had to admit respect and admiration for the last merchant ship of Donald McKay.

CHAPTER XVII

The Tragic Years

IN September, 1908, Captain Barneson delegated the direct management of *Glory* to the Seattle Shipping Company, a small shipping and commission firm based in Seattle, and owned wholly by an elderly woman, Mrs. Ella B. Morrison, and her partner, George Morrell. Their only claim to notoriety since their firm's founding three years before was the loss of two vessels under their ownership; the old 585-ton down-east bark *Nicholas Thayer,* which had been lost in Alaskan waters in early 1906 with all hands, and the 173-ton schooner *Martha W. Tuft,* which met her end in the region of the Gulf of Alaska in October, 1907. So far, their luck had not been of the best.

The Seattle Shipping Company was bound to have major problems finding a cargo for *Glory.* In September, nineteen vessels alone were laid up on Puget Sound, five of them steamers. Coast shipping was bad for both sail and steam and not expected to get better. There were still too many ships for the few available charters, and Mrs. Morrison had to rest content with one to Frank Waterhouse of Seattle for five months at the rate of 550 dollars per month plus 100 dollars a month for Henry Gillespie's wages as master. *Glory of the Seas* was to drough steamer coal as needed from British Columbia to the Waterhouse coal bunkers at Seattle.[1]

Up to January, 1909, *Glory* hauled two loads of coal from Nanaimo. In between cargoes she lay on the south side of Eagle Harbor on Bainbridge Island along with dozens of other vessels, patiently waiting for any

Tall ships laid up in Eagle Harbor, 1909. Courtesy Joe D. Williamson.

profitable charter. Gillespie had her securely anchored forward, with
stout manila lines made fast from her stern bitts to large trees ashore,
which kept her from swinging into the other tall ships alongside. Laid up
to port of *Glory* in the same manner was the stately down-easter *Benjamin F. Packard,* a wooden full-rigger about the same size as *Glory.* She
had quit the Cape Horn trade the past spring when her owners sold her
to the Northwestern Fisheries for use as an Alaska cannery tender. After
carrying a cargo of coal to the Navy Yard at Bremerton in May, 1908, the
Packard had been laid up at Eagle Harbor. Anchored near these two
deep-water aristocrats were the down-easters *Joseph B. Thomas* and *Jabez
Howes,* both California Shipping Company vessels, along with a half
dozen schooners, barkentines, a couple of old steamers, and the Hall
Brothers-built bark *Hesper,* all of which easily found moorages. The
latter part of January, the U.S. Revenue cutter *Thetis* entered Eagle
Harbor for major repairs at the well-known Hall Brothers shipyard situated on the north side. One of her sailor apprentices, young Henry Harlow, especially enjoyed his temporary stay in port. When on leave from
shipboard duties, he visited the various laid-up ships and became enam-
ored of old *Glory,* to him the most fascinating and beautiful ship in the
harbor. Several years ago, Harlow told the author of one particular experience he had while she lay at anchor. On a Sunday, after he had circled
her shapely hull many times in a small canoe, he mustered up enough
courage to tie up at her port quarter gangway and walk aboard. He encountered a most inhospitable Henry Gillespie, and asked permission
to look her over. The captain granted his request, but volunteered no
information. As Harlow slowly strolled her decks, taking in every detail,
he had the feeling that Gillespie was watching him like a hawk. He said
of the captain:

> He was not the talkative kind. He allowed me on deck to look, but was not
> communicative. She was very trim and very well kept up at that time. What
> impressed me greatly was her nice flare to the bow. All her rigging was trim
> and neat. Her topsail halyards (ties) were different from most other ships.
> Most of them had a sheave hole through the topmast and a chain that went
> down, but the *Glory of the Seas* had wire rope topsail halyards with an iron
> block, which was under the crosstrees going down through the block of
> the topsail yard and then brought up through a block alongside the top-
> mast and then on deck. Time and again I was about her. Mainly, I used to

Benjamin F. Packard on the ways, Eagle Harbor, ca. 1915. *Glory* underwent repairs to her keel at this same place in 1910. Courtesy Puget Sound Maritime Historical Society.

circle her in a canoe and watch her lines. Her hull looked well taken care
of and was painted. She was not shabby or dirty in any way.[2]

In February, a news dispatch from England appeared in the Puget
Sound newspaper under the title of "Vast Amount of Tonnage is Idle."
It explained why so many ships in every port in the world were inactive:

> Liverpool, Feb. 4 — Over 1,500,000 tons of shipping are laid up for want of
> employment and freights all over the world are lower than ever before. . . .
> The year, 1908, they say, like its predecessor, ended most unsatisfactorily
> for ship owners, ship builders, and every one else interested in shipping
> with few exceptions. It would be difficult for many to recall to memory any
> period so unfavorable as last year. We are not surprised that with 1,500,000
> tons of shipping laid up at home and abroad and freights all over the
> world lower than were ever known before, the advent of 1909 was hailed
> with the hope that the depression in shipping had about passed its worst
> phase. The American panic of October, 1907, has left its mark all over the
> world. It destroyed credit, restricted trade in every direction, and coming
> so unexpectedly on top of an oversupplied market, caught most of us un-
> awares.
> The time has now arrived when it is impossible to disguise the fact that at
> least 1,000,000 tons of old and obsolete tonnage must be broken up. It is
> good for no other purpose; and the sooner those interested face the inevita-
> ble and readjust their book values, the sooner freights will improve, for it
> it improbable that such tonnage can be worked again at a profit.[3]

The question was, who was going to give up first?

Come spring of 1909, the seasonal cannery tenders left Eagle Harbor
to go north, leaving *Glory*, the *Joseph B. Thomas*, the *Jabez Howes*, and
many other vessels behind. *Glory of the Seas* had carried her last load of
coal for Waterhouse in March to complete the five-month charter and
the immediate shipping prospects for her were poor. She had no chance
whatsoever for a coast lumber charter. For example, freight rates from
Puget Sound to San Francisco had been $8.25 per thousand in Febru-
ary, 1907, but the rate was now down to only $3.00.[4]

Back in San Francisco, John Barneson made arrangements to sell the
Sea King to an East Coast firm for conversion to a schooner barge. At the
time, the old down-easter was sailing back from Valparaiso to Puget
Sound in ballast. On arrival in May, she was docked at Hall Brothers
shipyard, loaded lumber, and sailed for Bath, Maine, via Cape Horn,
where she eventually arrived 169 days later. Strong rumors, meanwhile,

spread along the Pacific Coast that the California Shipping Company, once the owners of more than thirty square-rigged sailing ships, was to be dissolved and their fleet individually sold to the highest bidders. Some of their vessels had been unable to get a charter since the panic of 1907. In February, 1909, they still owned more than a dozen square-riggers, which the managers planned to sell off one by one as the market warranted. Poor charters, heavy ship losses, and general misfortune had dogged their last, great effort to compete against steam. The company had been formed just before the turn of the century, but now all their efforts were ending as one large, dismal failure. The *Joseph B. Thomas,* for instance, still a staunch craft although twenty-eight years òld, was sold in May for 20,000 dollars for coal barge duty on the East Coast. Other vessels in the fleet were eventually to follow suit or become Alaska cannery tenders. In November, twenty-five full-rigged ships, more than half the number of those remaining registered under the Stars and Stripes, were laid up on the Pacific Coast with almost no hope of cargoes for at least five months. Of that number, nearly a dozen were cannery tenders which made only one voyage a year to the Alaskan fishing grounds; moreover, ships like the proud bark *Shenandoah,* laid up since early 1908 in San Francisco, had one pathetic voyage left — to an East Coast shipyard for conversion to lowly coal barges.

At the turn of the year John Barneson decided that he had better get rid of *Glory of the Seas* before the market plummeted further. Unfortunately, if he expected to get anything out of her, she needed underwater repairs. During her long layup, she had dragged bottom and had lost two-thirds of her 5-inch keel shoe and badly scarred her 235-foot oaken keel. So, in February, 1910, Captain Barneson had her docked and repaired at Hall Brothers shipyard to the tune of nearly 1,800 dollars.[5] In April a Victoria syndicate bought her for only 10,000 dollars.[6] Because many of the remaining wood down-easters were up for sale at low prices at the same time, this was all he could get for her. The syndicate, consisting of Captain W. J. McDonnell, an old South Sea Island trader, Arthur Fellows, and several other men, also bought the old skys'l bark *Hesper* for a song. The new owners planned what seemed like a goldmine on paper — to send both vessels to the South Sea Island of Malekula to load hardwood. Because the inhabitants of the island were out-and-out cannibals known to have eaten a couple of missionaries and the crew of a French schooner not long before, they planned to carry crews of 250 men, heavily armed, to ward off any stew-pot ideas of the natives. Meanwhile, the *Hesper* badly needed rigging repairs so the syndicate arranged for Hall Brothers to work on her.[7]

To give them more legal leniency in operating *Glory*, the syndicate withdrew her from American registry and placed her under the Uruguayan flag. Their methods of operation were the usual shoestring variety. To help pay for the extensive repairs to *Hesper*, and provide more capital for the Malekula venture, they chartered *Glory of the Seas* to the Alaska Commercial Company to load coal for Unalaska. In July, 1910, she took on 3,000 tons at Ladysmith and was towed back to Victoria to ship a crew. A Captain Poindexter was placed in command and either because of his methods, inexperience, or lack of money, he could not get enough fo'c's'le hands to sign on to take her north. By the middle of August she had officers and several apprentices on board but the captain did not seem to be depending on "reliable" firms such as Simms and Levy of Port Townsend, the largest shanghai artists on Puget Sound, to round up a crew for him. Finally, to keep the terms of the charter, he arranged to have her towed up.[8] After spending two months at Dutch Harbor unloading, Poindexter shipped a crew of runners to take her back to Puget Sound in ballast. *Glory* sailed on November 25, making a fine passage of twelve days to sheltered Neah Bay. This brought to a close a forty-year career of more than one hundred voyages. She was never to make a voyage under sail again.

On arrival at Victoria, December 8, 1910, there was bad news not only from the owners, but also from Poindexter. The South Sea hardwood scheme had fallen through; they still owed the big repair bill on the *Hesper;* the voyage to Unalaska had been a financial flop; and the prospects for further employment for *Glory* were doubtful. Although they had paid the runners their pittance on arrival at Victoria, the officers, plus an apprentice, still stood by the ship, patiently waiting for four months' back wages. Early in 1911, the owners tried to sell *Glory* and an offer was received from Boston for 15,000 dollars on condition that she be delivered there.[9] The syndicate got a lumber cargo for her to pay for the voyage but to no avail. No insurance company was willing to insure her for the kind of money McDonnell, Fellows, and the others could afford to pay. In the last few years many wooden ships, among them some of the California Shipping Company fleet, had headed east via Cape Horn for conversion to barges, only to be badly damaged in some way in order to have heavy insurance claims. The *Alex Gibson,* one of the latest old vessels to attempt the passage, for example, had put in to a South American port for extremely costly repairs.[10] Now the marine underwriters refused to insure any wooden full-rigger over twenty years old for a Cape Horn voyage, so the idea of a lumber cargo to the East Coast for *Glory* was thoroughly squelched.

By February, 1911, the two mates, boatswain, carpenter, cook, steward, and an apprentice, who were still on board, were left no choice but to sue the ship as she lay in Esquimalt Harbor. In March the case went to Admiralty Court and the resulting decree was a judgment of 2,133 dollars against the ship; moreover, the *Hesper* was awarded to Hall Brothers for the unpaid repair bills.[11] This meant only one alternative left for the financially embarrassed owners of *Glory of the Seas:* to let her go under the hammer to the highest bidder. Her tragic future was soon to be decided. On March 30, 1911, a legal notice appearing in the Victoria *Times* read in part, "By order of this honourable court I [Marshal of Victoria] will sell by public auction the ship *Glory of the Seas* . . . at Post Office, Esquimalt, Vancouver Island, British Columbia on Friday at twelve o'clock noon the seventh day of April, 1911." On that day *Glory*'s reputation was further tarnished. Only several interested parties and a group of curious idlers assembled at the post office and the highest bid was only 1,750 dollars.[12] Marshall Siddall had to postpone the sale because the amount was not enough to pay crew wages and court expenses. During the following two weeks he made two more fruitless attempts. Obviously nobody wanted to pay the actual value of a ship on the block, but they were not even willing to pay the amount needed to satisfy the court. No one was really to blame; old square-rigged ships were known to have been sold at sheriff's auctions for as little as 500 dollars. Realizing that he would just fail again, the Marshal had 18-inch by 24-inch circulars printed up by a local firm stating in bold red type that *Glory* would definitely be sold on April 25. These were sent to all the major ports on Puget Sound, and one reached Frederick C. Johnstone, president of the Tongass Trading Company of Ketchikan and Seattle. Johnstone, whose main offices and residence were in Seattle, had recently decided that a new, unique kind of vessel was needed in the fishing grounds up North, a floating salmon cannery, which could be towed wherever the run of fish were. If he could get *Glory* for a low enough price, she just might enable him to prove his idea.

In the Exchequer Court of Canada.

BRITISH COLUMBIA ADMIRALTY DISTRICT

Berthel Petersen, et. al.

AGAINST

The Ship "Glory of the Seas"

By Order of this Honourable Court, JOSEPH H. LIST has received instructions to sell by Public Auction, without reserve, the American built Sailing Ship "Glory of the Seas," now lying in Esquimalt Harbour, together with all her standing and running gear, boats, tackle apparel and furniture, etc.

The dimensions of the vessel are as follows:

Length, 240 ft. 8 in.   Breadth, 44 ft. 1 in.
Total draft, 26 ft.   Depth, 20 ft.

TONNAGE:

Gross registered, 2102.   Nett registered, 1939.
Deadweight Capacity, 2,800 to 3,000 tons.

Staunchly built of oak and well equipped throughout.

Intending purchasers are requested to inspect the ship at any time prior to the sale.

The Sale will be held at the office of The Marshal Grand Theatre Building, Government Street, Victoria, British Columbia, on Tuesday, the 25th day of April, 1911, at 3:30 p. m.

Further particulars may be obtained of the Auctioneer, Joseph H. List, 738 Fort Street, Victoria, or Hinkson Siddall, the Marshal.

T. N. HIBBEN & CO.　　PRINTERS. VICTORIA. B C

Poster advertising the sale of *Glory* at public auction, April 25, 1911. Courtesy Robert C. Leithead.

Frederick C. Johnstone, president of Tongass Trading Company and Alaska Fish Company, purchaser of *Glory*. Courtesy of Robert C. Leithead.

On the date announced, seafaring men filled the office of Marshall Siddall — a big change from the three earlier attempts to sell *Glory*. The auctioneer started the bidding at 2,000 dollars. From there, "Do I hear a higher bid?" advanced the auction at monotonous 50-dollar jumps until the 3,000-dollar mark was reached. Then, the advances were quite rapid until 4,000 dollars was bid by the representative for Dodwell and Company, a large shipping firm, with offices both in British Columbia and Puget Sound. Frederick Johnstone now put in a bid of 4,050 dollars, the highest anyone would go. From there, all the auctioneer could say was, "Going once, going twice, sold to Mr. Johnstone for 4,050 dollars." It had taken a mere half-hour to spell downfall for *Glory of the Seas*.[13]

✳✳✳

CHAPTER XVIII

The Mark of Disgrace

O N May 12, 1911, without any fanfare, *Glory of the Seas* left her anchorage at Esquimalt harbor under tow bound for Seattle, where it would
be her turn to experience the ultimate in disgrace for an old square-rigger, that of being cut down to a barge. Several days later, Johnstone had
her thoroughly caulked and painted at the Heffernon floating dock in
West Seattle, where she remained for nearly a week.[1] Then a tug towed
her to the Arlington Dock at the foot of University Street in downtown
Seattle. In the following weeks workmen stripped *Glory* of all her yards,
save the lower mainyard, which Johnstone planned on using as a cargo
boom. Apart from this, everything above topmasts on the fore and main
was sent down along with all running rigging; on the mizzen, only the
lower mast was left standing, along with the spanker gaff and boom.
Her jibboom at the outboard end of the bowsprit was sawed off roughly
and fell into Elliot Bay with a splash.

Three weeks after her arrival at Seattle, she lay prepared for her new
status in life. A 54-foot by 18-foot house had been built atop her fo'c's'le
to house cannery hands, of which sixty were needed for the operation up
North. The new house not only provided additional sleeping quarters,
but in the after end also had a large mess hall in which to serve the crew's
meals. She was completely wired for electricity in her 'tween decks and
houses and literally tons of fish canning equipment were positioned on
board, much of it operated by gas engines.[2] With the conversion completed, Johnstone had her legally conveyed to a new Washington corpo-

The 'tween decks of *Glory* during her conversion to cannery operations, June 1911. Courtesy San Francisco Maritime Museum, J. Porter Shaw Collection.

Conversion work on *Glory*'s main deck, June 1911. Courtesy San Francisco Maritime Museum, J. Porter Shaw Collection.

ration that he and his business partners had formed, the Alaska Fish Company. *Glory,* valued at 4,050 dollars only one month before, was now sold to the corporation for 27,500 dollars.[3] Though over forty years old, she was still sound "with as little as eight and ten inches of water per week," Johnstone reported.[4] He had picked up an exceptional bargain. Though she lay at the bottom rung of the maritime social ladder, she at least had the distinction of being the first floating salmon cannery in existence in the United States.

At 2:00 P.M. on June 15, twenty-four days after the actual conversion work had begun, *Glory* sailed from Seattle under command of Fred Johnstone, bound for Hawk Inlet, Southeastern Alaska, under tow of the steam tug *Tatoosh*. The following contemporary account, which was written by one of Johnstone's office staff, tells of her 1911 venture North as a cannery. Although not written in nautical style, it relates in a personal manner some of the events that made this an interesting chapter in the lives of about fifty people.

At Ketchikan on the way up, a stop of a few hours was made to take on some fish gear. At this point Captain Johnstone was relieved by Captain King, who continued with her during the season and is still in command.

The crew upon leaving Seattle consisted of about sixty people, men and boys — residents of Seattle and Ballard. At Ketchikan two quit and [one] was taken to the hospital, having fell and suffered slight injuries. He later returned to the ship at Hawk's Inlet, being no worse for the experience.

On June 22nd, the ship was anchored in Hawk's Inlet and began immediately the work of canning fish. The fish at this place were of fine quality and being canned fresh and under the sanitary rules of the cannery, rigidly enforced, produced an A-1 class of canned salmon.

The ship remained at Hawk's Inlet until August 5th, when she was taken in tow by the steamer *Northland,* bound for Ketchikan. This was Saturday and on Sunday, anchors were dropped in Saratoga Harbour and the *Northland* left her to call in at a port near by. The day being ideal for a tramp in the woods, most of the crew went ashore to visit the different places of interest in that vicinity, among them being Murderer's Cave, where years ago, so the story goes, a party of whiskey peddlers were massacred by the Indians after having traded whiskey for all their furs, gold, and other things of value in the village.

The *Northland* returned Monday and the trip was resumed. The tow line on the launch *Alert* parted and after a chase of several hours was picked up by the *Occidental* and again made fast. Later, the main tow [*Glory of the Seas*] parted, and but for the quick work on the part of the

Northland and *Occidental,* it might have resulted seriously. [She almost went on the rocks in Stikine Strait.] After two or three hours everything was made fast and we again started on our way. The ship arrived at Ketchikan August 9th, and the work of canning began immediately. The supply of fish at this point being much greater than at Hawk's Inlet, and in anticipation of this extra supply of fish, the capacity of the plant had been considerably increased. This work had been done on the way down from Hawk's Inlet, thereby causing no delay upon arrival at Ketchikan.

The season's pack was completed here and a part of the Ketchikan's Cannery pack was taken aboard, and on October 3rd, in tow of the tugboat *Pioneer,* Captain Nelson in command, the ship started south to Seattle. In Fitzhugh Sound she ran into a seventy-five-mile-per-hour gale and was forced to return to Bella Bella, where she was anchored for sixty hours. A phonograph aboard added considerable pleasure to the trip and especially during this long delay. A stop of two days was made at Anacortes to unload the salmon brought down for the Ketchikan cannery, the tug awaiting alongside. Leaving Anacortes on the morning of the 13th, she arrived at Seattle eight P.M. the same day, having been gone three months and twenty-nine days. A stop of a few days was made at Pier #14 in order to unload cargo, the last of the season's pack. On October 27, she was taken to Eagle Harbor and anchored for the winter.[5]

The floating cannery experiment turned out a "phenomenal success," as the *U.S. Fish Commission Reports* put it.[6] Forty thousand cases of "Glory of the Seas Alaska Brand Salmon" were soon on the market nationwide, bringing a net profit of over 40,000 dollars to the Alaska Fish Company after voyage, shore, and conversion expenses.[7]

But in 1912, Johnstone had stiff competition. The ex-square-rigger *William H. Smith,* housed completely over and equipped with both canning and freezing facilities, operated in Saginaw Bay, southeastern Alaska, starting in June, a month following *Glory.* This vessel, formerly owned by the California Shipping Company, had also reverted to barge status. More than a year before, she had lost a bout with a rollicking storm off Cape Flattery, leaving behind her mainmast and other tophamper. She was purchased as she lay at Eagle Harbor in her storm-battered condition by Welding Brothers, a Puget Sound concern. They had not only copied but also improved upon Fred Johnstone's idea of a floating cannery by installing a reefer plant. Both ex-ships spent the summer and early fall of 1912 trying to capture a large percentage of the southeastern Alaska cannery profits. Changes had taken place on *Glory* before she had headed north for the second year. From the break of the poop and forward

Above. Another view of conversion work on *Glory*'s main deck, June 1911.
Courtesy San Francisco Maritime Museum, J. Porter Shaw Collection. Below.
Glory, under tow, leaving her berth for Alaska, June 15, 1911. Courtesy Robert
C. Leithead.

Glory heading north, towed by the tug *Tatoosh*. Courtesy Robert C. Leithead.

77 feet she had been housed over to a height of 9 feet above the main deck. This was so the cannery hands working on the receiving, cutting, and sliming end of the canning operation would be out of the Alaska cold and rain. During the 1911 fishing season, they had hung *Glory*'s old mainsail somewhat horizontally overhead the work area, but it had not proved especially satisfactory.

The year 1912 proved to be a poor one for floating canneries. Pink salmon were widely in demand, but the market price dropped to a point that reversed the 1911 results. Though Alaska Fish Company made a slight profit on the 20,000 cases canned, Johnstone saw that the future of floating canneries was uncertain. Years later he told his relatives he had become downright afraid of the growing competition from other floating canneries. Also he was nervous that *Glory* might be lost on a lee shore with all that expensive machinery aboard. Or perhaps "pirates" might make off with the large amount of money kept on board to buy fish from the small seiners.[8] Fred Johnstone was the worrying kind. So he and his associates decided to sell and be content with a shore plant. He bought out a small firm, the Oceanic Packing Company, which had a cannery at Waterfall on Prince of Wales Island, and made arrangements to enlarge their facilities. Meanwhile, *Glory* and all her machinery went to a new firm, the Glacier Fish Company, for 23,500 dollars in February, 1913.[9] The president of this corporation, Ed Simms, of the notorious Simms and Levy boardinghouse at Port Townsend, was the principal deep-water shanghai artist on Puget Sound. Though innumerable men had been shanghaied by this gentleman, the local newspapers still referred to him as the "Honorable" E. A. Simms. Despite his means of commerce, he had put a lot of money into the coffers of the Port Townsend city fathers.

After buying *Glory*, Glacier Fish Company formulated plans further to downgrade her and mar her beauty by converting her into a reefer barge. The latter part of February, her new owners had the old ship towed from her winter anchorage at Eagle Harbor to the foot of Spring Street at Seattle. There shipwrights housed her completely over like an old Navy prison ship, but worse. Because there was so much clutter now on deck — mainly a nearly 17-foot-high, irregularly shaped structure topped by a smoke stack just abaft the fo'c's'le head — Ed Simms decided that there was only one solution to steering her behind a tug: to have her wheel on the mizzen top. A structure like an outhouse was built aloft, containing her wooden wheel and an endless chain connected below to

her rudder head. To the Seattle waterfront fraternity, this was the
crowning indignity for the old clipper. In the *Seattle Times* appeared a
comment by the master of the seagoing punt *Ruddy Maru,* "It's a libel
on us old salts." Captain Alexis A. Paysee of the *Bonnie Jean,* the Colman
Dock launch king, said he would be arrested if he voiced his thoughts on
the matter A special meeting of the "ginger beer board" was held at the
foot of Spring Street. There, Captain Fred Lillico and his brother talked
about getting legislation passed to keep this inglorious modification
from being repeated on other vessels. However, in spite of the verbal
tirades, Simms said the steering mechanism would stay put.[10] *Glory* had
a job to do and it was going to be done his way. In the meantime, carpenters had sealed her up tight below decks by insulating her with slabs of
cork stripped from an old brewery that had been closed by the Washington State prohibition law. At the same time an ammonia freezing plant
with all the accompanying pipes had been run throughout the ship.[11]

Heading north in June under tow, she spent four months in Idaho
Inlet, Icy Straits (southeastern Alaska), and was towed back to Seattle
that October. As a reefer she proved a surprising success by packing
1,600,000 pounds of halibut and 200,000 pounds of salmon (a total of 900
tons), and broke all her competition for the year.[12] Although Ed Simms
was no poor man by any means before this venture, he made a small fortune out of *Glory* during 1913. "Shanghai" Simms soon decided that
there was no reason for him to work any longer; he sold his interest in the
corporation and took his wife on a world tour that was unfortunately cut
short by the start of World War I.[13]

During the year of 1914, *Glory of the Seas* remained on Puget Sound.
Several area packing firms so heavily pressed the price on halibut that
Glacier Fish could not afford to send *Glory* north.[14] In the long run,
laying her up proved to be a wise decision, for the war was creating a
global financial crisis.

In March, 1915, Glacier Fish made their headquarters at a dock on
the east side of the Middle Waterway at Tacoma. While *Glory* lay tied
up there, Jim Bashford, marine reporter for the Tacoma *Ledger,* went
aboard one day. He was deeply impressed by what he called in his notes
"Donald McKay's masterpiece." Besides describing her as a barge in detail, he wrote that she was "solid and good for forty years," which was
about as far from the truth as Bashford could get, though unintention-
ally so.[15] Being sealed up as a reefer meant "stinking dryrot" was slowly

Glory in Icy Straits, Alaska, June 1913. Courtesy Joe D. Williamson.

The fruits of *Glory*'s cannery operations. Labels of "Aristocrat" and "Glory of the Seas" salmon cans. Courtesy Robert C. Leithead.

but tenaciously eating into the old ship's vitals, imperceptibly rotting her ceiling and frame. But even though she had now reached the age of forty-five, *Glory* had not lost her value. To finance her venture to south-eastern Alaska in the year 1915, Glacier Fish Company mortgaged her for 50,000 dollars to the Fidelity Trust Company of Tacoma.[16] This included funds for having her docked and completely painted before going north. The copper paint on her underwater body, fresh when Simms first bought her, was oxidized enough that new paint was in order to keep the toredoes out of her. On May 15 and 16, Yarrows Limited docked her at the public facilities at Esquimalt for 485 dollars. The following estimate record made by the firm shows what the years have wrought in marine repair prices:[17]

"Glory of the Seas"		May 7th, 1915	
Estimate for Docking, Cleaning and Painting			
Particulars	Material	Labor	Cost
Docking and undocking		40.00	
Water for cleaning, say, 3000 gallons	1.80		
Use of brushes, scrapers, etc.	1.20		
Launch	2.00	5.00	
Preparation and washing		3.00	
Labour cleaning and painting			
22 men — 2 days		110.00	
	5.00	158.00	163.00
	12%	10%	
	.60	15.80	16.40
actual 18′0″ aft, 17′6″ for'd.	5.60	173.80	179.40
(Caulked to 17′0″ mark) Supervision			6.60
2 coats			186.00
		Profit 20%	38.00
2102 Gross 1st day 200.00 Lay day 105.00		Dock	305.00
With Owners Paint Quote			529.00
(in bond) With Woolsey's Paint Quote			829.00
With Bapco Paint Quote			829.00
With 25% on labour and 25% profit			
(in bond) With Woolsey's Paint quote			868.00
With Bapco Paint Quote			868.00
With Owners Paint Quote			568.00
$30.00 added to quotation for diver's work — packing up keel			

If the diver had not packed up the 16-inch hog in her keel, the repair costs to her underwater body would have been prohibitive. Glacier Fish

Company spent as little money as possible on her. They knew they had shortened her life by rotting her innards with dryrot, but their attitude remained that she had work to do, and she would do it their way.

On May 18, the ugly *Glory of the Seas* was towed out of Esquimalt Harbor behind the steam tug *Goliah,* bound for Icy Straits. As *Glory* headed up Haro Straits, three women and a little girl, ranging in age from three to seventy-nine years, viewed her from a three-story mansion high on a hill in Victoria, British Columbia. They were Lucy Freeman, her daughter Lucy, her granddaughter Marguerite, and her great-grand-daughter Barbara. Seeing this once great ship, which still meant so much to them, in such a pitiable state, they could do only one thing. Lucy Freeman broke down and wept, and the others including little Barbara could not help but join her.[18]

In March, 1916, two months before she was towed north again, Joshua Freeman made one last voyage to the coal ports that both he and his old command had known so well. For two years his health had been failing rapidly, and it was now a great effort for him to manage even simple tasks. Little Barbara, Marguerite Twigg's pretty daughter, remembered seeing her eighty-one-year-old great-grandfather come slowly sideways down the stairs in the Little home favoring his game leg, holding onto the staircase rail with both hands. His years were coming to a close.[19] The voyage that he took in March, 1916, was on board James Dunsmuir's yacht *Dolaura,* on which Dunsmuir and Frank Little had spent many a pleasant hour together. This time, Joshua, his good friend Captain Porter, and the regular crew, made the special trip up to Union Bay. Perhaps Dunsmuir and Porter, who had known Freeman since the days of the *Gold Hunter,* perceived that the old captain's time was near and wanted him to see the old ports once more. He was very happy this day, and told many a sea tale about *Glory* in these waters years before. The visit buoyed him and he appeared unusually bright and well, but just one week later Joshua Freeman died quietly in Victoria.[20] Another link to *Glory*'s past had been broken.

After spending one final season north, she returned to Tacoma with 638 tons of frozen fish in October, 1917, only to be requisitioned by the United States Government for war service. Every vessel of over 2,500 gross tonnage was being put into use because of the extreme shortage of ships. The bureaucrats in Washington, D.C., did not realize that her 2,737 gross tonnage was as a result of the structures on her main deck,

Members of *Glory*'s crew and their girl friends enjoy an informal dance on deck, 1915. Courtesy Gordon P. Jones.

Glory driven onto the beach, December 1922. Courtesy San Francisco Maritime Museum.

and nothing else. They kept her only a week, discovering that she had gone downhill too far for rerigging to be sensible.[21] By sealing her up four years before, Glacier Fish Company had ruined *Glory* for any other use except as a hulk. By plugging all her air vents and insulating her, they had allowed dryrot to spread like cancer below decks.[22]

Four dismal years passed in which the world in general suffered a postwar depression. Seeing that her chances for activity up north were slim, the owners let her go completely. About the only thing they had done, besides docking her once at Winslow to stem a leak, was to paint a big white sign on her starboard side in 6-foot-high letters: "GLACIER FISH COMPANY, COLD STORAGE SHIP NO. 1." This defacement was in full view of downtown Tacoma as she lay in the Middle Waterway. In 1921, the financial condition of Glacier Fish Company turned critical, not only because of bad management but also because of the serious economic recession in the United States.[23] They could no longer pay on the 1915 mortgage on *Glory,* and they were left with no eventual choice but to convey her for the pitiful sum of 1 dollar to the Tacoma branch of the Bank of California, the mortgage assignee.[24]

The bank officials had her surveyed and discovered there was no profitable way that *Glory* could be used. The official verdict was "unfit for further use."[25] They planned to dismantle the reefer plant and burn the hull for its scrap value, the final stage of the status that *Glory of the Seas* had suffered for ten long years.

During the short interval before the wreckers went to work on her, James A. Farrell, president of the United States Steel Corporation, visited Puget Sound and made it known that he would like to save *Glory's* figurehead from the funeral pyre. Farrell, best known for having owned and operated the American full-rigger *Tusitala* in the 1920's, had a rich maritime heritage. His father, Captain John Guy Farrell, had once commanded the schooner *Susan Scranton,* had been part owner of the brig *Monte Cristo,* and had also served in the famous brig *Pilgrim,* the central ship in Richard Henry Dana's masterpiece *Two Years before the Mast.*[26] It is understandable why the bank officials offered the marvelous Greek goddess to Farrell as a gift. They soon had it sawed from its once magnificent pedestal, carefully crated, and on its way to New York City, where Farrell planned to restore it and put the goddess on display in his private dining club, India House.

In January, 1922, the Bank of California engaged the Tacoma refrigeration firm Maingault and Graham to dismantle the reefer plant
from *Glory* as she lay alongside the Glacier Fish dock. During the next
few months the monstrous deckhouses were hacked open as the wreckers ripped out the boilers, ammonia plant, and the fully equipped machine shop.

After the ugly boiler stack was toppled just abaft the fo'c's'le head, a
mummified seagull, which had lain in the stack for ages, was discovered.
While the wrecking took place, John C. Graham's two sons, Oscar and
John, spent much of their free time on *Glory*. Twelve-year-old Oscar
(Okey) especially was fascinated with everything about the old ship. He
told the author how he went into every conceivable "nook and cranny."
This included going aloft to her unorthodox wheelhouse by way of the
"pretty rotten" ratlines. One of the first memorable experiences he had
was with the barge master, "Scow" Charlie (more likely he was the
watchman), a tall and lanky Norwegian, who stayed on board much of
the time Maingault and Graham wrecked her. Okey told of how Charlie
took him into *Glory*'s pantry back aft and fixed him what was his first cup
of coffee, mostly cream. Charlie remarked to Okey, "I t'ink you don't
like coffee." At the same time the old Scandinavian fixed himself a special
cup, half coffee and half whiskey. Affected by his "coffee" or otherwise,
"Scow" Charlie held young Okey in complete fascination with his sea
tales, one of which pertained to *Glory* in her hulk state. He remarked how
they used to set a couple of jibs on her in fair weather and several other
sails when heading north through the inside passage to Alaska. Though
the old ship was clipped like a grounded bird, she would sail away from
the tug. They would drop the towline and let her sail by herself for a few
miles; then pick her up again.[27]

At 3:00 A.M. one night in February, John C. Graham received a fright.
A telephone call from downtown Tacoma gave him the disheartening
news that *Glory of the Seas* was slowly sinking alongside the Glacier Fish
dock. He and his two sons drove down as quickly as they could, to see
what could be done. They found the old ship heeling far over onto the
dock. Though she had been far from completely dry before, there was
now enough water in her bilges to sink her if something drastic was not
done and *fast*. In fact, without the wharf to lean on, *Glory* would already
have capsized. John Graham, "Scow" Charlie, and John and Oscar hur-

riedly brought on board a large centrifugal pump and got it into action. In a matter of two hours, the crisis was past and *Glory* was on a nearly even keel.[28]

"Scow" Charlie said he knew why she leaked and that they'd never be able to find that big leak. Her figurehead, her "soul," was gone. Return it and she would stop leaking. Even the rats had left, Charlie maintained. John Graham tried to explain that this was not reasonable, but superstitious Charlie persisted and said that he had been on two ships where the rats had left and both of them went down. To him, she was a doomed ship. A more plausible point of blame was the toredoes. The large inroads they had made in her barnacle-encrusted outer skin had reached the destination of total ruin. John Graham and his sons now concluded that her days were numbered, and "Scow" Charlie's prophecy was about to be fulfilled. From that day on, they kept the pump on board in case of emergency, and connected a gas engine to her old, well-worn main pumps to speed up the routine daily pumping.[29]

Since she was to be completely demolished, the bank gave Graham permission to strip anything he wanted from the old ship. He had the insight to know that some day artifacts would be of historical interest, and he wanted to remove the entire after cabin and set it up ashore, but the task was too great. Okey and John ripped off two of her great, 14-foot-long nameboards, two locker doors, several lamps, and a pile of miscellaneous findings. Okey removed her brass mess hall bell. The two boys had just learned that it was an old custom for builders to place 20-dollar gold pieces under a square-rigger's masts. Wheels began turning in their young minds, and with great hopes they decided, "She looks like she has her original mainmast. Let's get that gold piece before she goes up in smoke." One weekend they took a flashlight and went below into her slime-covered lower hold. There they began sawing through the heel of her mainmast, using, as Okey said, a crosscut saw and a "dull" axe. After cutting sufficiently through, about 10 inches up from the heel, the boys methodically chopped out the sawed section and shone the light where the gold piece was supposed to be. For all their efforts, of course, they found only the four-bit piece George Ekrem had placed there in 1902. The boys were crestfallen, but at least they had the consolation that the money was valuable as a memento of the ship.[30]

At this point Cornelius J. Vanderbilt, IV stepped in to see what could be done to save *Glory* for posterity. During the last week in March, 1922, he sent a telegram from Tacoma to the city officials of Boston:

> Donald McKay's Boston-built *Glory of the Seas* will be dismantled. Appeal to pride, honor, and patriotism of Boston to save historic, record-breaking ship as an object of interest for Boston. One million of your people would welcome old *Glory* at her home town. The possible expense of vessel delivered at Boston would be $7,000. Vessel capable of facing Atlantic at slight expense. Her copper is said to be worth more than her cost when launched in 1869.[31]

The logical question, then asked, "Is she worth saving?" was tossed around all summer. A survey was made to determine whether she could carry a lumber cargo to Boston via the Panama Canal, but with the inspection came a jump in expense to 43,000 dollars. Could the people of Boston provide the "ransom" money? Meanwhile, the Bank of California officials grew tired of waiting for action and sold her stripped hull to Neider and Marcus, Seattle junk dealers, for final demolition. Although she was useless for any other purpose, her new owners held up burning her. They even made it known to the Boston parties that they would waive all profit on her hull if the money were put up to save her.[32] Chance for survival hung by a thread. National concern was beginning to be felt as is shown in an editorial that appeared on October 24, 1922, in *The New York Times*. It was entitled "Glory of the Seas":

> Whether the effort to save the famous *Glory of the Seas* is successful or not, it has demonstrated one thing and it is this: With all the materialism of the present age, America retains the saving grace of sentiment and veneration to the fullest degree. Old World critics refer to us as a materialistic people. If that were true, how explain the fine thrill that swept through every seaport of the United States when the news was flashed from Seattle that the *Glory of the Seas*, souvenir of America's great day on the ocean, had been granted a respite from the flames.
> Both coasts exulted.
> Why?
> Old hulks are burned or otherwise destroyed almost every week. Their passing causes little or no comment. They are merely so much wood or steel or iron that has outlived its usefulness in the form of a ship. In that respect, the old *Glory of the Seas* differs from no other hulk. Divorce her from the past and she is a thing for the junk pile.
> But this old ship incarnates something to America. She carried the flag of America in triumph up and down the great trade routes of the Atlantic

and the Pacific, in the days of the "iron men and wooden ships." She embodied the skill, the daring, the seamanship of a great age. In foreign ports, Americans far from home greeted her with brightened eyes. In American ports our people welcomed her home with pride and joy. She rode the gale with victorious masts.

Last masterpiece of Donald McKay, Boston's greatest builder of the clipper ship era — The *Flying Cloud,* the *Lightning,* the *Flying Fish,* and the *Sovereign of the Seas* were other testimonials of that — the *Glory of the Seas* invaded the ocean routes in 1869, as the days of sail were declining rapidly. But she held her own for years. As long as sail could combat steam, her wonderful hull with its graceful figurehead and its great clouds of white canvas, added beauty to the seas.

From a practical viewpoint, she is only so much junk.

But the junk in this case is ennobled by a fine national sentiment, by the veneration that a patriotic people give to historic monuments. She is one of the humbler monuments, it is true, as compared with "Old Ironsides," or the sword of Washington, or the home of Lincoln, but she embodies much that is worthwhile and she will live long in our maritime history.

But time was running out. Moorage costs at the Glacier Fish dock were too expensive for *Glory* to be left there, and in the middle of December, 1922, a tug towed her from Tacoma to a pebble beach about a half mile south of Brace Point in a community called Endolyne. At high water, to offset her leaky condition, she was run up on the beach in a small shallow cove. Here she awaited the verdict of the people of Boston — reprieve or a funeral pyre?

Meanwhile, Charles G. Tackaberry, an employee of the Alaska Junk Company, which had subcontracted the final junking of *Glory,* busied himself on two wooden hulls that were also to be burned for their fastenings, an uncompleted World War I "Ferris"-type hull and the half-wrecked motor ship *Coolcha.*

Through a fluke of chance, Frank Prothero, today a noted Seattle boatbuilder, found himself involved in the final hours of *Glory* and the other ships. One weekend in March, 1923, he and one of his school chums climbed aboard *Glory* and wandered curiously around her ancient decks. Tackaberry evidently caught sight of the boys from shore and went hastily on board to see if they were up to any mischief. He asked the two what business they had being on board. As a lame excuse, Prothero said, "I'm looking for work." Tackaberry softened and told them he would give them both jobs helping to strip and burn the ships. The friend said that he would have to ask his mother and disappeared, not to return. But Frank Prothero was in business for the next six months. Although the boy was still attending West Seattle High School, he began working on weekends for Tackaberry along with two men.

The old McKay ex-square-rigger struck a responsive chord in Frank Prothero. Tackaberry told him she was being held to the very last in hopes that somebody would offer to save her. At an especially low tide Frank would walk around *Glory* admiring her graceful lines, so vastly different from those of the boxy steel sailers built in the last days of commercial sail. He remembered standing in the gravel by her starboard bilge, looking at her great hull rising more than 30 feet above him. To his young mind she seemed to be a ship that had been passed by time.[33]

One by one, the "Ferris" hull and the *Coolcha* were burned for their metal fastenings. Then Tackaberry brought barges alongside to load the tangled metallic debris. Prothero remarked about their demolition, "We never had no trouble getting them to burn."[34] After stripping the burned-out hull of the *Coolcha*, they heaved her closer to shore for further burning, using two capstans from *Glory*, which had been removed and positioned ashore on heavy timbers. The lines were manila, 4 or 5 inches in diameter, and heaving was begun at dead high water in "high" gear. *Glory*'s capstans were the compound variety with double rows for the bars and could be shifted, depending upon the direction of rotation, to gain mechanical advantage. Prothero termed them "four speed," but said that low gear required eight revolutions of the head to make the barrel turn one revolution. They hauled the *Coolcha* farther up the beach, but were limited because of the heavy hull weight, and a considerable amount of the metal in her water-soaked remains was lost to them.[35]

In the meantime, Tackaberry was receiving letters almost every week asking him not to burn *Glory of the Seas*. He told Frank Prothero that he did not want to, and of how he hoped someone or some organization would come forward to save her, but that he was powerless to save her. The disposal had to be accomplished one way or another, either by having her claimed for posterity or by putting the burning torch to her, for him to come out financially.

By May, Neider and Marcus could see that nobody really cared enough to save her, and the order was given to Tackaberry to burn *Glory* on Sunday, May 13. That morning, about two hours before high tide, Tackaberry, Prothero, and the other two employees went on board her to start the cremation. This was a day that Charles Tackaberry had not wanted to come. The duty was painful to him. They four went below, gathered some scrap wood, and built an ordinary wood fire. Quickly, the blaze spread to her dry timbers. It ate its way through her decks and stalwart beams, sending a pall of smoke hundreds of feet high. In a matter of hours she was a raging inferno from stem to stern. Back aft in her beautiful cabin, the paint and varnish work blistered, then burst into flame as layer upon layer peeled off to uncover the exquisite workmanship that her creator had carefully put into her fifty-four years before at East Boston. Amidships, beams collapsed, causing her "built" mainmast to sway uncertainly for a few seconds and then topple slowly over her port side to smash on the remains of the gutted "Ferris" hull. The decks surrounding the foremast housing and its supporting shrouds were devoured by the holocaust, and the foremast, too, toppled over the side. *Glory*'s life force, the cellulose bonding agent in her aged timbers, turned into smoke as the fire raged furiously in her vitals. The only sounds coming from her were the roar and crackling of the fire and an occasional dull thud as beams and red-hot metal collapsed. *Glory of the Seas* was in her last death agonies.

Walter Francis, an elderly commercial artist living in Seattle, witnessed the final hours of the old vessel. She meant more to him, probably, than anyone present, for he had served in her under Joshua Freeman many years before. He wrote a letter to Frederick C. Matthews the following week telling of the end of *Glory:*

Well, old *Glory* has gone at last and by some curious working of the mind, I was inspired, directed, or allowed to be present at her finish.

Sunday, May 13, was gloomy and threatening so I stayed home until about 3 P.M., then suddenly determined to take a ride some place. Was just about to board a car for town as a starting place, when "something" directed me to return, get my sketch pad, and ride to Endolyne to see if anything had happened to the old ship since I last saw her six weeks before.

Nearing the beach, instead of her topmasts through the trees, I saw a thin cloud of smoke and felt that she might have been smouldering for a week and I would see nothing but her keel.

Down to the beach and found that she had been burning only a few hours but at that nothing was left of her but a fire-punctured shell, a section of which would occasionally fall into the water of Puget Sound with a dull explosion. Her badly charred fore and main masts were alongside, the mizzen hanging over the port quarter, the whole mixed up with bolts, wire, and remnants of another burned hull. The picture made one think of the effect of a tidal wave followed by fire. My sketch will let you visualize it.

The only spectacular bit I saw was when, from the weight of the bowsprit, the entire bow from catheads to stempost at the bobstays fell overboard in one huge chunk. I felt glad that the goddess, who formerly capped the stem, was saved the humiliation of being smashed to splinters by gravel and shallow water in a junk yard. She was an old friend and I had sketched her more than once.

That the old ship was to be burned that day was not made public, so only a few residents, mostly children, saw the end of what was to them merely a lot of wood bolted together and called a "boat." Had it been given publicity, probably thousands would have driven there to see the smoke and to most of them it would have been an entertainment.

Well, what with gloomy sky, silent water, and certain fire, I felt rather badly, but at the same time superior to the other few spectators in that I knew what it all meant. Also, for consolation that, after the death notice, we of the faithful will have some rest from the drivel that has been written about a fine old ship that was rather extravagantly named.

The place is Endolyne, on the Sound, about five miles from Seattle. Nothing is there but a tiny strip of pebble beach and the banks. Within a mile passed *Blue Funnel,* Admiral-Orient lines, and other big steamers to and from Tacoma.[36]

Late that Sunday afternoon, the 140-foot steamer *Nisqually* on her way down sound approached Brace Point with a noteworthy passenger on board — Captain George Ekrem, past master of *Glory,* who since retiring from the sea was operating a small shoe store in Olympia. This particular Sunday he returned home from a trip to Seattle. As the fast screw steamer came abreast of the point, Ekrem was on deck talking to the chief officer of the *Nisqually,* Volney Young. Together they viewed the smoking ruins of *Glory* afar off. It was a sad sight for Captain Ekrem, and he said with emotion to Young, "She used to be my ship."[37]

By Monday morning all that remained of her was a badly charred, blackened, smouldering wreck, about 9 jagged feet in height, with debris scattered all about.

Several days later, Frederick Pease Harlow of Seattle, who had played by her hull fifty-four years earlier in Donald McKay's shipyard, went to see her remains. Walking alongside the ruins he stooped over and picked up two blackened copper spikes lying in the gravel. In the coming years, these cherished relics, and a stateroom door from her after cabin he had previously removed, were to have an honored place in his home.

Above. Guy A. McKay and Hugh Robert McKay, son and grandson of her builder, view the remains of *Glory*'s charred hull, April 1926. Courtesy Captain Harold Huycke. Below. Model of the *Great Admiral,* made by Frederick Pease Harlow from one of *Glory*'s stateroom doors. Courtesy Gordon P. Jones.

Tackaberry and his men picked her bones that summer until all that was left were the remains of her bottom. There she lay on the beach forgotten by the world until April, 1926, when a dignified, white-haired, sixty-year-old man and his middle-aged son came to Seattle to view her fire-blackened remains. It was Donald McKay's son, Guy A. McKay, and grandson, Hugh Robert McKay, who now lived in the Middle West, coming to pay their final respects to the old ship. They walked along the shore until they found her charred bones high on the beach. A steel cable was made fast to the remnant of her stem to keep her from floating off. What they saw was a tragedy of the times, a result of the failure of an apathetic public to act in time. *Glory of the Seas* was dead.

CHAPTER XIX

Epilogue

NEARLY fifty years have passed since *Glory of the Seas* was burned on that forlorn pebble beach. Though her memory has generally faded into the past, a few relics from the old ship are scattered around the nation. Her Greek goddess figurehead is mounted in the entranceway of India House in New York City. Several people have malleable iron belaying pins that they removed prior to her destruction. Though Okey Graham still has some souvenirs, several have disappeared. The ship's brass mess hall bell was stolen years ago. The "four-bit" piece from her mainmast unaccountably vanished and, most ironically, her starboard bow name-board was chopped up for fire kindling unbeknownst to its owner. In carrying out his father's wishes, Graham was to put the remaining port bow nameboard on display before the general public; late in 1966, he let the San Francisco Maritime Museum purchase the 14-foot relic for permanent exhibition. Jim Gibbs, editor of the *Marine Digest* in Seattle, procured her port running light from Neider and Marcus and proudly displays it in his home. Frederick Pease Harlow's family in Vancouver have a unique model of *Glory* that Harlow built about 1940. He used copper from the ship herself for the model's anchors. The family also has a 3-foot model of the ship *Great Admiral*. Harlow built the hull, its hand-laid main deck, and its spars from the stateroom door he saved from *Glory of the Seas*. The author has a gavel that Okey Graham made from a wooden belaying pin and part of the mahogany rail which once led

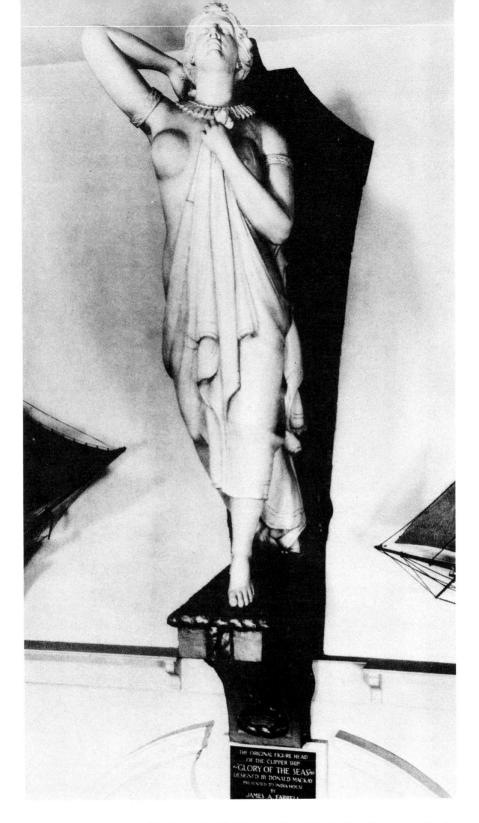

THE ORIGINAL FIGURE HEAD
OF THE CLIPPER SHIP
"GLORY OF THE SEAS"
DESIGNED BY DONALD MCKAY
PRESENTED TO INDIA HOUSE
BY
JAMES A. FARRELL

Glory's figurehead on display at India House, New York City. Courtesy Washington State Historical Society, Curtis Collection.

down from her companionway in the after cabin. However, almost everything else from the ship has gone with time.

At the foot of Border Street in East Boston, there is nothing to remind one that many of the great clipper ships in American maritime history had their beginning there. The Boston Towboat Company is situated on the site of Paul Curtis's yard, but directly north of it on the McKay shipyard site is only a barren, nondescript wharf. Probably the only monument in the entire Boston area calling attention to Donald McKay and his creations is a simple but impressive shaft on the north wall of Fort Independence on Castle Island, which overlooks the approaches to Boston Harbor. Listed on this shaft are the names of his clippers, including, of course, *Glory of the Seas*.

The New York water front until the recent birth of a maritime historical association had next to nothing to remind people that dozens of lofty sailing ships including *Glory* once lined the now drab wharves on the East River. Across the Atlantic Ocean in the British Isles, her memory is forgotten except in the minds of a few maritime historians. Cape Horn, that often dangerous, windswept region with its raging, frothy, everlasting waves, is no longer conquered by magnificent full-rigged sailing ships plowing through its waters.

However, in San Francisco, thousands of tourists are transported daily to that bygone age when hundreds of square-riggers and fore-and-afters busily cleared and entered the great port. The full-rigged *Balclutha* lies at Fisherman's Wharf; the schooner *C. A. Thayer* is moored at the foot of Hyde Street; and the Maritime Museum at the foot of Polk Street with its many exhibits helps people appreciate our deep-water heritage. The old Howard Street coal wharves are gone. At Port Costa on Carquinez Straits all that remains of the great grain docks are a series of stubby, burned-off pilings.

Further up the coast, the lookout station and lighthouse on Tatoosh Island, which once helped to guide *Glory* into the Straits of Juan de Fuca, is still intact; and further inland, a few memories of her coal-droughing days remain. In the mind's eye she can still be pictured heaving to and dropping her hook at Royal Roads at Victoria as the masterful backdrop of the Olympic Mountain range to the south accentuates her towering masts and "patched and patched" sails. On the other hand, at Ladysmith, British Columbia, the great coal wharf is today but a few broken-off pilings, though at Nanaimo the bastion that once housed her inebriated crew is still standing on the waterfront. A few miles north at Departure Bay all that remains of the Dunsmuir coal wharf is half a dozen stubby pilings almost completely buried in a large heap of ship ballast and coal slag. At Union Bay, though, the old coal wharf is still partially intact, though slowly going to pieces.

Farther down sound, the coal wharf at Tacoma has been dismantled for years. The Glacier Fish Company dock has been destroyed by fire. At Eagle Harbor, there is nothing left to remind one that this sheltered harbor was once filled with sailing ships. Even the Hall Brothers yard has been dismantled and partially serves as a boneyard for the Washington State Ferry fleet. The only large sailing ship left on Puget Sound is the dismasted ex-lumber, ex-codfish schooner *Wawona*. At Fauntleroy, docking point for several vessels in the Washington State Ferry fleet, the streetcar no longer runs out to its "Endolyne" from downtown Seattle. From the ferry dock to a spot almost a mile south of Brace Point, houses now cover much of the shoreline. Following curved, narrow, 47th Avenue Southwest in a southerly direction, one comes to a very steep road that leads off the main avenue down to the beach where a number of new apartments have been built. Then, walking along the beach farther south, a little cove is reached. High evergreen-covered cliffs on the east and the beautiful blue waters of Puget Sound on the west make this restful scene memorable. A modern freighter bound for Tacoma to load cargo for the Orient passes by. The peaceful beach is the grave site of a once proud sailing ship. Mingled with the sands and gravel are her remains. Nothing of her can be discerned. The elements of nature have taken away every trace that she was ever there. The *Glory of the Seas* is no more. She rests in peace.

APPENDICES

****

The New Clipper Ship *"Glory of the Seas"*

An account of the ship which appeared in Boston and San Francisco newspapers in 1869 and 1870

This is a magnificent vessel of 2102 tons register, with capacity to carry double that amount of California freight. She has three decks, with all her accommodations on the upper deck, and is of a splendid model to carry and sail. Her bow has a bold, dashy rake, with lightly concave lines below, but convex above, and terminates in a full female classical figure, with flowing drapery. The stern is curvilinear, finely formed, and the run is long and clean, and sets gracefully into the fullness of the hull. The stern is tastefully ornamented with gilded carved work on a black ground. Viewed broadside on she has all the imposing majesty of a ship of war, combined with the airy buoyancy of a clipper. Every seam of her planking harmonizes beautifully with her sheer, and sets her off to the best possible advantage. Everyone who has any idea of nautical beauty and grandeur combined, cannot fail to admire her. Her talented builder, Mr. Donald McKay, has produced many splendid vessels, but we consider this one an improvement on them all; not only on account of her matchless beauty, but also on account of her great strength, and the completeness of her equipment.

She is 250 feet long, on the line of the wales, between perpendiculars, and 265 feet from the knight-heads to the taffrail; has a 44 feet breadth of beam, 28 feet 6 inches depth of hold, with three full decks, including 8 feet 2 inches height between each deck; has $8\frac{1}{2}$ inches dead rise at half floor, and 7 feet sheer, which is graduated her whole length, with sufficient spring towards the ends to impart an air of lightness and buoyancy to her general outline. Her frame, pointers, breast-hooks and many of her knees are white oak; her keelsons, deck frames, ceiling, lower and main decks, and planking are Southern pine, and her upper deck is white pine.

The keel is white oak, sided 16″ and moulded 24 inches, with 5 inches depth of shoe or false keel, is in 6 pieces with sarphs of 12 feet, all bolted with copper. The floor timbers are sided 15 and moulded 20 inches on the

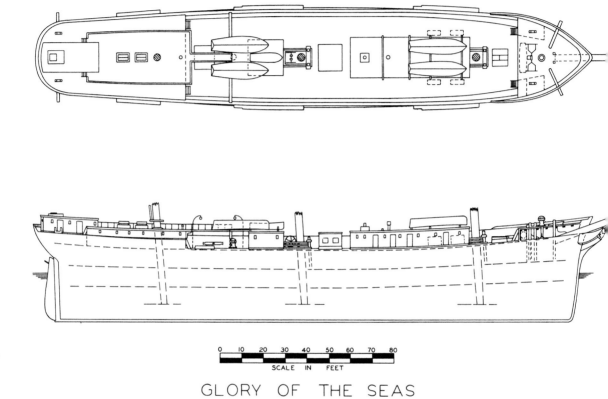

GLORY OF THE SEAS

General arrangement plan, *Glory*, as of 1875. Drawing by the author.

keel, with 28 inches space of frames from center to center, and as the frames ascend they vary from 12 by 14 to 8 by 11 inches, and the bulwark stanchions at the plank-sheer are sided 11 and moulded 8 inches. She has 3 midship keelsons, each 16 inches square, and two tiers of sister keelsons on each side, each of the same size, and fastened with refined iron and copper, the copper driven through the timbers and clinched on the base of the keel. The sister keelsons are bolted vertically and horizontally—vertically through the timbers and horizontally through the midship keelsons and each other.

The ceiling on the floor is 7 inches; on the bilge there are 3 tiers of thick work 15 inches and the rest of the ceiling varies from 10 to 9 inches thick, all scarphed, keyed, square fastened and bolted edgeways. The beams under the lower and main decks are 16 inches square, and those under the upper deck 16 by 11 and 12 inches; the water ways between the lower and main decks are 16 inches square, with strakes inside of them 10 by 15 inches, and a standing strake on the main deck of 12 by 15 inches. The ceiling is 7 inches thick, scarphed, keyed, square fastened and bolted edgeways.

The upper deck water-ways are 12 inches square, the strake inside of them is 9 by 12 inches, the deck planking 3½ by 6 inches of white pine, clear of every appearance of blemish. The other two decks are hard pine of the same substance neatly and strongly fastened.

The coveringboard and planksheer is 7 inches thick, the main rail is 6½ by 16 inches, and the monkey rail is solid; the bulwarks are neatly tongued and grooved, and from the deck are about 6 feet high.

She has four pairs of pointers in each 65 feet long on each side, filled in with massive hooks and beamed, the beams kneed and strongly bolted. These pointers cross the cants diagonally, and are bolted through all. Her stem, stemson, apron, sternpost, false post and stern knees are very strong and heavily bolted. The hooks between the decks forward and aft take in the full curves of the ends, and are securely beamed and kneed. The deck hooks, the hooks above and below the bowsprit, the hatch combings, mast partners, and rudder case are all of choice oak, fitted and fastened with extra care. The stanchions are 16 by 10 inches, clasped with iron below and in the wake of all the decks, and are also doubled kneed on the beams of the lower and middle decks, and firmly fastened.

Her lodging knees are sided 8 and moulded 16 inches in the angles, the hanging knees are 11 and 12 by 22 inches, and have on an average about 22 bolts and 4 spikes in each. The hanging knees under the middle or main deck extend 4½ feet along the beams and their lower ends rest on the water-ways.

In addition to the hanging and lodging knees she is diagonally trussed between the hanging knees of the upper and lower decks; the trusses or braces bolted through the ceiling and the timbers.

The steps of the fore and main masts are trussed, and the pump-well, the chainlockers, the foundation for her water tank (for she has an iron tank of 4000 gallons capacity), and the carlings and ledges of her decks are very

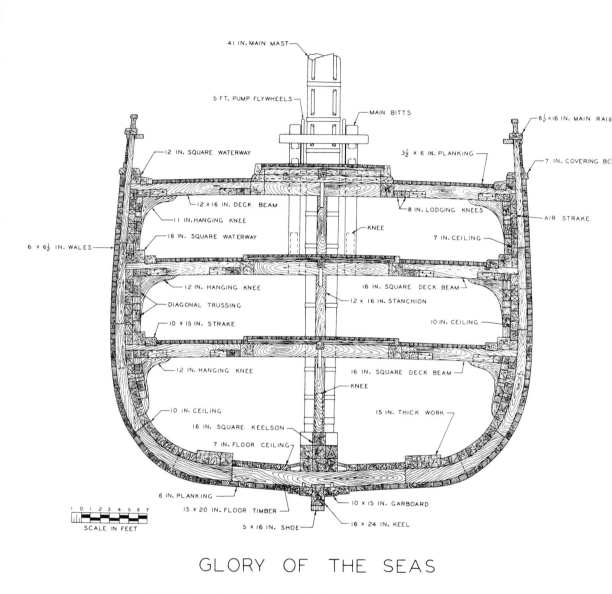

41 IN. MAIN MAST

5 FT. PUMP FLYWHEELS

MAIN BITTS

6½ × 16 IN. MAIN RAIL

12 IN. SQUARE WATERWAY

3½ × 6 IN. PLANKING

7 IN. COVERING BO

12 × 16 IN. DECK BEAM

8 IN. LODGING KNEES

11 IN. HANGING KNEE

AIR STRAKE

16 IN. SQUARE WATERWAY

KNEE

7 IN. CEILING

6 × 6½ IN. WALES

12 IN. HANGING KNEE

16 IN. SQUARE DECK BEAM

DIAGONAL TRUSSING

12 × 16 IN. STANCHION

10 × 15 IN. STRAKE

10 IN. CEILING

12 IN. HANGING KNEE

16 IN. SQUARE DECK BEAM

KNEE

10 IN. CEILING

15 IN. THICK WORK

16 IN. SQUARE KEELSON

7 IN. FLOOR CEILING

6 IN. PLANKING

10 × 15 IN. GARBOARD

15 × 20 IN. FLOOR TIMBER

5 × 16 IN. SHOE

16 × 24 IN. KEEL

1 0 1 2 3 4 5 6 7
SCALE IN FEET

GLORY OF THE SEAS

Midship section, *Glory*, as originally built. Drawing by the author.

substantial and well secured. The whole of the inside below the upper deck is bright and varnished, so that nothing is concealed by putty or paint. The size of her frames and the substance of her ceiling can also be seen through the open air strakes which extend fore and aft.

The garboards are 10 by 15 inches; the next strake is 8 by 15, the bottom plank is 5 inches thick, and she has 27 strakes of wales, averaging 6 by 6½ inches, finished smoothly as the joiner work of the bulwarks. She is sheathed with yellow metal up to 22 feet draft, and above there is painted black, and inside she is pearl color relieved with white, except the outlines of the bulwark stanchions, which are bright and varnished. She is square fastened throughout, butt and bilge bolted with copper, through treenailed, seasoned with fine salt; has ventilators along the line of her plank sheer, trunk ventilators through the houses, the poop and the forecastle.

She has cargo ports between decks; the main hatchway in the upper deck is 12 by 10 feet; in the lower deck it is 12 by 14 feet, and the fore and after hatchways are in proportion. She has double bowsprit bitts, double bitts before the foremast, and massive windlass bitts, all of white oak and strongly bolted.

The chainplates are secured with double preventer bolts through flat iron straps, and vary in size from 1½ to 2 inches. The iron work about the cutwater and stem and in the bows for the bobstays, bowsprit shrouds, backropes and jibboom guys, is of extra strength secured with great care.

Around the bow and stern she is built solid on the upper deck; she has a top-gallant forecastle 35 feet long amidships and 6 feet high with wing closets and lockers under it. Abaft the foremast she has a house 54 feet long by 18 wide and 8 feet 3 inches high, which contains spacious quarters for the crew, in separate apartment for each watch, the galley and several storerooms, and covers an entrance aft which leads to the deck below. She has a half poop 60 feet long with a house built into it 45 feet long, 24 wide and 8 feet high. It contains two cabins; the after one is elegantly finished with mahogany, maple and other fancy woods; has stained glass windows, a recess sofa on each side and is neatly furnished. The forward cabin or dining saloon is painted and grained and the staterooms, pantry and other apartments are all that could be desired for convenience or comfort. There is a companion entrance aft, and double doors forward. The outlines of the poop and house are protected by rails on turned stanchions. She has a wheelhouse; the rudder stock is 20 inches in diameter and she has one of Robinson's best steering machines with purchase enough for one man to steer her under any circumstances.

She has a patent windlass worked by a capstan on the top-gallant forecastle, another capstan also on the forecastle for general use, and still another on the main deck. The windlass capstan which was invented by Mr. Wm. Goodman, is of great power, very compact, yet simple in its operation, and will, no doubt, be generally applied when its merits are appreciated. Her ground tackle consists of two bower anchors of 5700 and 5500 pounds, a stream anchor of 1800 and a kedge of 700 lbs. Her chains are 90 fathoms long each, and are of 2⅛ inch, the stream chain is 75 fathoms of 1½ inch, and she has stout Manila hemp hawsers for towing or warping ship.

She has a force pump forward for washing decks, which can also be used in the event of fire to extinguish it. Close by the mainmast she has two iron hold pumps with fly wheels and 8 inch boxes, then two other pumps, also iron, on each side, which are worked with engine brakes and have 6 inch boxes. Thus she has in all six iron pumps for the hold, all of Edson's patent, and capable of throwing a vast quantity of water. She has four large boats, with quarter davits of iron on each side, and these are provided with everything necessary for the safety of the crew in the event of shipwreck. In all the details of her construction and equipment she is as nearly perfect as a ship need be.

She has a splendid set of spars finely proportioned and well made. The lower masts and bowsprit are built of hard pine, caged with lignumvitae, and hooped with iron; and the topmasts and jibbooms are also of Southern pine without knots or blemishes of any kind. She has double topsail yards, and the yards upon the fore and main masts are alike. In a suit of sails she has about 8000 yards of cotton duck, and the sails she has are not only roped along the reef and bellybands, but along the bands which cross from the clews to the earings. They were made by Mr. B. F. Palmer, of East Boston, who has made most of the sails for the clippers built by Mr. McKay. The spars were made by Mr. George E. Young, who ranks first among the foremost of sparmakers in the Island Ward. She has hemp standing rigging of 11 and 11½ inch, with extra backstays to the topmasts and top-gallant masts, chain topsail sheets and tyes, chain bobstays, ropes, and all her head stays set up inboard. The topmast rigging is set up with dead eyes and lanyards like the lower rigging, topmast, and topgallant backstays. Her rigging is of the best quality, manufactured by the Plymouth Cordage Co. The following are the dimensions of her masts and yards: *

MASTS	Length Feet			Mastheads. ft.		DIAMETER Inches	
Foremast ... Length ... Feet	91			17		40	3'4"
Topmast	54	53	6⅝	10		20	1-8"
Topgallantmast	29			00		14	1-2"
Royalmast	19			00		12	1
Pole	8			00		8	
Mainmast	94			17		41	3'-5"
Topmast	54	53		10	1¼	20	1-5"
Topgallantmast	29			00		14½	1-2½
Royalmast	19			00		12	1
Skysailmast	14			00		8	
Pole	8			00		6	
Mizzenmast	85			14		32	2'8"
Topmast	44			8		16½	1-4½
Topgallantmast	24	23		00		12	
Royalmast	14			00		8	
Pole	6			00		6	

YARDS				DIAMETER
Fore and Main 91	Yardarms	3½		24
Lower Topsail Yards 80		2		20
Upper Topsail ” 74		3¾		18
Topgallant ” 60		4		16½
Royal ” 44		2		14
Main Skysail ” 32		2		12
Cross-jack Yard 70		3		19
Lower Topsail Yard 64		2		17
Upper Topsail ” 57		3		14
Topgallant ” .:...... 43		2		13
Royal ” 32		2		12
Spanker Boom 66	Spanker Gaff	45 feet long.		

* Corrections in italics taken from original spar book of Donald McKay.

The bowsprit is 24 feet outboard and 34 inches in diameter, the jiboom and flying jiboom are in one spar 15 and 16 feet long (of the bowsprit). Aloft as well as below she appears splendidly and she has been thoroughly rigged by Mr. Albert Low.

APPENDIX 2

Disbursement Account of Ship *Glory of the Seas,*
at San Francisco, December 1871–January 1872

			Dollars
December, 1871	Customhouse fees	Currency (98.80) all over (4.25) (89.45)	93.70
"	Quarantine (2.50)	Reporting ship (5.00)	7.50
"	Inward pilotage		209.08
"	Towing to wharf at Oakland		100.08
"	Inward portage bill 1,148.93 @ 1,051.27 Gold coin 773.80		1,825.07
January, 1872	Board officers & crew (127.14) (18.00)		145.14
"	Lining ship (125.00) Dray (0.52)		125.52
"	Lumber (452.18) (20.00) (80.75) (25.00)		577.93
"	Medicines (8.25)		8.25
"	Old canvas (87.60 + 11.50)		99.10
"	C.P.R.R. Co.		73.10
"	Sbl Oil		64.30
"	Hand Move (69.41) rails (11.75)		81.16
"	Coombs—Carpenter work		681.07
"	Stevedore discharging cargo—2,811 Tons		2,670.45
"	Labor—hauling, ship painting		99.00
"	Repairs on bark *Oakland*		301.04
"	N. B. Edgerdy, ship chandlery		78.54
"	Shipping crew and advance		1,672.85
"	Davis & Cowell pressed brick for galley & engine room		15.00
"	Stores (31.75) (232.15)		263.90
"	Blacksmith		13.10
"	Survey		20.25
"	Dockage		141.25
"	Towing from San Francisco and to sea		250.25

"	Clearance	47.12
"	Lighterage (120.00) Fins to Oakland and stores in stream	144.00
"	Flour—four barrels	276.75
"	Loading cargo of wheat—2,994 tons	1,422.65
"	Potatoes and vegetables	241.39
"	Water	75.00
"	Commission on charter to Liverpool	1,956.50
"	Boatmen attending to ship	50.42
"	Watchman	50.42
"	Butcher—sea stock	136.12
"	Ruling chronometer	6.00
"	Advances to cook and police officer's fees	20.00
"	Cash advanced officers and crew by J.N.K.	210.00
"	Car fares—horse	42.50
"	Washing ship linen	4.00
"	Captain Knowles's board	123.50
		$14,630.54

February 7, 1872   [Signed]   J.N.K.

January 8   Remittance   L. and S. F. Bank
By Exchange   3rd Ro. Bank, Boston
From J. Henry Sears
10,000 Premium ¾ + 75.00 .... $10,075.90

February 6–   This amount placed to the credit of
Ship *Titan,* Capt. B. F. Berry 4,076.22
By amount freight on cargo railroad iron
from Cardiff and new port as from charter
party dated June 12, 1871

1007 $\frac{881}{2240}$ (Rate)   42/6 $\frac{2140/14/2}{}$
                                          $\frac{3607/6/10}{}$
                                          5748/1/

1803 $\frac{1506}{2240}$ (Rate)   40/

@ $4.84 .... $27,870.56

FRIEGHT ON MERCHANDISE

less commission 2½% 143.64
1¼% $1946.64 returned commission on
charter to Liverpool 699.10
                                                    486.66
Cash for sales moving chain and other 340.75
Cash half passage 100.00
Cash balance 589.25
                                                  $28,781.70

APPENDIX 3

Cargo manifest, *Glory of the Seas,*
for her record 96-day voyage from New York to San Francisco, October
13, 1873, to January 16, 1874. Voyage valued at $47,303.

New York—Per *Glory of the Seas*

7 cs. axles, 23 bxs. burial cases, 76 bbls. 10 bx. blacking, 324 bdls. binder's
board, 835 empty barrels, 17 trusses batts, 7 bxs. castings, 548 cs. chairs, 131
cs. chair stock, 300 cs. cider, 5 plcgs. carriage, 4 csks. cherry juice, 3 crates
crockery, 500 bbls. cement, 77 empty casks, 203 tons coal, 100 clay tile, 6 crts.
croquet, 49 cs. extracts, 2 crts. earthenware, 181 cs. 7 pkgs., 3 csks., 84 bxs.
glassware, 3 bbls. glue, 171 bxs. glass, 85 bbls do, 2 cs. gun stocks, 16 bales
cambrics, 18 bxs., 19 pkgs. hardware, 141 pcs. hickory, 3 csks. holloware, 1313
pkgs. 207 bds. iron pipe, 2202 bars iron, 221 pkgs. lead, 252 pcs. lumber,
100 cs. matches, 29 cs. mirrors, 2 trunks, 7 bbls. 1237 bxs. 58 bbls., 16,365
pkgs., 1313 cs. mdse., 9 pcs. machinery, 180 pkgs. nails, 405 kegs, 4 bdls. nails,
50 bxs., 50 bbls. oil, 233 pcs. oak, 16 cs. oilcloth, 6 cs. bars, 150 bbls. oakum,
13 cs. paper hangings, 737 bdls., 10 cs., 125 bdls., 165 pkgs. paper, 56 bbls.
putty, 3 cs. perfumery, 100 bbls. pitch, 20 empty pipes, 3565 pkgs. powder, 23
coils rope, 300 cs. Schnapps, 755 bxs. sewing machines, 139 bags sumac, 850
pkgs. starch, 14 cs. spokes, 520 cs. soap, 14,544 pcs. staves, 4 cs. sand paper,
100 stoves, 19 bxs. soda, 18 pkgs. twine, 80 cs. tobacco, 50 bbls. tar, 649 pkgs.
tinplate & pipe, 420 bxs. tinplate, 14 bdls. treenails, 18 bbls, varnish, 1326 ps.
walnut, 18 bxs. wagons, etc., 881 bbls. whiskey, 100 hf-bbls. do, 75 pkgs. do.

APPENDIX 4

Abstract log, *Glory of the Seas,*
San Francisco to Sydney, Australia, March 14 to April 19 1875

Sunday March 14, 1875   Sea Account
At six A.M. tug *Rescue* took us in tow and proceeded to sea with a strong NW. wind. At 8:30—cast off tug and made sail. At 9:30 pilot left just outside bar. At 12 midnight South Farallones bore N. 24 miles from which we take our departure. Strong N.W. wind. Going 12 knots. Made 50 miles from anchorage. Sailed 50 miles.

Monday March 15, 1875   One Day at Sea
Strong winds from N.W., cloudy. Ship very crank. Cannot carry as much sail as otherwise would. Ends—fresh breezes from N.N.W. Cloudy.
Made 278 Miles   Lat. 33°27′N. D.R.
Sailed 278 Miles   Long. 126°50′W.

Tuesday March 16, 1875   Two Days at Sea
Moderate breezes from N. to N.N.E., cloudy most all.
Made 216 Miles   Lat.30°50′N.
Sailed 216 Miles   Long. 128°50′W.

Wednesday March 17, 1875   Three Days at Sea
Moderate breezes from N.N.E., overcast, cloudy most all, poor sight.
Made 196 Miles   Lat. 28°04′N.
Sailed 196 Miles   Long. 131°18′W.

Thursday March 18, 1875   Four Days at Sea
Moderate breezes from N.N.E., overcast, cloudy most all, poor sight.
Made 193 Miles   Lat. 25°34′N.
Sailed 193 Miles   Long. 133°53′W.

Friday March 19, 1875   Five Days at Sea

Moderate trades from N.E., cloudy. Middle—very squally pleasant. Current
setting W. ¾ Kn. per hour.
Made 215 Miles   Lat. 22°28′N.
Sailed 215 Miles   Long. 135°20′W.

Saturday March 20, 1875   Six Days at Sea
Fresh trades from N.E. all. Middle—very squally. Carried away foretopmast
stunsail boom.
Made 235 Miles   Lat. 18°52′N.
Sailed 235 Miles   Long. 137°10′W.

Sunday March 21, 1875   Seven Days at Sea
Moderate trades from N.E. All. Occasional squalls. Ends—smooth sea and
pleasant.
Made 223 Miles   Lat. 15°18′N.
Sailed 223 Miles   Long. 138°13′W.
Made 1606 miles last week.

Monday March 22, 1875   Eight Days at Sea
Moderate trades from N.E.—All pleasant.
Made 236 Miles   Lat. 11°30′N.
Sailed 236 Miles   Long. 139°15′W.

Tuesday March 23, 1875   Nine Days at Sea
Moderate trades from N.E.—All pleasant, smooth, hot.
Made 233 Miles   Lat. 7°45′N.
Sailed 233 Miles   Long. 140°15′W.

Wednesday, March 24, 1875   Ten Days at Sea
First and Middle—Light baffling trades from N.E. to E.S.E., cloudy, rainy.
Latter—moderate from S.E. to East, clear pleasant.
Made 138 Miles   Lat. 5°30′N.
Sailed 138 Miles   Long. 140°51′W.

Thursday March 25, 1875   Eleven Days at Sea
First. Light breezes from East, frequent rain squalls. Middle and Latter—
Fresh trades from East to South and East, occasional rain squalls.
Made 180 Miles   Lat. 3°01′N.
Sailed 180 Miles   Long. 142°31′W.

Friday March 26, 1875   Twelve Days at Sea
Moderate S.E. trades—All, occasional rain squalls. Between pleasant and
hot.
Made 216 Miles   Lat. 0°29′N.
Sailed 216 Miles   Long. 145°06′W.

Saturday March 27, 1875   Thirteen Days at Sea
Light trades from E.S.E.—All—clear, pleasant, hot. Strong current setting
W.S.W. 1½ knot per hour.
Made 198 Miles   Lat. 1°39'S.
Sailed 198 Miles   Long. 147°36'W.

Sunday March 28, 1875   Fourteen Days at Sea
First and middle—fresh trades from East to E.N.E., heavy rain, squally—
latter—clear and pleasant. Trades from S.E.
Made 235 Miles   Lat. 4°20'S.
Sailed 235 Miles   Long. 14°36'W.
Made past week 1436 Miles.

Monday March 29, 1875   Fifteen Days at Sea
Moderate S.E. trades—All—clear, pleasant, current 14 mi. S.W.
Made 238 Miles   Lat. 7°11'S.
Sailed 238 Miles   Long. 153°10'W.

Tuesday March 30, 1875   Sixteen Days at Sea
Moderate S.E. trades—All—pleasant and smooth sea. Current 15 miles west.
Made 192 Miles   Lat. 9°20'S.
Sailed 192 Miles   Long. 155°34'W.

Wednesday March 31, 1875   Seventeen Days at Sea
Light trades—All—pleasant. Latter. Occasional rain squalls. Log distance 163
miles.
Made 152 Miles   Lat. 11°03'S.
Sailed 152 Miles   Long. 157°27'W.

Thursday April 1, 1875   Eighteen Days at Sea
Light baffling trades N.E. to East, pleasant, smooth sea, hot.
Made 141 Miles   Lat. 12°40'S.
Sailed 141 Miles   Long. 159°10'W.

Friday April 2, 1875   Nineteen Days at Sea
Light baffling winds and rain squalls—First part Middle Latter—Moderate
trades from S.E., pleasant and hot.
Made 175 Miles   Lat. 14°40'S.
Sailed 175 Miles   Long. 161°20'W.

Saturday April 3, 1875   Twenty Days at Sea
Light baffling trades from S.E. to N.E., occasional rain squalls—Hot.
Made 145 Miles   Lat. 15°58'S.
Sailed 145 Miles   Long. 163°26'W.

Sunday April 4, 1875   Twenty-one Days at Sea
Light baffling trades from S.S.E. to S.E.—First and Middle parts. Latter—
strong trades, pleasant.
Made 188 Miles   Lat. 17°30'S.
Sailed 188 Miles   Long. 166°17'W.
Past week made 1231 Miles.
Monday April 5, 1875   Twenty-two Days at Sea
Strong trades from S.E. to S.S.E.—all. Squalls and cloudy. At eight A.M.
Savage Island bore north 10 miles distant.
Made 261 Miles   Lat 19°38' S.
Sailed 261 Miles   Long. 170°18'W.

Tuesday April 6, 1875   Twenty-three Days at Sea
Strong trades from S.E.—All, squally. At noon Eooa Island bore north 23
miles distant.
Made 284 Miles   Lat. 21°53'S.
Sailed 284 Miles   Long. 174°44'W

Wednesday April 7, 1875   Twenty-four Days at Sea
Fresh trades from S.E., pleasant, occasional rain squalls. At six P.M. island
bore south 12 miles distant.
Made 278 Miles   Lat. 22°58'S.
Sailed 278 Miles   Long. 179°38'W.

Thursday April 8, 1875   Twenty-five Days at Sea
Fresh trades from S.E., pleasant, occasional rain squalls. Passed 180th Merid-
ian so make a change of a day.
Made 270 Miles by log.
            Lat. 23°58' DR
            Long. 175°36'E.

Saturday April 10, 1875   Twenty-six Days at Sea
Fresh trades from east. First part—squally. Middle and latter—pleasant.
Made 264 Miles   Lat. 25°05'S.
Sailed 275 Miles by log.   Long. 170°55'E.

Sunday April 11, 1875   Twenty-seven Days at Sea
Moderate from E.N.E. to East, clear and pleasant.
Made 252 Miles   Lat. 26°06'S.
Sailed 252 Miles   Long. 166°23'E.

Monday April 12, 1875   Twenty-eight Days at Sea
Moderate from E.N.E. First part—pleasant. Middle—light and heavy rain
squalls. Latter—moderate from E.N.E., pleasant. Made 1801 miles past week.

Dist. Made   192 Miles   Lat. 26°58′S.
Made by log 201 Miles   Long. 163°E.

Tuesday April 13, 1875   Twenty-nine Days at Sea
Light breezes from N.E. to E.N.E., clear and pleasant. Very warm current setting south 10 miles.
Made 148 Miles   Lat. 27°48′S.
Sailed 148 Miles   Long. 160°22′E.
Made by log 154 Miles.

Wednesday April 14, 1875   Thirty Days at Sea
Light baffling airs from E.N.E to N.E. Ends north, cloudy, overcast—poor sight.
Made 94 Miles   Lat. 28°22′S.
Sailed 94 Miles   Long. 158°42′E.

Thursday April 15, 1875   Thirty-one Days at Sea
First part—Light baffling airs and occasional rain squalls. Middle—clear and pleasant airs from south. Latter—moderate from S.E.—pleasant.
Made 94 Miles   Lat. 28°46′S.
Sailed 100 Miles   Long. 156°58′E.

Friday April 16, 1875   Thirty-two Days at Sea
First part—Strong breezes from S.E. to S.S.E. Middle—light airs. Latter—calm and pleasant, baffling airs from S.E. to East, current W.N.W.
Made 124 Miles   Lat. 29°47′S.
Sailed 130 Miles   Long. 154°55′E.

Saturday April 17, 1875   Thirty-three Days at Sea [Birth of Thomas Knowles]
First and middle—Light baffling airs from S.S.W. to S.E., pleasant. Latter—strong gales from S.E., current strong to N.N.E
Made 47 Miles   Lat. 30°25′S.
Sailed 146 Miles   Long. 154°22′E.

Sunday April 18, 1875   Thirty-four Days at Sea
First and Middle—Strong breezes from S.E., squally. Latter—Moderate from E.S.E., pleasant.
Made 78 Miles   Lat. 31°42′S.
Sailed 149 Miles   Long. 154°12′

Monday April 19, 1875   Thirty-five Days at Sea
First part—moderate from E.S.E. to East, cloudy and frequent rain squalls. At 12 midnight Port Stephens Light bore W.N.W. 20 miles distant. At five, Newcastle Light bore N.W. distant 20 miles. At eight A.M. made North

Head and at nine A.M. took Sydney pilot. At 11:30 A.M. anchored in Sydney Harbor making our passage in 35 days.
Made past week 770 Miles   Sailed 952
Total made 6844   Total sailed 7026
Average 8–1/8 miles per hour
Passage anchor to anchor, 35 days, 11 hours, 15 minutes
Passage Pilot to Pilot, 35 days, five hours, 15 minutes

APPENDIX 5

Slop Chest Inventory, *Glory of the Seas,*
as kept by Captain Josiah N. Knowles, August 1876

12 leather jackets	1/8	= $7		6 pr. tweed pants	10/	$2.50
8 pilot jackets	15/6	= $4		9 pr. pilot cloth pants	10/	= $2.50
2 short & 4 long pilot				12 hickory shirts striped		.50
coats, velvet collars	45/ = $12, 63/	= $16		28 blue flannel shirts	4/	$1
9 coats & 10 pants,				4 caps		.25
oil suits	10/	= $2.50		28 bars soap		[illegible]
4 jackets		$2		10 sheath knives		.25
7 cardigan jackets		$1		24 jack knives		.25
5 Bendy caps	1/6 =	.37		9 pr. slippers	2/11	.75
13 Scotch caps	11/8 =	.50		6 pr. boots	16/6	$4.25
16 Crimean shirts	5/	= $1.25		13 pr. bluchers	5/9	$1.50
20 pr. drawers	3/	.75		72 doz. boxes wax		
8 mufflers		.25		tapers 10/	12/5 =	.15
7 pr. mittens		.25		lot of pipes		$1
5 belts & 2 sheaths		$1 for all		Tobacco		
21 undershirts	3/	.75		2 s.westers		.25
30 pr. woolen socks	1/	.25		12 felt hats	2/10	.70
7 pr. cotton socks	1/	.25		52 lbs. common tobacco		.40
1 pr. common pants		$1.50		49 lbs. extra tobacco		.60
15 pr. dungaree pants	2/6 =	.62½		28 lbs. soap, salt water		$7.50
11 pr. dungaree jumpers	2/6 =	.62½		10 used ¼ used		
19 pr. serge pants		$1.75				

NOTES

Notes

CHAPTER I

1. *Boston Evening Traveler,* October 19–21, 1869.
2. Insolvent estate of Donald McKay, October 14, 1856, Records of Suffolk County, Massachusetts, Book 706, p. 123.
3. E. P. Alexander, *Iron Horses, American Locomotives, 1829–1900* (New York: Bonanza Books, 1941), p. 147.
4. Richard C. McKay, *Some Famous Ships and Their Builder, Donald McKay* (New York: G. P. Putnam's Sons, 1928), p. 362.
5. *Ibid.*
6. George Abdill, *Pacific Slope Railroads* (New York: Bonanza Books, 1959), pp. 20, 24, 33, 157.
7. Henry Hall, *Report on the Shipbuilding Industry of the United States* (Census Monograph, Tenth Census Vol. VIII, 1882), p. 87.
8. *Ibid.,* pp. 107, 112.
9. October 29, 1864.
10. *Norway* (Official No. 18261) 2,107.43 gross tons, 210.5 x 46.5 x 30; *Andrew Jackson* (Official No. 1136) 2,005.94 gross tons, 215 x 41 x 30; *Shakespeare* (Official No. 23838) 2,069.36 gross tons, 217 x 42 x 30.
11. Ship

	Glory of the Seas	Helen Morris	Sovereign of the Seas
Net tons except main deck enclosures	1,948.70	1,072.85	1,367
Builder's tonnage $\dfrac{\text{L. x B. x D.}}{100}$ (0.75)	2,162.50	1,035.51	1,346.81
Ratio, length–breadth	1/5.45	1/4.78	1/4.87

Note: All three ships were three masted, had round sterns, and figureheads.

Register No. 206 issued to *Glory of the Seas* on April 18, 1871, at Boston; Register No. 61 issued to *Helen Morris* on March 20, 1868, at Boston; Register No. 243 issued to *Sovereign of the Seas* on December 21, 1868, at Boston.

12. J. Robinson and George F. Dow, *The Sailing Ships of New England* (Salem, Mass.: Marine Research Society, 1921–1928) Series II, pp. 9–51.

13. This figure is an approximation based on the $75.50 per ton figure paid for *Sovereign of the Seas,* per bill of sale recorded at New York on January 15, 1869, Bureau of Customs, NARS, Book 55, p. 27.

14. Massachusetts Title Insurance Co. (Boston), February 17, 1967.

15. Benjamin C. Wright, *San Francisco's Ocean Trade, Past and Future* (San Francisco: A Carlisle and Co., 1911), pp. 162–164. In 1868, 193 vessels were in the California grain trade. In 1869 there were 240.

16. The original builder's model for *Glory of the Seas* is at the Mariners Museum, Newport News, Virginia.

17. The outfitting of *Sovereign of the Seas* took place in the latter part of November, 1868, and the early part of December, 1868.

18. *Boston Post,* December 8, 1868.

19. *Op. cit.,* December 9, 1868.

20. Alexander, *op. cit.,* p. 146.

21. *Seattle Times* Information Bureau Letter, April 15, 1964.

22. Bill of sale for *Sovereign of the Seas* recorded at New York on January 15, 1869, Bureau of Customs, NARS, Book 55, p. 27.

23. Bill of sale (security instrument) dated April 27, 1869, Records of Suffolk County, Massachusetts, Book 1040, pp. 5–11.

24. John B. Hutchins, *American Maritime Industries and Public Policy, 1789–1914,* (Cambridge, Mass.: Harvard University Press, 1901), p. 386.

25. *San Francisco Bulletin,* June 12, 1869.

26. William Armstrong Fairburn, *Merchant Sail* (Center Lovell, Maine: Fairburn Marine Educational Foundation Inc., 1944–1955), Vol. III, p. 1,717.

27. *Merchant Vessels of the United States* lists *Monarch of the Sea* (Official No. 16933) 2,183.62 tons, up until 1880. However, the endorsement on the document issued to said vessel on January 9, 1866, at New York says, "Lost on a voyage from Liverpool, never heard from." (The year of the loss was 1866 according to F. C. Matthews.) This document was finally surrendered on June 30, 1880, NARS.

28. *Boston Evening Traveler,* October 20, 1869.

29. *Great Republic,* 4,555 tons; *Donald McKay,* 2,594 tons; *James Baines,* 2,525 tons; *Champion of the Seas,* 2,447 tons; *Sovereign of the Seas* (built 1852) 2,421 tons. These figures are all according to the old tonnage rule prior to the Act of 1864. Although *Empress of the Seas* was rated 2,200 tons (old measurement), as remeasured, her correct gross tonnage was 1,647.

30. Hall, *op. cit.,* p. 87.

31. Enrollment No. 273 issued to schooner *Frank Atwood* on October 30, 1869, at Boston Bureau of Customs, NARS.

32. Marion V. Brewington, *Shipcarvers of North America* (Barre, Mass.: Barre Publishing Company, 1962), p. 78.

33. McKay, *op. cit.,* pp. 193–194.

34. *San Francisco Bulletin,* June 15, 1870.

35. *Ibid.* The spar dimensions are from the records of Frederick Pease Harlow, who acquired them from Guy A. McKay in the 1920's. See Appendix 1 for full text of *Boston Evening Traveler* and *San Francisco Bulletin* description of ship together with corrections.

36. Unpublished autobiography of Frederick Pease Harlow.

CHAPTER II

1. *Boston Evening Traveler,* November 15, 1869.

2. Frederick C. Matthews, *American Merchant Ships* (Salem, Mass.: Marine Research Society, 1930–1931), Series II, p. 145.

3. "Assignment for Benefit of Creditors" recorded March 24, 1871, in Book 1040, pp. 5–11, Records of Suffolk County, Mass., refers to this as being "United States Lloyds." However, she was first listed in the 1869 *Record.*

4. Insurance regulations for *American Lloyds* dated July 30, 1874.

5. "Assignment for Benefit of Creditors," *loc. cit.*

6. This figure is an approximation based on figures in *The American Maritime Industries and Public Policy, 1789–1914,* p. 389.

7. Enrollment No. 289 issued to *Glory of the Seas* and mortgage recorded in Book 38, p. 225, both on November 25, 1869, at Boston, Bureau of Customs, NARS.

8. *Ibid.* Moreover, the official number 85065 was assigned her.

9. *Boston Evening Traveler,* November 27, 30, 1869.

10. *American Clipper Ships,* p. 690.

11. Mortgage recorded January 24, 1870, at Boston in Book 39, p. 81, Bureau of Customs, NARS.

12. "Assignment for Benefit of Creditors," *op. cit.*

13. Register No. 75 issued to *Glory of the Seas* at New York on February 9, 1870, Bureau of Customs, NARS.

14. McKay, *op. cit.,* p. 324.

15. *Ibid.*

16. *San Francisco Bulletin,* June 15, 1870.

17. *Op. cit.,* June 15, 1870.

18. *Op. cit.,* June 25, 1870.

19. *Op. cit.,* June 15, 1870.

20. Comparison with incoming cargoes to San Francisco during year of 1870 in January, 1871, annual list in *San Francisco Commercial Herald.*

21. Bill of sale for ship *Glory of the Seas* recorded May 18, 1870, in Book 39, p. 246, *Bureau of Customs, Boston,* NARS.

22. "Assignment for Benefit of Creditors," *op. cit.*

23. *Ibid.*

24. Interview with Horace W. McCurdy (September, 1959).

25. "Assignment for Benefit of Creditors," *op. cit.*

26. *San Francisco Bulletin,* July 28, 1870.

27. Crew list dated July 30, 1870, at San Francisco, Bureau of Customs, NARS. The first entry on this list is for the chief mate on June 15, 1870.

28. Hall, *op. cit.,* p. 87.

29. Cargo manifest, *San Francisco Commercial Herald,* August 5, 1870. Regarding her draft laden with cargo, the *Record* for 1869 lists her fixed draft as 23 feet.

However, the *San Francisco Bulletin* on June 15, 1870, lists it as being 24 feet laden with "4,000" tons of general cargo. In *Some Famous Ships and their Builder, Donald McKay,* p. 325, Richard C. McKay lists her draft as being 25 feet (she was laden with a 3,022.63 long ton grain cargo per manifest).

30. "Assignment for Benefit of Creditors," *op. cit.* Cargo manifest, *San Francisco Commercial Herald,* August 5, 1870.
31. Protest recorded October 7, 1870, in Book 40, p. 96 at Boston, Bureau of Customs, NARS.
32. "Assignment for Benefit of Creditors," *op. cit.*
33. *Ibid.*
34. Hall, *op. cit.*
35. Letter to Junius S. Morgan from Richard C. McKay dated July 5, 1928.
36. McKay, *op. cit.,* pp. 329–347, 364.

CHAPTER III

1. "Confirmation of Title," recorded March 25, 1871, in Book 41, p. 136, at Boston, Bureau of Customs, NARS.
2. Satisfaction of mortgage on instrument recorded April 14, 1871, in Book 39, p. 81, at Boston, Bureau of Customs, NARS.
3. Transfer of mortgage balance on instrument recorded April 14, 1871, in Book 38, p. 225, at Boston, Bureau of Customs, NARS.
4. "Assignment for Benefit of Creditors," *op. cit.*
5. Massachusetts Title Insurance Co. (Boston) report February 17, 1967.
6. William F. King, Jr., "The Sailmakers and Ship Chandlers of 79 Commercial Street, Boston" *The American Neptune* (July, 1955), p. 226.
7. Register No. 206 issued to *Glory of the Seas* on April 18, 1871, at Boston, Bureau of Customs, NARS.
8. *New York Maritime Register* (April 19, 1871).
9. Register No. 206 issued to *Glory of the Seas, op. cit.*
10. J. H. Sears Company fleet — 1870–1873: *Gold Hunter* of 1,258.34 tons (Official No. 10871); *Titan* of 1,229.40 tons (Official No. 24770); *Mogul* of 1,365.32 tons (Official No. 90068); *Kentuckian* of 1,233.59 tons (Official No. 14172); bark *Aurelia* of 561.07 tons (Official No. 1450); *Centaur* of 1,255.10 tons (Official No. 5668); *National Eagle* of 1,368.05 tons (Official No. 18069); and *Roswell Sprague* of 923.11 tons (Official No. 21122).
11. Bill of Sale recorded April 14, 1871, in Book 41, p. 162 at Boston, Bureau of Customs, NARS.
12. Register No. 206 issued to *Glory of the Seas, op. cit.*
13. Knowles papers.
14. *Ibid.*
15. *Ibid.*
16. Letter from Josiah N. Knowles, III, dated June 3, 1964.
17. Interview (taped) with H. A. Harlow in July, 1959.
18. Interview with Josiah N. Knowles, III, January 8, 1963; interview with Mrs. Alice Knowles Roberts, April 1, 1963.
19. Knowles papers.
20. *Ibid.*

21. Bill of Sale for ship *Glory of the Seas* recorded February 19, 1872, at Boston, Bureau of Customs, NARS.
22. Knowles papers.
23. *Ibid.*
24. *San Francisco Commercial Herald,* December 22, 1871.

CHAPTER IV

1. Knowles papers.
2. *Ibid.*
3. *Ibid.* See Appendix 2 for accounts dated December 18, 1871, through February 5, 1872.
4. Reprinted by permission from "The Crusoes of Pitcairn's Island; An Account of the Wreck of the *Wild Wave* from the Diary of Captain Josiah Nickerson Knowles of Brewster," Barnstable, Mass., Henry Sears Hoyt and J. King Hoyt, Jr., 1938.
5. Knowles papers.
6. *San Francisco Bulletin,* November 25, 1872.
7. Certificate of Desertion attached to February 7, 1872, crew list at San Francisco, Bureau of Customs, NARS.
8. Knowles papers.
9. *Ibid.*
10. *Ibid.*
11. *Ibid.*
12. *Ibid.*
13. *San Francisco Bulletin,* November 26, 1872.
14. Register No. 183 issued to *Helen Morris* on December 11, 1872, at New York is endorsed "lost at sea November 29, 1875." A note in the *Official Number Book* at the National Archives at Washington, D.C., has a note in the margin indicating that she was burned off the coast of Chile.
15. Interview with Mrs. Alice Knowles Roberts, April 1, 1963.
16. Interview with Mrs. Marguerite Little Twigg, September, 1965.

CHAPTER V

1. William W. Bates, *American Marine, The Shipping Question in History and Politics* (Boston and New York: Houghton, Mifflin Co. 1892), p. 162.
2. John G. B. Hutchins, *The American Maritime Industries and Public Policy, 1789–1914* (Cambridge, Mass.: Harvard University Press, 1941), pp. 418–419.
3. Knowles papers.
4. Reprinted by permission from "The Crusoes of Pitcairn's Island," *op. cit.*
5. Knowles papers.
6. *Ibid.*
7. *Ibid.*
8. *Ibid.*
9. *Ibid.*
10. Basil Lubbock, *The Down Easters, American Deep-Water Sailing Ships 1869 1929* (Glasgow, Scotland: Brown, Son and Furguson Ltd., 1929), p. 264.
11. Hall, *op. cit.,* pp. 27–28, 118.

12. Cargo Manifest, *San Francisco Bulletin*, January 18, 1874. See Appendix 3 for manifest.
13. *Trow's New York City Directory* for 1873–74, p. 67, refers to Sutton's Line as being at Pier 19. Knowles's reference to Pier 18 appears to be an error on his part.
14. Knowles papers.
15. *Ibid.*
16. McKay, *op. cit.*, p. 324. Frederick C. Matthews, "The Glory of the Seas," *Pacific Marine Review*, May, 1923, p. 277, states that "the passage was 94 days land to land; 95 days 2 hours from New York Anchorage to San Francisco bar and 96 days from anchor to anchor."

CHAPTER VI

1. Bates, *op. cit.*
2. Registry No. 78 issued to *Ericsson* (Official No. 7723) at New York on February 18, 1868, Bureau of Customs, NARS.
3. Frederick C. Matthews, "The Glory of the Seas," *Pacific Marine Review* (May, 1923), p. 277.
4. Knowles papers.
5. *Ibid.*
6. Crew list dated February 5, 1874, at San Francisco, Bureau of Customs, NARS.
7. Interview with Mrs. Marguerite Twigg, September, 1965.
8. *Ibid.*
9. Knowles papers.
10. *Ibid.*
11. *Ibid.*
12. Lubbock, *op. cit.*, p. 64.
13. Erich W. Zimmerman, *Ocean Shipping* (Englewood Cliffs, N.J.: Prentice-Hall, Inc., 1921), p. 226.
14. Matthews, "The Glory of the Seas," *op. cit.*, p. 276.
15. *Victoria Daily British Colonist*, January 4, 1875.
16. Knowles papers.
17. *San Francisco Daily Alta California*, December 26, 1874; Matthews, *American Merchant Ships, op. cit.*, Series II, p. 150.
18. Matthews, "The Glory of the Seas," *op. cit.*, p. 277.
19. The June 20, 1874, statute on reporting damage in excess of 300 dollars to the Government evidently did not apply to *Glory*. The National Archives have no record of any damage report ever being submitted. Per letter March 4, 1965.
20. Matthews, *American Merchant Ships, op. cit.*, Series II, p. 247.

CHAPTER VII

1. Hutchins, *op. cit.*, pp. 418–419.
2. Bates, *op. cit.*, p. 162.
3. Crew list issued at San Francisco on March 13, 1875, Bureau of Customs, NARS.
4. The cargo manifest for 1870–1885 indicates that *Glory* had between 500 and 600 tons of coal for ballast on four different occasions. No figure is extant of the amount of rubble ballast she carried.
5. Matthews, "The Glory of the Seas," *op. cit.*, p. 276.

6. Frederick C. Matthews papers.
7. Interview with Josiah N. Knowles, III, January 8, 1963.
8. Frederick C. Matthews papers.
9. *San Francisco Bulletin,* June 15, 1870, stated: "The French bark *La Paix* arrived from Newcastle, N. S. W. on Monday, in a passage of 59 days, one of the shortest for some time, though the *Borrowdale* made it in 56 days, the *Glengaber* in 59 days, the *Ravenscrag* in 60 days, and others in 62, 63, 64, and 65 days each."
10. Frederick C. Matthews papers.
11. Bates, *op. cit.,* p. 162.
12. Interview with Mrs. Alice Knowles Roberts, April 1, 1963.
13. Letter from Josiah N. Knowles, III, June 3, 1964.
14. *Ibid.*
15. Knowles papers.
16. Interview with Mrs. Alice Knowles Roberts.
17. Matthews, *American Merchant Ships, op. cit.,* Series I, p. 325.
18. Knowles papers (for log); memoranda from *San Francisco Bulletin,* August 24, 1876.
19. Knowles papers.
20. *Ibid.*
21. *Ibid.*
22. William Craig, not Colby, was mate on this voyage. Per crew list issued at San Francisco on October 7, 1875, Bureau of Customs, NARS.
23. Frederick C. Matthews papers.
24. Knowles papers.
25. Title Insurance and Trust Company (Oakland Branch) report, June 1, 1965.
26. Lloyd C. M. Hare, *Salted Tories* (Mystic, Conn.: Marine Historical Association, Inc., 1960), p. 77.

CHAPTER VIII

1. Letter from Gerrish House Society, Grand Manan Island, dated November 21, 1964; *Pen Pictures from the Garden of the World* (Fresno, California: Fresno County Historical Society [no date]); Donald C. Brown, "Eastport: A Maritime History," *The American Neptune* (April, 1968), p. 121.
2. Crew list dated October 23, 1876, at San Francisco, Bureau of Customs, NARS.
3. M. F. Purcell, *History of Contra Costa County* (Berkeley, Calif.: Gillick Press. 1940) p. 416.
4. *Contra Costa Gazette,* September 16, 1876.
5. *Ibid.*
6. Crew list dated October 23, 1876, at San Francisco.
7. *San Francisco Bulletin,* August 23, 1877.
8. Bates, *op. cit.,* p. 162.
9. *San Francisco Commercial Herald,* November 10, 1877.
10. *Portland Oregonian,* November 5, 1878.
11. Color scheme for *Borrowdale* from Mr. William Hartman in letter and watercolor sketch dated November 25, 1964.
12. *San Francisco Commercial Herald,* September 30, 1878.
13. *San Francisco Commercial Herald,* January 30, 1879.
14. Crew list dated April 7, 1879, at San Francisco, Bureau of Customs, NARS.

15. Matthews, *American Merchant Ships, op. cit.,* Series I, p. 281.

16. On December 3, 1879, Enrollment No. 148 was issued to *Glory* by the Bureau of Customs at Boston. The following day Register No. 217 was issued to her at New York. The *New York Maritime Register* for the period October 12 through December 9, 1879, notes no evidence that *Glory* was in Boston, yet the record still stands.

17. According to the insurance regulations for *American Lloyds* dated July 30, 1874, ". . . in all cases if the bottom has been caulked within three years, docking may be dispensed with."

18. *San Francisco Bulletin,* April 4, 1880.

CHAPTER IX

1. Crew list dated May 29, 1880, at San Francisco notes the following information about William B. Joseph: home state, Massachusetts; age, eighteen; rate, boy; complexion, light; hair, dark; height, 5 feet, 6 inches.

2. Interview with Mrs. Fred Homer, February 28, 1963.

3. *Ibid.*

4. McKay, *op. cit.,* p. 325.

5. Abstract of wreck reports, Volume 7, Records of U.S. Coast Guard, Record Group 26, NARS.

6. Interview with Mrs. Fred Homer.

7. *San Francisco Daily Alta California,* May 6, 1881.

8. Matthews, "Glory of the Seas," *op. cit.,* p. 278.

9. Lubbock, *Down Easters, op. cit.,* p. 3.

10. George Harlan, *San Francisco Bay Ferryboats* (Berkeley, Calif.: Howell-North Books, 1967), p. 113; George Harlan. *Of Walking Beams and Paddlewheels* (Oakland, Calif.: Bay Books Ltd., 1951), p. 30, lists it as being December 28.

11. Purcell, *op. cit.,* pp. 411–412, 415.

12. Title Insurance and Trust Company (Fresno Branch) report, February 3, 1965.

13. Abstract of wreck reports, Volume 8, Records of U.S. Coast Guard, Record Group 26, NARS.

14. The crew list dated July 9, 1881, lists no William Gribble. Evidently Gribble used an alias, which was not uncommon for seamen to do.

15. Frederick C. Matthews papers.

16. *Pen Pictures from the Garden of the World, op. cit.*

17. Frederick C. Matthews papers.

18. *Ibid.*

19. *Pen Pictures from the Garden of the World, op. cit.*

20. Abstract of wreck reports, Volume 8, Records of U.S. Coast Guard.

21. Hutchins, *op. cit.,* pp. 418–419.

22. Title Insurance and Trust Company (Fresno Branch) report, *op. cit.*

23. Frederick C. Matthews papers.

24. Title Insurance and Trust Company (Fresno Branch) report, *op. cit.*

25. Letter from Gerrish House Society, Grand Manan Island, dated November 21, 1964.

CHAPTER X

1. Bates, *op. cit.,* p. 162.

2. Hutchins, *op. cit.,* pp. 418–419.

3. Suffolk County, Massachusetts, Registry of Deeds in Book 1652, p. 388, dated June 16, 1884.

4. Bills of sale recorded June 16, 1884, at Boston, Bureau of Customs, NARS.

5. *Boston Evening Transcript,* December 3, 1897.

6. Bills of sale recorded September 29, 1884, at Boston, Bureau of Customs, NARS.

7. Freeman family papers.

8. *San Francisco Bulletin,* March 26, 1859: "March 25, ship *Christopher Hall,* Freeman, 127 days from Boston, merchandise to Stevens, Baker, and Co. [memorandum concerning ship] . . . was 56 days to Cape Horn; off the Cape three days with fine weather; crossed the equator in Pacific February 26, Long. 110°W.; was becalmed five days off this port."

9. Freeman family papers.

10. Attachment to Washington, D.C., office copy of Register No. 60 issued to ship *W. B. Dinsmore* of Boston on March 9, 1865, Bureau of Customs, NARS.

11. Interview with Mrs. Marguerite Twigg, September, 1965.

12. Freeman family papers.

13. Abstract of wreck reports, Volume 7, Records of U.S. Coast Guard, Record Group 26, NARS.

14. Interview with Mrs. Marguerite Twigg and Mrs. Lucy Sutherland, September, 1965.

15. Interview with Mrs. Alice Knowles Roberts, April 1, 1963.

16. *San Francisco Bulletin,* February 12 and 21, 1885.

17. Bill of sale recorded February 11, 1885, at Boston, Bureau of Customs, NARS.

18. *1962 Annual Report, Contra Costa County* (February 1, 1963), p. 19.

19. Letter from Liverpool Consulate to J. D. Porter, Asst. Secretary of State, dated August 18, 1886, NARS.

20. *Ibid.*

21. *Glory of the Seas* was not listed in *British Lloyds* until the 1889 issue.

22. *Report of the Chief of Engineers, U.S. Army,* Vol. II, Part I, 1885, p. 385.

23. Hutchins, *op. cit.,* pp. 423, 438.

24. *Ibid.,* pp. 418–419.

25. James Griffiths papers.

26. Interview with Mrs. Marguerite Twigg and Mrs. Lucy Sutherland, September, 1965.

CHAPTER XI

1. John Cass (undated) article from *Nanaimo Free Press;* Matthews, *American Merchant Ships, op. cit.,* Series I, p. 186.

2. Interview with John Cass, September, 1965.

3. *Ibid.*

4. Provincial Archives reference letter, August 28, 1964.

5. Interview with Mrs. Marguerite Twigg, September,1965.

6. Register No. 5 issued to bark *Ocean King* at San Francisco on July 27, 1886, Bureau of Customs, NARS; Matthews, *American Merchant Ships, op. cit.,* Series II, p. 247.

7. Washington territorial laws passed in 1877 and 1881 prohibited discharging ballast in less than 20 fathoms except under certain circumstances, *Revised Code of Washington Annotated,* Title 88.28.060.

8. Tacoma Mill Company records.
9. *Tacoma Daily Ledger,* May 26, 1886.
10. Interview with Mrs. Marguerite Twigg and Mrs. Lucy Sutherland, September, 1965.
11. Reference report by John Cass (no date).
12. Matthews, *American Merchant Ships, op. cit.,* Series I, p. 263.
13. *New York Marine Register,* February 22, 1887; Matthews, *American Merchant Ships, op. cit.,* Series I, p. 30.
14. Interview with Mrs. Marguerite Twigg, September, 1965.
15. E. W. Wright (Ed.), *Lewis and Drydon Marine History of the Pacific Northwest* (Portland, Ore.: Lewis and Drydon Publishing Co., 1895), p. 341; *Marine Digest,* September 23, 1922.
16. *Nanaimo Free Press,* February 7, 1889.
17. Based on freight rate figures in James Griffiths papers.
18. "*Glory of the Seas* Long on Coast," *Marine Digest* (June 9, 1923), p. 9.
19. Interview with Mrs. Marguerite Twigg, September, 1965.
20. *Ibid.*
21. *Ibid.*
22. *San Francisco Bulletin,* December 24, 1888.
23. "*Glory of the Seas* Long on Coast," *op. cit.,* p. 9. The San Francisco Marine Exchange Lookout Station reported *Glory* as being "17 days from Nanaimo, 3,300 tons coal for John Rosenfeld," not six days.
24. *San Francisco Bulletin,* December 24, 1888.

CHAPTER XII

1. Freeman family papers.
2. James Griffiths papers.
3. Provincial Archives Reference Report, August 19, 1965.
4. Statement of Mr. Henry Rusk, January, 1963, quoting his father.
5. Provincial Archives Reference Report, *op. cit.*
6. *Boston Herald,* June 21, 1922.
7. Interview with Mrs. Marguerite Twigg and Mrs. Lucy Sutherland, September, 1965.
8. *Ibid.*
9. Letter from Mrs. Marguerite Twigg, February 8, 1963.
10. Freeman family papers.
11. John Cass Reference Report (undated).
12. Matthews, "The Glory of the Seas," *op. cit.,* p. 277; letters from Mr. Charles E. Mohle, May 23, 1959, and March 11, 1963.
13. Letter from Captain P. A. McDonald, March 3, 1960.
14. Ralph Cropley, "Bully Freeman," *The Binnacle,* Volume I, No. 7 (September, 1956), p. 3.
15. *Ibid.*
16. Interview with Mrs. Marguerite Twigg, September, 1965.
17. *Ibid.*
18. Letter from Mrs. Marguerite Twigg, February 8, 1963.
19. Letter from Mrs. Marguerite Twigg, June 20, 1965.
20. *Ibid.*

21. Letter from Mrs. Marguerite Twigg, February 8, 1963.
22. Letter from Mrs. Lucy Sutherland (undated, 1963).
23. *Nanaimo Free Press,* February 12, 1892.
24. The original story was written by John Cass based on the Nanaimo Police Court records.
25. James Griffiths papers.

CHAPTER XIII

1. Interview with Mrs. Marguerite Twigg, September, 1965.
2. Provincial Archives Reference Report, December 9, 1965.
3. Letter from Mrs. Marguerite Twigg, February 8, 1963.
4. *Report of the Chief of Engineers,* U.S. Army, 1893, Vol. IV, pp. 3,217–3,220.
5. Letter from Mrs. Marguerite Twigg, February 8, 1963.
6. Interview with Mrs. Marguerite Twigg and Mrs. Lucy Sutherland, September, 1965.
7. Letter from Mrs. Lucy Sutherland (undated, 1963).
8. Josiah Knowles papers.
9. Probate Iventory for Josiah Knowles dated August 18, 1896, Records of Alameda County, California.
10. Reference Report from National Archives, October 19, 1965; Provincial Archives Reference Report, December 9, 1965.
11. Interview with Mr. Josiah N. Knowles, III, January 8, 1963.
12. Interview with Mrs. Alice Knowles Roberts, April 1, 1963.
13. *Oakland Tribune,* June 10, 1896.
14. From Esquimalt Naval Dockyard Records, her draft forward was 14 feet, aft 11 feet, per letter from Commodore Deane, Commandant, dated October 2, 1958.
15. Thomas Wiedemann, *Cheechako into Sourdough* (Portland, Ore.: Binfords and Mort, 1942), p. 21.
16. Enrollment No. 179 issued to *Sovereign of the Seas* at New York on March 20, 1900, was endorsed, "Lost at sea, February 19, 1903."
17. Log entry for Nov. 30, 1899, U.S.S. *Adams.*
18. This occurred prior to 1896 because a photograph of her figurehead dated 1896 in the "Wind and Wave" collection, San Francisco Maritime Museum, shows the bracing.

CHAPTER XIV

1. The original manuscript was handwritten in pencil by Walter Ehrhorn in 1954 and has been edited by the author. The crew data is taken from the shipping articles dated July 5, 1901, at San Francisco, Bureau of Customs, NARS. The cargo data was copied from the entry August 28, 1901, at the Lookout Station, San Francisco Marine Exchange.
2. *The Olympian,* February 22, 1937.
3. Interview with Captain Volney Young, December 12, 1962; interview with Mr. and Mrs. Carl Woodard, January 2, 1966.
4. Provincial Archives Report, August 19, 1965.
5. Interview with Mr. and Mrs. Carl Woodard, January 2, 1966.
6. Marine Disaster Report, Lookout Station, San Francisco Marine Exchange, March 1, 1902.
7. Interview with Mr. Okey Graham, July 3, 1965. Captain Ekrem told him this in the late 1920's.

8. *The Olympian,* February 22, 1937.
9. Bill of Sale recorded March 7, 1902, Bureau of Customs, Federal Records Center, Seattle.

CHAPTER XV

1. As shown on the shipping articles 1902–1904 for the Port of San Francisco for *Glory of the Seas.*
2. Interview (taped) held September 2, 1961, with Mr. George Webb.
3. *Victoria Daily Colonist,* October 20, 1903.
4. Disaster Report, Lookout Station, San Francisco Marine Exchange, March 9, 1904; *Victoria Daily Colonist,* March 18, 1904.
5. *San Francisco Chronicle,* March 11, 1961.
6. Load lines were not established by law on American ships until 1929. However, insurance companies fixed load lines for special class vessels.
7. Interview (taped) on October 4, 1958, with Fingal Larson on deck of *Balclutha.*
8. Freeman family papers.
9. *Report of the Merchant Marine Commission,* Vol. I, 1905, p. 402.

CHAPTER XVI

1. E. A. Woods, "A Merchant Venturer," *Sea Breezes* (June, 1939), pp. 102–105.
2. Bills of sale recorded May 10, 1906, at San Francisco, Bureau of Customs, Federal Records Center.
3. *Ibid.*
4. Title Insurance and Trust Company (Oakland Branch) report, July 14, 1965, shows that the conveyance was made prior to her death. Bill of sale No. 399 at San Francisco, dated May 23, 1903, and recorded May 10, 1906, was executed also prior to her death.
5. Interview with Josiah Knowles, III, January 8, 1963, in which he related how much data including logs and photographs were destroyed in the fire.
6. James Griffiths papers.
7. "Captain Gillespie Honored For 40 Years Service" (San Francisco) *Sextant,* January, 1960; Master's commission No. 3944 was issued to Henry J. Gillespie who may have been the father of the master of *Glory.*
8. James Griffiths papers.
9. Shipping articles dated July 19, 1906, at San Francisco, Bureau of Customs, NARS.
10. James Griffiths papers.
11. *Ibid.*
12. Shipping articles dated July 19, 1906, at San Francisco, Bureau of Customs, NARS.
13. James Griffiths papers.
14. Bellingham Public Museum reference report, February 15 and February 22, 1963.
15. Wreck report dated February 25, 1907, at San Francisco, Bureau of Customs, Federal Records Center.
16. James Griffiths papers.
17. Bellingham Public Museum reference report, *op. cit.*
18. Interview with Mr. William H. Beeman, March 11, 1961.
19. James Griffiths papers.

20. *Victoria Daily Times,* May 27, 1907.
21. Interview with Mr. William H. Beeman, March 11, 1961.
22. *Ibid.*
23. *Ibid.*
24. *Seattle Times,* December 4, 1907.
25. Shipping articles dated November 21, 1907, at Port Townsend, Bureau of Customs, Federal Records Center, Seattle.
26. Official logbook dated November 21, 1907, at Port Townsend, Bureau of Customs, Federal Records Center, Seattle.
27. Shipping articles dated November 21, 1907, at Port Townsend.
28. *"Glory of the Seas* Long on Coast," *op. cit.,* p. 16; "Captain Gillespie Honored For 40 Years Service," *Sextant, op. cit.*
29. Official Log Book dated November 21, 1907, *op. cit.*
30. Shipping articles dated November 21, 1907.
31. *Ibid.*

CHAPTER XVII

1. James Griffiths papers.
2. Interview (taped) held with H. A. Harlow, July, 1959.
3. James Griffiths papers.
4. *Ibid.*
5. Hall Brothers Shipyard records.
6. Freeman family papers.
7. Hall Brothers Shipyard records.
8. Seattle Marine Exchange records.
9. Frederick Johnstone papers.
10. Matthews, *American Merchant Ships, op. cit.,* Series II, p. 13.
11. *Victoria Daily Times,* March 25, 28, 30, April 8, 13, and 26, 1911; Frederick Johnstone papers.
12. *Ibid.*
13. Frederick Johnstone papers.

CHAPTER XVIII

1. Frederick Johnstone papers.
2. *Ibid.*
3. Bill of sale recorded June 8, 1911 at Seattle, Bureau of Customs, Federal Records Center.
4. Frederick Johnstone papers.
5. *Ibid.*
6. Report of the Bureau of Fisheries, Alaska and Fur Industries, *Fishery and Fur Industry of Alaska in 1912,* (1912), p. 46.
7. Frederick Johnstone papers.
8. Interview with Mr. Robert Leithead, December 6, 1965.
9. Seattle Marine Exchange records.
10. Gordon Newall, *H. W. McCurdy's Marine History of the Pacific Northwest, 1896–1964* (Seattle, Wash.: Superior Publishing Co., 1966). Unpublished portion was used.
11. Frederick Johnstone papers.
12. Reference report by Captain L. H. "Kinky" Bayers, September 22, 1958.

13. Interview with Mr. Jack Olinder, October, 1959.
14. *Ibid.*
15. James Bashford papers.
16. Mortgage recorded in Misc. Book, p. 301 (mtg. 5) recorded June 14, 1915, at Tacoma, Bureau of Customs, NARS.
17. Records of Yarrows Limited, Victoria, B.C.
18. Interview with Mrs. Marguerite Twigg, September, 1965.
19. Interview with Mrs. Barbara Bumpus, September, 1965.
20. *Victoria Daily Times,* April 3, 1916.
21. Reference report by captain L. H. "Kinky" Bayers, September 22, 1958.
22. Interview with Mr. Okey Graham, July 3, 1965.
23. Interview with Mr. C. Arthur Foss, October, 1959.
24. Interview with Mr. Okey Graham, July 3, 1965.
25. Endorsement on final register issued to *Glory of the Seas* on March 3, 1921, at Tacoma, Bureau of Customs, Federal Records Center, Seattle.
26. Letter from Mr. James A. Farrall, December 5, 1962.
27. Interview with Mr. Okey Graham, July 3, 1965.
28. *Ibid.*
29. *Ibid.*
30. *Ibid.*
31. Copy in author's collection.
32. "*Glory of the Seas* Long on Coast," *op. cit.,* p. 9.
33. Interview with Mr. Frank Prothero, September, 1963.
34. *Ibid.*
35. *Ibid.*
36. Frederick C. Matthews papers.
37. Interview with Captain Volney Young, December 12, 1962.

BIBLIOGRAPHY

✶✶

Bibliography

I. Official Documents of the United States

Customhouse Records, National Archives and Records Service.

U.S. Coast Guard Records, National Archives and Records Service.

Hall, Henry. *Report on the Shipbuilding Industry of the United States,* 1882, Census Monograph, Tenth Census, Vol. VIII.

Report of the Bureau of Fisheries, Alaska and Fur Industries, 1911–1916.

Report of the Chief of Engineers, U.S. Army. 1871–1897.

Report on the Merchant Marine Commission with the Testimony Taken at the Hearings. Washington, D.C. Senate Document 2755, 58th Congress, Three Sessions, 1905.

U.S. Coast Pilot, Atlantic Coast, Section A, St. Croix River to Cape Cod. 1918.

U.S. Coast Pilot, Atlantic Coast, Section B, Cape Cod to Sandy Hook. 1918.

U.S. Coast Pilot, Pacific Coast, California, Oregon and Washington. 1909.

U.S. Statutes at Large.

U.S. Department of Commerce annual *List of Merchant Vessels of the United States,* 1868–1925.

II. Official Records of Counties in the United States

Suffolk, Massachusetts (Boston).

Alameda, California (Oakland).

Fresno, California (Fresno).

III. Marine Exchange Records and Shipping Registers

American Lloyds and *American Record.* Penobscot, Maine: Penobscot Marine Museum.

British Lloyds. San Francisco, Calif.: San Francisco Maritime Museum.

New York Marine Register. Mystic, Conn., Mystic Seaport; The New York Public Library.

San Francisco Marine Exchange Records. San Francisco, Calif.: 1885–1920.

289

Seattle Marine Exchange Records, 1906–1925. Puget Sound, Wash.: Puget Sound Maritime Historical Society.

iv. Works on Maritime Economics and Policy

Bates, William W. *American Marine, The Shipping Question in History and Politics.* Boston and New York: Houghton, Mifflin Co., 1892.

Hutchins, John G. B. *The American Maritime Industries and Public Policy, 1789–1914.* Cambridge, Mass.: Harvard University Press, 1941.

Zimmerman, Erich W. *Ocean Shipping.* Englewood Cliffs, N.J.: Prentice-Hall, Inc., 1921.

v. General Works on Sailing Ships and Their Histories

Carse, Robert. *The Twilight of Sailing Ships.* New York: Grosset & Dunlap, 1965.

Chapelle, Howard I. *History of American Sailing Ships.* New York: W. W. Norton & Company, Inc., 1935.

———. *The Search for Speed under Sail, 1700–1855.* New York: W. W. Norton & Company, Inc., 1967.

Clark, Arthur H. *The Clipper Ship Era.* New York: G. P. Putnam's Sons, 1911.

Davis, Charles G. *The Ways of the Sea.* New York: Rudder Publishing Co., 1930.

Fairburn, William Armstrong. *Merchant Sail.* 5 vols.
Center Lovell, Maine: Fairburn Marine Educational Foundation, Inc., 1944–1955.

Harlow, Frederick Pease. *Making of a Sailor.* Salem, Mass.: Marine Research Society, 1929.

Hawthorne, Daniel. *Clipper Ship.* New York: Dodd, Mead & Company, Inc., 1928.

Howe, Octavius T. and Matthews, Frederick C. *American Clipper Ships, 1833–1858.* 2 vols. Salem, Mass.: Marine Research Society, 1926–1927.

Kittredge, Henry C. *Shipmasters of Cape Cod.* Boston: Houghton, Mifflin Company, 1935.

Laing, Alex. *American Sail, A Pictorial History.* New York: E. P. Dutton & Co., 1961.

Lubbock, Basil. *The Down Easters, American Deep-Water Sailing Ships 1869–1929.* Glasgow, Scotland: Brown, Son and Furguson Ltd., 1929.

———. *The Last of the Windjammers.* 2 vols. Glasgow, Scotland: Brown, Son and Furguson Ltd., 1927.

McKay, Richard C. *Some Famous Ships and Their Builder, Donald McKay.* New York: G. P. Putnam's Sons, 1928.

Matthews, Frederick C. *American Merchant Ships.* 2 vols. Salem, Mass.: Marine Research Society, 1930–1931.

Mattieson, Peter J. R. *Master of the Moving Sea.* Flagstaff, Ariz.: J. F. Colton and Co., 1959.

Robinson, J. and Dow, George F. *The Sailing Ships of New England.* 3 series. Salem, Mass.: Marine Research Society, 1921–1928.

Sears, J. Henry. *Brewster Ship Masters.* Yarmouth Port, Mass.: C. W. Swift, 1906.

Underhill, Harold A. *Deepwater Sail.* Glasgow, Scotland: Brown, Son and Furguson Ltd., 1952.

———. *Masting and Rigging.* Glasgow, Scotland: Brown, Son and Furguson Ltd., 1946.

Periodicals and Pamphlets

Caldwell, George B. Jr., "Building the *John Adams*," *Nautical Research Journal* (October, 1950).

Clark, Admont G., "They Built Clipper Ships in Their Back Yard," *The American Neptune* (October, 1962).

"*Glory of the Seas* Long on Coast," *Marine Digest* (June 9, 1923).

"*The Glory of the Seas*," *Standard Oil Bulletin* (March, 1922).

Matthews, Frederick C., "The Glory of the Seas," *Pacific Marine Review* (May, 1923).

VI.   General Works on Shipping and the Shipbuilding Industry

Brewington, Marion V. *Shipcarvers of North America*. Barre, Mass.: Barre Publishing Co., 1962.

Desmond, Charles. *Wooden Shipbuilding*. New York: Rudder Publishing Co., 1919.

Hare, Lloyd C. M. *Salted Tories*. Mystic, Conn.: Marine Historical Association, Inc., 1960.

Harlan, George. *Of Walking Beams and Paddlewheels*. Oakland, Calif.: Bay Books Ltd., 1951.

————. *San Francisco Bay Ferryboats*, Berkeley, Calif.: Howell-North Books, 1967.

Howe, William H. *History of Maritime Maine*. New York: W. W. Norton & Company, Inc., 1948.

Kemble, John H. *San Francisco Bay, A Pictorial Maritime History*. Cambridge, Maryland: Cornell Maritime Press, 1957.

Newall, Gordon. *H. W. McCurdy's Marine History of the Pacific Northwest, 1896–1964*. Seattle, Wash.: Superior Publishing Co., 1966. (An unpublished portion of manuscript was also used as reference.)

Pinckney, Pauline A. *American Figureheads and Their Carvers*. New York: W. W. Norton & Company, Inc., 1940.

Tyler, David Budlong. *Steam Conquers the Atlantic*. New York: Appleton-Century-Crofts, Inc., 1939.

Wright, Benjamin C. *San Francisco's Ocean Trade, Past and Future*. San Francisco: A. Carlisle and Co., 1911.

Wright, E. W. (ed.) *Lewis and Drydon Marine History of the Pacific Northwest*. Portland, Ore.: Lewis and Drydon Publishing Co., 1895.

Periodicals and Pamphlets

Brown, C. Donald. "Eastport: A Maritime History," *The American Neptune* (April, 1968).

Cropley, Ralph. "Bully Freeman," *The Binnacle*, vol. I, no. 7 (September, 1956).

King, William F. Jr. "The Sailmakers and Ship Chandlers of 79 Commercial Street, Boston," *The American Neptune* (July, 1955).

Marine Digest (September 23, 1922; June 9, 1923; April 17, 1965).

"Old Wooden Ships Burned to Salvage Metal," *Popular Mechanics* (March, 1935).

Sterling, Robert E. "Donald McKay—Dreamer," *The Mentor* (August, 1929).

Woods, Capt. E. A. "A Merchant Venturer," *Sea Breezes* (June, 1939).

VII. Local Histories

Abdill, George. *Pacific Slope Railroads*. New York: Bonanza Books, 1959.

Abraham, Dorothy. *Romantic Vancouver Island*. Victoria, B.C.: Hebden Publishing Co. Ltd., [no date].

Alexander, E. P. *Iron Horses, American Locomotives, 1829–1900*. New York: Bonanza Books, 1941.

Purcell, M. F. *History of Contra Costa County*. Berkeley, Calif.: Gillick Press, 1940.

Sumner, William H. *A History of East Boston*. Boston: J. E. Tilton & Co., 1858.

Wiedemann, Thomas. *Cheechako into Sourdough*. Portland, Ore.: Binfords and Mort, 1942.

Special Publications and Periodicals

"Captain Gillespie Honored For 40 Years Service," *Sextant,* January, 1960 (San Francisco)

The City of Ladysmith, 50th Anniversary, 1904–1954, Ladysmith, B.C.: Ladysmith Chamber of Commerce, 1954.

"The Crusoes of Pitcairn's Island; An Account of the Wreck of the *Wild Wave* from the Diary of Captain Josiah Nickerson Knowles of Brewster." Barnstable, Mass.; Henry Sears Hoyt and J. King Hoyt, Jr., 1938.

Harrington, Eugene I. "The History of General Petroleum Corporation," (New York), Mobil Oil Company, [no date].

Nesbitt, James K. "California Press Toured Victoria in 1897," *The Daily Colonist* (Victoria, B.C.), May 1, 1966.

1962 Annual Report, Contra Costa County. Contra Costa County, Calif.: February 1, 1963.

Pen Pictures from the Garden of the World, Memorial and Biographical History of the Counties of Fresno, Tulare and Kern California. Fresno, Calif.: Fresno Historical Society, [no date].

"Seattlelites Recall Cable Car Days," Seattle *Times,* September 19, 1965.

"75 Years of Safety and Service," Seattle, Wash.: Washington Mutual Savings Bank, 1964.

VIII. Private Papers of Individuals and Business Firms

Bashford, James. Tacoma, Wash.: Washington State Historical Society.

Ehrhorn, Walter. San Francisco.

Freeman, Captain Joshua. Mrs. Barbara Bumpus and Mrs. Lucy Sutherland, Victoria, B.C.

Griffiths, Captain James. Seattle, Wash.: Seattle Historical Society.

Harlow, Frederick Pease. Harlow family, Vancouver, Wash.

Hall Brothers Shipyard. Captain Harold Huycke.

Johnstone, Frederick. Robert Leithead, Seattle, Wash.

Knowles, Captain Josiah N. Josiah N. Knowles, III, San Francisco, Calif. Harry Chase, Oakland, Calif. California Historical Society.

Matthews, Frederick C., San Francisco, Calif.: San Francisco Public Library.

Puget Mill Company. Seattle, Wash.: University of Washington.

Tacoma Mill Company. Tacoma, Wash.: Washington State Historical Society.

IX. Interviews

Beeman, William H. March 11, 1961.

Bumpus, Mrs. Barbara. September, 1965.

Cass, John. September, 1965.

Foss, C. Arthur. October, 1959.

Graham, Oscar. July 3, 1965.

Harlow, H. A. July, 1959 (tape recording).

Homer, Mrs. Fred. February 28, 1963.

Knowles, Josiah N., III. January 8, 1963.

Larson, Fingal. October 4, 1958 (tape recording).

Leithead, Robert. December 6, 1965.

McCurdy, Horace W. September, 1959.

Olinder, Jack. October, 1959.

Prothero, Frank. September, 1963.

Roberts, Mrs. Alice Knowles. April 1, 1963.

Rusk, Henry. January, 1963.

Sutherland, Mrs. Lucy. September, 1965.

Twigg, Mrs. Marguerite Little, September, 1965.

Webb, George. September 2, 1961 (tape recording).

Woodard, Mr. and Mrs. Carl. January 2, 1966.

Young, Captain Volney. December 12, 1962.

X. Special Reference Reports

Applebee, Robert B. (Librarian), Penobscot, Maine: Penobscot Marine Museum (general ship data).

Bayers, Captain L. H. "Kinky," Juneau, Alaska (cannery and reefer data on *Glory*).

Boston Public Library (construction data on *Glory* and period data on Boston).

Casaleggio, John, San Francisco Public Library (data on *Gold Hunter* and *Christopher Hall*).

Cass, John (Historian), Nanaimo, B.C. (Vancouver Island coal shipping).

Conklin, Florina, *Seattle Times* Information Bureau (general historical data).

Dolbear, Mrs. Inez, Contra Costa Public Library, Martinez, Calif. (grain shipping).

Franklin, W. Neil, National Archives and Records Service, Washington, D.C. (general ship data).

Hartman, William, Birmingham, England (*Borrowdale* information).

Hoyt, Henry Sears, Barnstable, Mass. (J. H. Sears and Knowles family data).

Ibbotson, Mrs. Anna, Washington State Historical Society, Tacoma, Wash. (*Dashing Wave* data).

Ingersoll, L. Keith, Gerrish House, Grand Manan Island, New Brunswick (Daniel McLaughlin family data).

Ireland, Willard (Provincial Archivist), Provincial Archives, Victoria, B.C. (data on Freeman family, ships *Bristol, Wellington, America,* and *Ericsson*).

John Hancock Life Insurance Company, Boston, Mass. (data on Donald McKay and the McKay Monument).

Johnson, Mrs. Dorothy H. (Director), Bellingham, Wash.: Bellingham Public Museum (1906 data on *Glory*).

Kochanek, Miss Jean, Massachusetts Title Insurance Company, Boston (Donald Mc-Kay's property holdings 1849–1880).

Kortum, Karl (Director), San Francisco Maritime Museum (data on museum *Wild Wave* display and general ship data).

Lochhead, John (Librarian), Mariners Museum, Newport News, Virginia (builder's model of *Glory*).

McDonald, Captain P. A., Santa Monica, Calif. (data on windmill pumps, ship ballast).

Mohle, Charles E. (Librarian), Cabrillo Marine Museum, Los Angeles, Calif. (data on 1891 stranding of *Glory*).

Nesdall, Andrew (Historian), Waban, Mass. (owners of *Glory* — 1869–1871.

The New York Public Library (1873–1874 record voyage, New York to San Francisco).

Otsuki, James, National Archives and Records Service, San Francisco, Calif. (general ship data).

Parsons, Susan, Boston Atheneum (Donald McKay, his family, and Charles Brigham).

Peters, Anita, Fresno, Calif.: Title Insurance and Trust Company (McLaughlin real estate holdings.

Pollard, Dan R. (Administrator), Fresno, Calif.: Fresno County Historical Society (McLaughlin family data).

Prather, Howard, Oakland, Calif.: Title Insurance and Trust Company (Knowles's real estate holdings).

Reiger, Morris, National Archives and Records Service, Washington, D.C. (documents and voyages of *Glory*, 1900–1925).

Schultz, Charles (Librarian), Mystic, Conn.: Mystic Seaport (general ship data).

Smith, Jane F., National Archives and Records Service, Washington, D.C. (general ship data).

INDEX

Index